As more and more Christians answer God's call to serve the orphan, it is vital that we relentlessly bind together action with understanding and zeal with knowledge. *The Global Orphan Crisis* helps us do that, offering an impressive array of data, a primer on key issues and thorny debates, and a wealth of ideas for personal involvement. All orphan advocates stand to benefit from the extensive information Diane Elliot shares.
—JEDD MEDEFIND, president, Christian Alliance for Orphans

The Bible tells us that we "have the mind of Christ" (Philippians 2:5). Jesus' mind is more than His intellect. When united to Christ, we think, feel, hurt, and act right along with Him. Throughout the Bible our Christ is burdened by the plight of the fatherless. Sharing His Spirit, we must be as well. This book prompts Christians to the enormity of the global orphan crisis, and calls us to action.
—RUSSELL D. MOORE, dean, The Southern Baptist Theological Seminary and author of *Adopted for Life*

This book reaches deep into my "inner Robin Hood" and calls me to action for the sake of Christ and His children. Kids pay the highest price when the issues of economic, physical, and spiritual oppression go unaddressed. *The Global Orphan Crisis* is packed with research that informs us, photos that convince us, and stories that move us.
—SCOTT OLSON, President/CEO, International Teams

While the evangelical church should be commended for its growing commitment to orphan ministries, there remains a wide chasm between our zeal to care for the fatherless and a true understanding of their plight. *The Global Orphan Crisis* is a must-read for all who want to truly obey God's call to care for orphans. Diane Elliot helps us not only understand the scope of the orphan crisis throughout the world but also presents practical and biblical solutions to the crisis. A great resource to go through individually or with a group.
—DR. DANIEL BENNETT, pastor and author of *A Passion for the Fatherless: Developing a God-Centered Ministry to Orphans*

Diane Lynn Elliot has written a well-researched, thoughtful, and balanced work. This is not a book for the faint of heart but for those who are serious about being in the center of God's will for the orphan. She takes the reader on a journey fraught with heartache, struggle, sorrow, pain, sadness but also filled with the possibility of hope, joy, redemption, healing, grace, and unconditional love. It is a journey that begins and ends in the heart of God, and if you are faithful to His voice—will change you and the children you serve in His name forever.
—Michael Douris, president, Orphan Outreach

Diane Elliot in her book has uncovered and exposed the dirty, complex, and messy problems that define the lives of millions of vulnerable children around the world. *The Global Orphan Crisis* aids the reader in knowing the mind and heart of God relating to orphans and vulnerable children. This resource opens the reader's mind, heart, and hands to developing and implementing solutions. Those of us on the ground in orphan care ministry anxiously await God's blessings on this phenomenal tool!
—ED SCHWARTZ , founder and president, Loving Shepherd Ministries

She did it! Diane Elliott answered the big question "I want to help, but what can I do?" with clear and powerful ideas that will surely make an impact.
—MATTHEW STORER, president of VisionTrust, chairman of Christian Alliance for Orphans, chairman of Food for Orphans

P9-DFH-578

I wish I had read *The Global Orphan Crisis* years go! For far too long, I read Scripture but missed God's heart for the orphan. Not only does this book offer an inside look at the causes of the crisis, it also equips you to live out the call to practice true religion and make a lasting difference in the lives of the most vulnerable.
—PETER GREER, president and CEO, HOPE International and coauthor of *The Poor Will Be Glad*

For 25 years, I've prayed that God would call someone to shine a spotlight on the issue of orphans. He answered that prayer through Diane Elliot and her book *The Global Orphan Crisis*. Her writing begs you to take a hard look, perhaps for the first time, at the staggering statistics of how many children, worldwide, are orphaned. Then she inspires you, as a child of the God—who calls Himself "the father to the fatherless"—to do something for the orphans in your town, your state, your country, your world!
—CHRISTA M. MARCH, founder and president, Teen Mother Choices International and author, *Light to Lead the Way*.

This book is a must-read for all who want to be informed about and involved in the global orphan crisis. I know firsthand the life-changing impact we can make in the lives of these vulnerable children, as we respond to this invitation of engagement. With a wealth of data, challenging questions, and practical ways to participate, the book is a valuable resource in the struggle to be God's love to these needy orphaned children. As you read, I pray your heart will be open to how God wants you to be part of the solution.
—EMILY D. VOORHIES, president, Tirzah International

The Global Orphan Crisis is a masterful blend of awareness and engagement. Inviting us to not leave these children in the ignored, abused, or unwanted state they find themselves in, but calls us to help right the wrongs, and to be about action, compassion, justice, purpose, respect, leadership, and commitment. Rejecting passivity and fulfilling the call God has given us to help bring relationship, renewal, and reconciliation—for Christ.
—ANDY LEHMAN, vice president, Lifesong for Orphans

The Global Orphan Crisis is an inspiring, well-articulated, wake-up call. As the title suggests, there is a literal crisis in our world—children without means who desperately need love and care. With overwhelming compassion, Diane Elliot reminds us of the world's least fortunate, their dire needs, and what we can do to help. She also shows the dangers faced by orphans around the world, including the ever-increasing problem of human trafficking. The problem is heartbreaking, yet Diane addresses this challenging topic with hope providing a call to action for people striving to live as Christ did. The book offers a number of ways to get involved and emphasizes that no contribution is greater than another. It is impossible to read this book and not be moved to make a difference.
—REBECCA MCDONALD, president of Women at Risk, International

The Global Orphan Crisis is a well-researched and careful handling of a complex issue, including interviews and insights from some of the orphan care community's top leaders/thinkers, that leave the reader with multiple tangible suggestions for ways to respond and get involved.
—SCOTT VAIR, president of World Orphans

Diane Elliot has written a powerful guide that is more than informative; it is a call to action. She did not assume she had all of the solutions; rather she prayerfully and diligently researched the issues involved and sought best practice solutions. This book provides much more than a helpful clear description and analysis of the underlying problems; it provides answers. I think book clubs, church leaders, Bible studies, and all who share God's heart for orphaned and fatherless children will be blessed by the material.
—CLAYTON WOOD, president of Allies for Orphans and director for the SOAR mentorship program

The Global Orphan Crisis

Be the Solution; Change Your World

DIANE LYNN ELLIOT

MOODY PUBLISHERS

CHICAGO

Edited by Annette LaPlaca
Interior design: Ragont Design
Cover design: Beryl T. Glass
Cover image: Rwandan Orphan by Matthew James
Author Photo: Dave Elliot

All websites and phone numbers listed herein are accurate at the time of publication, but may change in the future or cease to exist. The listing of website references and resources does not imply publisher endorsement of the site's entire contents. Groups and organizations are listed for informational purposes, and listing does not imply publisher endorsement of their activities.

Library of Congress Cataloging-in-Publication Data

Elliot, Diane Lynn.
The global orphan crisis : be the solution, change your world / Diane Lynn Elliot.
   p. cm.
Includes bibliographical references (p.   ).
ISBN 978-0-8024-0954-6
1. Orphans. I. Title.
HV965.E47 2012
362.73--dc23

2012023828

We hope you enjoy this book from Moody Publishers. Our goal is to provide high-quality, thought-provoking books and products that connect truth to your real needs and challenges. For more information on other books and products written and produced from a biblical perspective, go to www.moodypublishers.com or write to:

Moody Publishers
820 N. La Salle Boulevard
Chicago, IL 60610

1 3 5 7 9 10 8 6 4 2

Printed in the United States of America

Outside a schoolhouse in northeast India, these children couldn't contain their smiles and giggles as the photographer playfully made faces at them. *Bill Wegener photographer,* copyright © *Evangel Bible Translators, Int'l*

For orphaned, fatherless, abandoned,

and vulnerable children around the globe,

who even today need protection, sustenance,

help, and encouragement.

Fear not, for the Lord your God is with you!

Cry out to Jesus; He will hear your cry.

The troops are being assembled. Help is on the way.

126456

Contents

Gaielle's quiet spirit and smiling eyes immediately stole my heart at a children's village in Port-au-Prince, Haiti. A family from Argentina is adopting Gaielle to give her the love and stability she needs.

Diane Lynn Elliot, photographer © Diane Lynn Elliot

Foreword

What I would have done for a book like *The Global Orphan Crisis* when I first responded to my orphan care calling in 1997. At the time I knew the verse James 1:27, and maybe a random statistic or two, but nothing like the thorough research and faith-based analysis you will find here. It would have made a big difference as I bumped and bruised my way through the learning curve and our progression from a relief organization to a developmental one. This resource offers substance to the eager, the passionate, and the called but not-yet-experienced. The author will guide you to possible solutions beyond adoption and into permanence. For someone like me, who is still eager, passionate, and called—but now experienced—this book provides a view outside the world I frequent. It offers a perspective on events from the bird's eye point of view.

As is common, I can spend too much time with my head down and focused on my own field. It's helpful to be able to gain the perspective the author offers through her research and the insight gained from countless hours spent in interviews. As a result, Diane Elliot has written a book with good ideas and solid, realistic outcomes. In the orphan care community, we are learning, and growing exponentially. God is depositing His heart for the orphan into church leaders, young people, adoptive parents, mission trip participants, researchers, foundation presidents, missions boards, and little children. He is giving wisdom, and we need good communicators to gather that wisdom and help us share one with another.

We need workable solutions that are spread over a spectrum. Sometimes the solution is adoption, sometimes it's foster care, sometimes it's residential, sometimes it's kinship care. To know what and when takes analysis of the situation, the culture, the funding, the support, the personnel, and the need. It takes knowledge, and books like this one, to put some of those tools in the hands of the decision makers.

The Global Orphan Crisis will walk you through some of the biblical promises with stories that shout the simple promise of Colossians 1:17: "He is before all things and in Him all things will hold together." He has gone before us in this global orphan crisis, not just in your adoption story, or in the lives of the missionaries you support, but every day, in every relationship, experience, or eyewitness. All are done by Him and are not due to our cleverness or great programs.

This last year, I was studying about Miriam, a Jewish woman whose story we can read in Exodus. She was a slave, whose mother was a slave, whose mother was a slave, and so on. She had no reason to believe anything different was ahead. And yet . . . after Moses's famous confrontation with Pharaoh when Moses said, "Let my people go!" . . . after the plagues that we can hardly imagine, Pharaoh—that evil captor—finally relented. Imagine how a message of that magnitude got out, in a world without texting or the Internet, or any way of mass communicating.

"We are free, we can go!"

It must have just looked like chaos, people running through the streets, shouting door to door. Somehow, Miriam heard that message and took off with her people to a place she couldn't imagine, to a land she had never seen. She had no idea, couldn't have fathomed yet how they were going to get through the enormous sea that separated her from the freedom they were hoping to taste. On her way out of the only dwelling she had ever known, what did she grab for this journey? If it had been me, I might have considered an extra pair of shoes, a family document, a kilo of flour, I don't know.

How does one prepare for a God-journey you can't picture?

Miriam follows her people across the dry land of the split sea, and when she arrives on the other side, Exodus 15:20 says, "and then Miriam, the prophetess, taking out her tambourine, leads the people in song..."

What? A tambourine?

She thought to pack up a musical instrument in her rush to leave slavery? Why would she do that? Because she knew what we are now desperate to believe, that in the midst of chaos—or a global orphan crisis—that we don't understand, we can trust that He has gone before us. We need to be prepared in a moment's notice to praise Him when He provides a rescue.

This year, hold a tambourine in hand. Praise Him for your own stories of split seas and gifts of freedom. Praise Him for giving you a role in chasing after orphans in His name. There's a long history of God's people witnessing this holding-it-togetherness. Join us! Be a part of the global orphan solution and bring your tambourine!

BETH GUCKENBERGER
Co-executive director of Back2Back Ministries

Ashley Nieuwsma holds her new son for the very first time. In answer to their prayers for the blessing of additional children, God brought Ashley and her husband to Haiti. Because the adoption process is long and difficult, they are trusting God to bring their two new sons home to their family soon. *Diane Lynn Elliot, photographer*
© Diane Lynn Elliot

Introduction

It has been more than a week since I returned from Haiti, and I have to say that I have left my head and heart there. I'm a mess! Since I have been home I have slept more than I realized I needed, lost a credit card, lost a driver's license, spent hours to replace the license, found the old license right where I left it, am still taking anti malaria meds and itching a dozen mosquito bites even though it is twenty degrees in Chicago, wrote a chapter in two-and-a half days (a record for me), edited 3,500 Haiti pictures, answered a box full of emails, tried to get back to "normal" life, and still I just can't seem to "get over" Haiti. This is not like me. After visiting twenty different countries, seldom have I ever longed to go back even before I left the country. There is a big world out there, and I'm usually ready to move on to the next adventure. This time it's different! This time I'm different!

Even stepping onto the plane in Haiti I knew I wasn't ready to leave. We accomplished our mission, explored ten different children's homes, met with dozens of leaders who shared their inspiring visions, and we saw more than a hundred orphaned and abandoned children (the real highlight). Oh, the faces—so beautiful! It is hard to believe the children who we fell in love with are orphaned or abandoned. Some will be adopted, some permanently placed in local children's homes or orphanages, but the majority of children orphaned and abandoned

globally will never be freed for adoption and will be stuck in this limbo-
land childhood where they will not experience the reality of a permanent
family.

I'm also trying desperately to wrap my mind around the thought that
while we saw somewhere around 150 children, this is a drop in the bucket
of the nearly half million children currently orphaned or abandoned in
Haiti, and the more than 153 million orphaned and abandoned children
around our globe.[1,2] The immensity is overwhelming! I'm more convinced
than ever that these children's only hope is the life-changing love of Jesus
and people willing to sacrifice comfort and "normalcy" to make a
difference one child at a time.

Oddly, as I sit here, tears running down my cheeks, I'm also very
grateful. Grateful that God has the answers that are well beyond my
comprehension. Grateful God adopted me into His family. Grateful that
God loves every orphaned and abandoned child far more than I will ever
understand. Grateful that I have parents who sacrificed and worked hard
to raise five children and stick with us no matter what. I'm grateful that
there are people already answering the cries of orphaned and abandoned
children (my heroes). And I'm grateful that you are willing to read my
rambling thoughts, ask the tough questions, and join me on this heart-
wrenching, soul-searching journey.

Comfortable is the word that best describes many of us fortunate enough
to live in a developed country. Growing up in North America, I enjoyed
a peaceful, safe, and idyllic childhood with all the benefits of middle-
class living. Sure, in my lifetime there have been political, economic,
and certainly personal challenges, but with a few notable exceptions, I
have experienced comfort, freedom, stability, safety, affluence, opportunities, and blessings.

I live in a comfortable, suburban home my builder-husband built for us. We have two nice cars, we have unlimited sparkling-clean water from multiple faucets, and we have never been without access to nutritious, fresh food. Electricity flows freely to our house, and except for the occasional storm, the power has never been out for more than a few hours. Because of the general affluence of my country, I have access to education, employment, good roads, police protection, and garbage pickup right at the end of my driveway. And, although some of my fellow countrymen have experienced more difficulties than I, in general life in a developed country is *comfortable*.

So what's the problem? When we are surrounded by everyday comfort and convenience it is easy to overlook the fact that just a short distance away there are people starving, impoverished, distraught, and hopeless. To make matters worse (if that is even possible), at the core of this human tragedy innocent children bear the brunt of the devastation as they watch their parents succumb to disease, starvation, natural disaster, and human evils. These children are left orphaned, alone, and utterly hopeless. This crisis is seen all over the globe, but the most tragic situations are found in the least developed countries. The bottom line is that globally more than 153 million children—a staggering number—are considered orphaned, abandoned, and vulnerable.[3] This crisis is not new; in fact it has been with us for all the ages and, in spite of our technology and upward mobilization, has now reached epic proportions.

I first became aware of the orphan problem years ago when traveling to Siberia, South Africa, and Jamaica. However, I didn't grasp the global significance at that time. Visiting a Mexican orphanage opened my eyes a little more, as I saw the faces and held the hands of orphaned, abandoned, and at-risk children. More recently, I've been inspired by several compassionate people encouraging me to take the time to really understand the passion God has for orphaned children. Through deeper awareness and study, my passion to advocate for orphaned children who cannot speak for themselves has grown and now burns brightly. I have been convicted that if others knew the gravity of what is at stake with these precious children, they would become advocates for orphaned children as well.

Researching this book has been a process of discovery, drawing me into the heartbreaking reality of the global orphan crisis. I have seen the result of poverty, neglect, and evil in the little faces of those who endure the worst humankind has to offer. But in the midst of the tragedy, God has brought glimmers of hope through the outpouring of compassionate, idealistic people who are not willing to accept convention, but rather choose to create around them the world that should be. These amazing people are the hope and promise that will continue to bring solutions to the crisis and inspire many more to become involved as well. It is my prayer that you, too, will see a glimpse of God's heart and respond to the cries of orphaned children.

The Global Orphan Crisis is designed to help you and those around you to enter this journey of response. In Part 1, we will explore the orphan crisis and discuss the ramifications geographic location has on the predicaments of at-risk children. We will also look at the contributing factors and key risks inherent to a child who has become orphaned. In Part 2 we will take an in-depth look at how we as Christ-followers, by our willingness and service, can participate in bringing God's Kingdom to earth. In addition, by studying forty-four passages in the Bible that have to do with orphaned and fatherless children, we will uncover God's orphan-care blueprint. Finally, we will explore practical suggestions that you, your family, your local church, and other organizations can use to be part of the global orphan solution.

I am so glad that you are willing to join me on this challenging journey. It is my hope that this book will open your eyes and compel you to action. The need is overwhelming. In a small or a great way, if you are willing, you can be part of the solution. It won't be easy or without pain and sacrifice. It is a decision that will change your life, for the rest of your life. It is a journey well worth the effort in countless blessings along the way both now and for all eternity. I invite you to dive into the rest of the book. Together, with God's strength, we can make a difference in the life of an orphaned child.

Part 1

Understanding the Global Orphan Crisis

This smiling, orphaned boy in Haiti has AIDS. Through receiving medicine, care, and love in a small residential, home-style setting, he has hope for a happy childhood and the promise of vocational training to help him become self-supporting. *Diane Lynn Elliot, photographer © Diane Lynn Elliot*

1

The Orphan Crisis: A Cause Bigger Than Ourselves

A father to the fatherless,
a defender of widows,
is God in his holy dwelling.
Psalm 68:5

Globally, more than 153 million children have lost one or both parents and are, by definition, considered orphaned.[1] Added to that number are millions more street and trafficked children with no parental influence in their lives, easily making the estimated number of orphaned and abandoned children well into the hundreds of millions. Orphan's Hope ministry paints a powerful picture:

> It is hard to grasp such large numbers, so picture being on a very long road trip. If you had these orphans hold hands in a line, you would see more than 1,700 orphans per mile. If you were to follow that line of Orphans holding hands, driving 60 mph, you could drive 24 hours a day seeing 1,700 orphans every mile, hour after hour, day after day without stopping for over two months.[2]

Our lives are busy. We have obligations. We have to work. We need to play. It takes so much time to manage all the activities and "things" in our lives; time just seems to slip away. The 153 million orphaned children are somewhere out of view. Except for the occasional late-night, fund-raising infomercial that invades our home with pictures of emaciated children with distended bellies, orphaned children seem somehow remote, in countries we will never visit. We don't see them. We don't hear their cries.

How do we see orphaned children through the eyes of our Heavenly Father?

Sometimes it can be hard to imagine the hardships that go on around the world. We sit in our comfortable homes, with pantries full of necessities, and it seems strange that most of the world doesn't have a pantry, let alone food to fill it. However, for millions of children in Africa this is their reality. Hunger is a part of their daily lives. Then add the fact that many of these children are also orphaned, either by death or abandonment . . . it's almost more than we can bear. It's hard to go there mentally and we protect our hearts by pretending it doesn't exist. But it does. Children are suffering.[3]

We, as Christians, are called to be more than just observers in this global crisis. We are the body of Christ, called to care for the orphaned children in our world. We are called to be the voice for those who cannot speak for themselves. We are to rescue orphaned children and be willing to jump into the muck and mire to help lift these treasured ones out of hopelessness. Not everyone can sell all their belongings and move to Bangladesh to serve orphaned children (although some will be called to do so). But God *is* calling each of us to help orphaned children in their distress.

Response requires commitment and sacrifice. It requires active participation. Exploring the global orphan crisis will touch your heart and cause you to want to do something—anything—to make the life of an orphaned child a little easier and to give him or her the opportunity to see Christ through the acts of kindness and love.

All of Me

When I started writing this book and talking about how to help orphaned children, a friend jumped to a speedy conclusion and said to me, "So you are going to tell me that you want my money, right?" as if that alone would solve the orphan crisis. I didn't think quickly enough in the moment to reply with anything notable, but after praying about it, I thought that perhaps God might have responded with something like this:

I don't want your money—the orphaned children want your heart!

I want you to see the face of the six-year-old boy who lost both his parents to AIDS and lives all alone in the bush of Uganda. I want you to feel the pain of a nine-year-old orphaned girl who is unable to escape from her captor and is forced to have sex with faceless "johns" multiple times each day. I want you to be heartbroken when you hear the sobs of the lonely, disabled girl as she cries herself to sleep night after night because she knows that no one will ever "pick" her. I want you to feel the gripping fear of the young man aging out of a government-run orphanage as he realizes that once he walks out the door he has no earthly possessions, no home, no job skills, and no one in this world to turn to.

When your heart breaks, like my heart breaks, when your eyes are opened to the things you don't want to see, when you feel my children's pain and it becomes unbearable, then—and only then—can I use you to change the life of an orphaned child. No, I don't want your money—I want your heart!

Defining the Orphaned Child

The term *orphan* can be quite confusing. In the past, *orphan* described a child who had lost both parents. The AIDS crisis changed that. More than a decade ago, the World Health Organization and the United Nations determined that, due to the AIDS epidemic, when a child loses one parent to the disease (leaving the child as a "single" orphan), it is only a matter of time before the surviving parent becomes sick and could succumb to the disease as well, resulting in the child becoming a "double" orphan.

The words *fatherless* or *motherless* describe the child who has lost one parent. Particularly in developing countries, if a child loses one parent, the life of that child can be significantly altered, putting the child at considerable risk. If the father dies, often the mother and children lose rights to ownership of land and other possessions. Conversely, if the mother dies, the father who has to work to provide for the family isn't able also to care for the children, so there is a significant caregiver void. Being a single parent in any culture is difficult, but being a single parent in a least developed country often brings dire consequences.

The term *orphan* is common in much of the world but feels awkward and strange in a developed country. In a suburban setting you would probably not call a child an "orphan" if a child's father dies but the child still has a mom. What about a single mom or dad? By global definition, a child of a single, divorced mom is technically considered an *orphan*. A single mom in a developed country might be offended at the thought; it doesn't exactly hit the descriptive nail on the head. But in a least developed country, where a single mom experiences severe economic hardships, designating her children as *orphans* might be very appropriate. Such is the blanket nature of definitions: They fit well in some situations and not so well in others. In any case, the situation surrounding the orphaned child will look very different in a developed country versus a least developed country, which we will look at in the pages ahead.

For ease of use, we will use the words *orphaned child* when we are talking about a child who is left orphaned, fatherless, motherless, or abandoned. I tend not to say that a child is an orphan, as I really dislike that label. I prefer to say, "a child is orphaned." It is a slight difference, but I want the term to describe the child, not to become the child. Being orphaned is a state of circumstances, but it doesn't define who the child is.

Unique Challenges for Orphaned Children

Numerous complicated issues result from a child losing one or both parents, which might include: a lack of protection, neglect, abuse, mental health issues, lack of education or resources, poverty, higher rate of suicide, and increased susceptibility to disease. In the best circumstances, relatives step in to care for the orphaned child. Some children find shelter in an orphanage or foster home. Worst case, they are abandoned, left to fend for themselves or die trying.

In many developed countries, except for a small contingent of private and Christian child welfare organizations, we have largely depended on the government to care for our country's vulnerable children. As helpful as this is in developed societies, systems are often flawed and can cause more complications for children who are already in a vulnerable state. Part of the problem of depending on government systems is that it gives us the false assumption that we are absolved from responsibility. This could not be further from the truth. As human beings, and specifically as Christians, we have a responsibility to be part of the global orphan solution, and governmental policies are no substitute for our wholehearted involvement.

The global orphan crisis is so enormous that we need an "all hands on deck" approach to orphan care. Globally, government organizations, nongovernment organizations (NGOs), and various religious groups are engaged in the orphan crisis. Hundreds of thousands of benevolent people and organizations are mobilized, fighting on the front lines in many capacities. Within the global Christian community, thousands of organizations are already engaged. Through their faithful and visionary leadership, their numbers are growing and more churches and individuals within the body of Christ have started to respond. In total, what these organizations are doing is admirable and inspiring, but it's not enough. More needs to be done to solve the crisis. Millions and millions of children are still in desperate need.

Christ-Centered Worldview

To understand the philosophy I base my beliefs on, you need to know that I am a follower of Jesus Christ. I came to know Jesus at a very young age and have spent my life as a devoted follower. I have not built my spiritual beliefs around a "religion," but rather have a personal relationship with God that has become the foundation of my worldview. God created the universe with precision and intentionality, with nothing random in His design. In a God-centered worldview, every person has infinite value. God uniquely created every individual, throughout all of history, and for the rest of time, and He values each person. God, the Creator of all things, has a purpose for each and every human being.

Those with a Christ-centered worldview also subscribe to the idea that the sins of humankind created a great divide between humanity and God. Because of our Creator's love and compassion for us, God sent His Son, Jesus, to stand in our place to pay for our sins and die on our behalf. We have been given the choice to choose God's forgiveness or to choose our own way. That choice determines our values and beliefs in this age and our future in the age to come.

A person who holds to a Christ-centered worldview believes the Bible is a unique book, inspired by God and relevant for all of life.

Because of God's Word, we have everything we need to live a life that is honoring to Him and to be a blessing to others. When a person who holds to a God-centered worldview struggles to understand a complicated issue, the God-inspired Bible provides clarity and direction.

The Bible is an instruction book for everyday life but in specific areas as well. In the Bible, more than two thousand general verses deal with compassion and justice. Forty-four verses specifically use the words *orphan* or *fatherless*, giving us instruction and clarity in our role with the orphan crisis. Not every verse addresses how to care for orphaned children, but most do. Through my study, I realized that all people with a God-centered worldview, not just those who are "interested," have a responsibility to look after orphaned children. I am more convinced than ever that we live in a time when the orphan crisis is truly a "crisis," and by the very definition of the word, we are at a "critical stage or turning point" compelling us all to take action.

We all know that evil is pervasive in our world. Unfortunately, we will have to look evil right in the face, because it is evil that exploits orphaned children. That doesn't mean that the evildoers have no value. They need God, just as we all do. However, if they choose evil and harm innocent children, they must be stopped. Throughout this book we will look at what we can do for orphaned children and recognize the tremendous evil that threatens to harm them. Though the odds are against us, this battle for the lives of orphaned children cannot be lost.

There are, of course, those who do *not* adhere to a God-centered worldview; perhaps you are one of them. The call to action in this book is written for all people, and I invite you also to be a part of the orphan solution. Sometimes I will address those who hold to the same worldview as I, times when I call Christ-followers to action. It is my hope that you will not throw out the intentionality and significance of this book just because we differ in our worldviews. This cause is bigger than any single person, community, country, or religion. Thank you for respecting my choice to write from my perspective.

You Have a Role in the Global Orphan Solution

Are you feeling overwhelmed by the crisis? Let me assure you that we are just one part of the overall solution. The big picture is God's.

We are the willing vessels that can be used by God to be one piece of a much larger puzzle. We have different roles. Some will adopt. Some will foster. Some will be in a ministry on the front lines. Others will be in the background supporting those on the front lines. Regardless of the role you play in the big picture, you can significantly support an or-phaned child. No one role is more significant than another. Every role, regardless of visibility, is as important as another.

In our culture we tend to have a "rock-star" mentality and view those in the up-front roles as more important than those in the support roles. That is certainly not God's view as evidenced in the Bible. I had a wonderful moment of clarity on this topic some years ago.

In the late '90s I was working as the director of operations in a student ministry at Willow Creek Community Church. It was a large ministry of about seven hundred students and more than a hundred volunteers. My role was to support the ministry's infrastructure in planning activi-ties, events, fund-raising, etc. Ironically, if I was doing my job well, I would make it look so easy that no one would know I was doing my job.

In one moment of blazing clarity I realized the importance of the team concept and my role within it. It was during a large event one evening and the auditorium was filled with hundreds of people. I stood at the back of the auditorium and marveled at the presentation going on. Dozens of people had developed the program, shot the video, prac-ticed the worship music, coordinated the message, practiced the pres-entation, and organized every detail from beginning to end. In the big picture, my role in this event would never be noticed by anyone in the auditorium, but without my part the event would have been chaotic. I felt complete fulfillment knowing that my part was a small part of the big picture, though I never stepped on the stage.

While few of us will ever step on "stage" to declare the importance of caring for orphaned children, your role, large or small, is part of God's plan. I encourage you to step out in faith and fulfill the role God has for you in the life of an orphaned child.

Where Do We Start?

It's very simple: We all need to do our part. Not too many years ago we were all overwhelmed with the idea of recycling. Now it is second nature. If I throw a plastic bottle in the garbage, I feel guilty. Addressing the global orphan crisis is a matter of retraining ourselves to make small changes that eventually have large consequences.

Every person can make a positive contribution toward improving the life of an orphaned child by taking these four critical steps:

1. Understand the global orphan crisis (you're reading this book, so you are on your way),

2. Know God's heart, and embrace His instructions for orphan care,

3. Evaluate your strengths, talents, and resources to be part of the bigger plan,

4. Create an action plan, implement the plan, and stay open to God's leading.

As we unpack these steps, you will find that *you* are uniquely gifted to participate in alleviating the suffering of orphaned, abandoned, and at-risk children. Your involvement won't look like someone else's involvement. Whether you contribute by creating jobs for orphaned teens or stick postage stamps on fund-raising letters, each and every contribution is important and will serve to change the life of an orphaned child. This side of heaven it is difficult to grasp the importance of our roles in this venture. I really hope you will open your heart and mind and actively ask God to make His will clear to you. You might be thinking you have some skills and experience that would be a perfect fit, and that is wonderful.

You might also be thinking you have no idea how to help or what you might do. Believe me, I've been on both sides of that equation! As skilled and prepared as I am in some areas of my career and life, I feel inadequate to guide you on this global orphan journey. While my story is still evolving, what I have found so far is summed up in this truth: "God doesn't always call the equipped; He equips the called." God has given me a passion and a heart for children, especially those who are most vulnerable. I'm excited to see where God takes me on this journey, and I hope you are open to joining me on this exciting adventure as well.

You also have the opportunity to bring others along with you in your journey. My husband, David, has a real soft spot for ministries that offer donation matching programs. He enjoys the benefit of doubling his investment for a good cause. The same can be true for you. You can double, triple, and significantly multiply your efforts by bringing other individuals, churches, and organizations along with you. You have the opportunity not only to change one child's life, but to change a multitude of lives. *The Global Orphan Crisis* is designed as a guide for your personal journey or as a small group study so that you can learn together and encourage one another.

Remember as we continue to learn about the global orphan crisis, the overarching point is simple: Just do something!

QUESTIONS TO PONDER

1. What has been your global or local experience with orphaned, abandoned, and at-risk children?

2. When you think of an orphaned child, what do you picture in your mind? What is the setting? What does the child look like? What is the child's situation?

3. How do you think an orphaned child's life looks different in a developed country from how it looks in a least developed country?

4. What comes to mind when you think of 153 million children being orphaned, abandoned, and at-risk?

5. What information in this chapter especially caught your attention?

ACTION POINT: SEE THE FACES

Many orphanage websites contain listings of children waiting for adoptive parents. Most of those children will go through their whole childhood waiting. Although I can't personally adopt these precious children, something that I *can* do will impact their lives significantly and that is to pray. Out of the hundreds of children whose profiles I viewed, I chose two to pray for. Ivan is an eleven-year-old boy with haunting eyes. Ana is a fourteen-year-old girl who has a sweet smile. Both are from Russia and look just like kids I would see in my neighborhood.

You, too, can do an Internet search for child sponsorships, adoptable children, kids in foster care, or children in orphanages. Pick a country of interest. Then explore the sites to see the children who are currently adoptable or who need sponsorship in that country. Look at the faces of the children, read their stories, and allow God to speak to your heart through their eyes. Then choose one or two children and print out their pictures and stories. Put their photos in a place of prominence by your computer or in your office, and commit to pray for them every time you see their faces.

Note: If you are in a small group study, bring your photos with you to your next discussion so you can share your children-in-prayer with the group. Tell everyone why you chose the particular children you did.

Debbie Ruzga was glad to be the shoulder little Rosamunde could lean on. Rosamunde, like so many other older children, needs a family. Somewhere, there's a family praying for a child, maybe even one named Rosamunde. *Diane Lynn Elliot, photographer © Diane Lynn Elliot*

2

On Becoming an Orphan: Contributing Factors

For the Lord your God is God of gods and Lord
of lords, the great God, mighty and awesome,
who shows no partiality and accepts no bribes.
He defends the cause of the fatherless and
the widow, and loves the foreigner residing
among you, giving him food and clothing.

Deuteronomy 10:17–18

She was stunned. The news of her parents' death shot through her body like a numbing current. She just sat there, not knowing what to do or how to respond. Tears welled up in her eyes and spilled out uncontrollably. Her foggy mind played tricks on her: *It can't be true. I just saw them a few hours ago. How could this have happened?* She buried her face in her hands. Moments felt like hours.

A flurry of people, some she didn't even know, put a few of her things in a backpack and whisked her into a car and away to an unfamiliar part of the city. She was old enough to understand but young enough not to have any control over her fate. Her heart hurt so badly that she didn't care what happened anymore.

The car pulled up in front of an old block building with wide concrete stairs going up to an oversized wooden door. Her uncle stepped out of the car and opened her door. He handed her a backpack and greeted a woman that met them at the bottom of the stairs. He said, "Go with this nice lady. Don't be afraid—she will take care of you now. You know I'd like to keep you, but I'm out of work and can't even afford my own children right now. This will be best. You'll be fine. I'll come and visit when things settle down." The car door slammed, and she watched in disbelief as her uncle drove away.

The hallway sounded hollow and echoed with every step. She saw no pictures and no furniture. Windows were slightly opened along the left, and a long blank wall with wooden doors was on the right. Through the open windows she heard the distant sound of children playing outside but the noise seemed out of place. She entered a large room with a dozen or more beds and saw a bed off on its own in the far corner of the room with a stuffed animal on it. The lady pointed to the bed and said, "This is where you will be sleeping. Dinner is in an hour, so you have time to settle in. The girls will be coming in shortly. Introduce yourself when they come in. Don't bother crying. It doesn't do any good anyway. You'll be fine. Trust me; I've seen this before. You'll get over it." The lady walked out, and the door slammed loudly, echoing through the open room. She was alone. Sitting on the bed, the young girl opened her backpack. Lying right on the top was a picture of her and her parents taken the year before in their garden. She held the picture in her arms, drawing it close to her heart, stunned at the events of the day. She lay down on her bed, buried her face in the musty-smelling pillow, and sobbed. The new normal had begun.

It's Complicated

This story is fictitious, but versions of it have been played out tens of thousands of times for generations. And while this story could be one out of the early 1900s, scenes like this still occur in various parts of the world today.

A child becomes an orphan primarily in one of three ways: death, displacement, and abandonment. The death of one or both parents through any circumstance is final and not reversible. Displacement it is not a choice of the parent or parents but rather an unplanned separation due to war, natural disaster, or other situation. Abandonment or relinquishment usually happens out of desperation, and in some cases with good intention, but with potentially disastrous results.

In cases of displacement and abandonment, a family may potentially be reunited in the future. In one situation, in a least developed country, a mother had lost her husband and sometime later remarried. Her new husband didn't like the idea of having a child from the woman's former husband and forced her to sell her daughter. The mother was devastated but felt that she had no other option. She sold her daughter as a servant to a family with economic means. A few years later the daughter was rescued from her domestic servitude and returned to the mother. The mother, after lamenting over the lost years with her daughter, stood up to her husband, who ended up leaving. The decision was a difficult one with many implications, the least of which was economic, but mother and daughter were reunited.

In our ever-changing world the way that a child loses one or both parents is often complicated. More than likely it is multiple intertwining issues rather than just one catastrophic event. Geography plays a significant role, often determining the type of risks a family faces. Included within the geography issue are also cultural and political issues.

A country's global status is another key component to understanding the risks associated with various countries. Countries can be classified in many ways, but economics is not necessarily the most important factor, as was once assumed. Sweeping generalizations, such as the term *third world country*, are no longer specific enough, nor do they define where the country is in relation to other countries. The most accurate country measurements to serve our discussion is the human capital approach to country ranking called the Human Development Index.

HDI was developed by an economist in 1990 and adopted for use by the United Nations and serves to "shift the focus of development economics from national income accounting to people centered policies."[1]

"HDI is a comparative measure of life expectancy, literacy, education and standards of living for countries worldwide. It is a standard means of measuring well-being, especially child welfare. It is used to distinguish whether the country is a developed, a developing, or an underdeveloped country, and it is also used to measure the impact of economic policies on quality of life."[2] This method assigns a number to each country from .1 (lowest HDI) to .9 (highest) and uses three classifications: developed, developing (or emerging), and under-developed (or under resourced). For example, the country with the highest HDI in 2011 was Norway at .943. The country with the lowest HDI was the Congo at .286.[3] In later chapters we will talk in more detail about the HDI and its impact on orphaned children around the globe as well as evaluate the strategies that are most effective in various areas.

These next few chapters might be difficult to read, yet they also provide the foundational building blocks for future opportunities. So hang in there with me, as we discover the gripping realities of how children become orphaned, starting with the death of a parent.

Orphaned by the Death of a Parent or Parents

The death of a parent is a traumatic event for a person at any age, but especially for a child. Children depend on their parents on a daily basis, and their absence changes everything. We all know many of the circumstances that take parents from their children, such as cancer, heart disease, and accidents. However, in a developed country we might not see important issues that are pervasive in other parts of the world.

Poverty, Hunger, and Starvation

Today 25,000 people will die of starvation—that is one person every 3.5 seconds.[4] Approximately seven billion people live in our world today. Of those people, one in seven (13.1 percent) are considered hungry.[5] Poverty is the major cause of hunger. As we start peeling back the causes of the global orphan crisis, poverty will come up repeatedly. Here is the irony about starvation in our world: Sources indicate that we have enough food in our world to satisfy everyone's hunger. Unfortunately, our global resources are not evenly distributed or accessible, so we will continue to face enormous poverty and deaths due to starvation.

HIV/AIDS

By the end of 2009, 30.8 million adults and 2.5 million children had HIV/AIDS.[6] That same year 2.9 million people became infected with HIV. Of that number, 270,000 children were infected, largely due to mother-child transmission during the pregnancy, labor, and delivery. Although there are drugs available to minimize the dangers of mother to child transmission, drugs are often not available where most desperately needed.

There were 1.8 million deaths from AIDS-related causes in 2009, which was slightly down from 2004 due to antiretroviral drug therapy availability. In total, by the end of 2009 the disease resulted in 16.6 million AIDS orphans, children under the age of eighteen.[7]

Another stunning statistic is that 68 percent of all infected people live in sub-Saharan Africa making that the most concentrated HIV/AIDS population in the world. Second, but not even close, is east, south, and southeast Asia at 12 percent of HIV/AIDS infected people.[8] The numbers are staggering, and even with technology, drug therapy, and education, the numbers are likely to continue rising especially in sub-Saharan Africa. Coupled with other critical issues such as poverty, starvation, and conflict, Africa is long on problems and short on solutions.

Charles lost his father to AIDS in 2005, and a year later, he lost his mother. At just 13 years old, Charles was left to care for his four younger brothers.

With nobody to care for them, Charles and his brothers were forced to beg for food from neighbors to survive and often spent two or three days without eating anything. The boys struggled to meet their basic needs of food, health, and medicine.

Charles and his brothers eventually received some governmental assistance to grow manioc and beans, but this assistance was not enough to guarantee the children would not go hungry or be malnourished. Thanks to the support of an organization operating in the community, Charles and his brothers received medical and nutritional support, an opportunity to go to school, and assistance with income-generating activities.[9]

Death in Childbirth

Maternal death, also called obstetrical death, is the death of a woman during or shortly after pregnancy. The leading causes of maternal death are severe bleeding after childbirth, infections, hypertensive disorders, and unsafe abortion.[10] Less than 1 percent of the deaths occur in developed countries and the majority of deaths occur in least developed countries in Africa, Southeast Asia, several countries in South America, and a few countries in the Middle East. The highest incidence of maternal death is in Sierra Leone closely followed by Afghanistan. The lowest maternal death rates are found in Ireland followed by Austria.[11]

Around the world, unplanned pregnancy is a difficult challenge for man women, especially those struggling economically. Abortion has been considered a solution, and many countries have made abortion legal. However convenient it seems, the act of taking a child's life at any stage of development pricks at the very heart of God and His followers. Apart from the moral implications, many women die because of unsafe practices and resulting complications.

"Unintended pregnancy is a major cause of maternal deaths. Worldwide, unintended pregnancy resulted in almost 700,000 maternal deaths from 1995–2000 (approximately one-fifth of the maternal deaths during that period). The majority (64%) resulted from complications from unsafe or unsanitary abortion."[12] Since 1990 maternal deaths have decreased by about one third.[13] Poverty, lack of access to skilled medical care, and general poor nutrition and health contribute to the high death rate.

In many cases when a mother does not survive pregnancy, caring for the child or children falls to the father and extended family. The families struggle to recover from the strain, and some families don't have the resources to make the transition. I have heard countless stories of heartbroken fathers taking their children to orphanages to find a better home for the children than what they can provide.

Orphaned by Displacement

Displacement is a term used to describe having to leave one's home, and sometimes even one's nation. While there are other reasons (such as war) for displacement, most displacement occurs because of natural disasters.

Displaced by Natural Disasters

Our world is full of natural disasters, and 2010 was a very active year, leaving 260,000 fatalities and millions of people displaced.[14] The severity of the disaster itself, as well as the fallout and recovery, is often determined by the condition of the country's infrastructure prior to the disaster. Haiti, for example, was so broken before the earthquake on January 12, 2010, that the devastation affected more people than it would have had the earthquake struck a more developed country with stricter building codes. The earthquake struck around 5 p.m. when it was still light, and many people were still outside rather than in their homes. Had the earthquake happened in the middle of the night, the nation's death toll could have been substantially higher. Ironically, the poorest people living in tin shacks experienced fewer injuries and less general damage than their economically advantaged neighbors with homes made of poor-quality brick and mortar, which collapsed in the quake.

One Haitian boy was ten years old when the earthquake hit. In all the devastation and confusion he found his father's body but was never able to find his mother or any other living relative. A few days after the quake he decided to try to find an orphanage his mother had spoken about that was a few hours' bus ride from Port-au-Prince. With no money and nothing to his name, he convinced a bus driver to take him to the orphanage. For days he watched the orphanage from across the street, making sure they were treating children well and not beating or abusing them. Eventually he mustered the courage to approach one of the staff and tell about his situation. He was taken in, fed, and given a bed. Eventually he was able to attend school. Although life will never be how it was before the earthquake, this brave boy now has a new home and family.

All around the world natural disasters rocked our planet that year. The volcano Mount Merapi erupted in October of 2010, and the Indonesian government was able to successfully evacuate 35,000 people, although 386 died from respiratory complications due to the gas and ash clouds. Pakistan experienced the worst flooding that country has ever seen with almost 2,000 people killed and 20 million people affected. South China had torrential rains and flooding, and Yushu, Qinghai, China, was shaken by an earthquake with a 6.9 magnitude. Thousands of people in China died, and many others were displaced and impacted.[15]

The summer of 2010 brought an unusual heat wave to Russia that caused forest fires resulting in 15,000 deaths. In addition, the drought and deadly fires "displaced thousands more people."[16] Natural disasters and the chaos that accompanies them will continue to affect children by taking the lives of parents, caregivers, and family members. First responders are critical for rescue and recovery, but it is the ongoing relief and eventual development are critical for helping displaced people to recover.

Displaced by War and Violence

War and violence are an all-too-familiar part of our world, and where there is conflict, there are orphaned children. Mexico, a country we don't often think of as being at war, is currently embroiled in a drug war that affects thousands of children every year. "In 2009 alone, 10,000 children were orphaned due to the Mexican drug war in the U.S border city of Ciudad Juárez. The city has the distinction of being the most violent in Mexico . . . 'We live in a state of war and children are left to drift.' Of the 90 children housed at the orphanage, [in Ciudad Juárez] 63 have lost their parents to organized crime."[17]

Mexico's Drug Orphans

Marisol was a pretty seventeen-year-old when a big-league local drug lord seduced her and took her as a permanent mistress. He kept her shut up in one of his houses and took to beating her before he was killed by a hired gun from a rival gang. She married a lower-level trafficker and they had a baby girl. But since he was murdered she sits at home, depressed and bloated from drinking all day. To stop her infant daughter from screaming, she bottle-feeds her with beer.[18]

Countries experiencing fallout from war and violence usually have a low State Fragility Index. A State Fragility Index (SF) is a score assigned to a nation, rating its government's effectiveness and legitimacy based on performance in "security, governance, economics, and social development."[19] The State Fragility Index of 2010 establishes that the majority of African nations are considered fragile, followed by several Asian countries and a few others scattered around the globe. In fact, International Rescue Committee (IRC) estimates that there are 150,000 war orphans in Africa, 60,000 of them from Sierra Leone.[20]

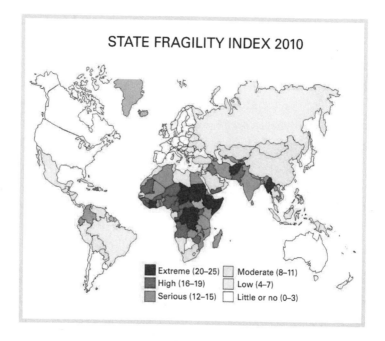

STATE FRAGILITY INDEX 2010

Extreme (20–25)　Moderate (8–11)
High (16–19)　Low (4–7)
Serious (12–15)　Little or no (0–3)

Conflict orphans will continue to be an issue, especially in Africa, Asia, and parts of the Middle East. Although there isn't one statistic that gives us the total number of orphaned children due to war, conflict, and violence, the number is likely significant.

Displaced Due to Gender Inequity

I have heard it said that the most dangerous three words in our world today are *It's a girl!* In much of the world, it is safer to be a boy child than a girl child. Gender inequity is a huge global issue when it comes to a child's well-being, care, and ultimate survival. Because many cultures value boys more than girls, boys have a greater statistical chance for survival during their earliest years. As children age, it is more likely that an adolescent girl will be given as a child bride and married off much earlier than a boy. The possibility of pregnancy—and complications due to the pregnancy, as well as the risk of unsanitary abortions—is high. "Girls are the world's most squandered gift. They are precious human beings with enormous potential, but across the world, they are generally the last to have their basic needs met and the first to have their basic rights denied."[21]

Gender inequity has been a fact for most of the world's history, although it didn't start out that way. Adam and Eve were created with different roles but equal in value in God's eyes. However, sin has distorted the relationships of all people, and it has become the norm for stronger members to dominate weaker members of a society.

The tide for women started to turn in a positive direction in the late nineteenth century with the rise of the movement for women's suffrage. Today many developed countries experience relative gender equality. Unfortunately the same is not true in many emerging or least developed countries where equality is anything but equal.

We as Christ-followers are aware of the unbiased love God has for all people, so we should be leading the parade to value and protect the rights of all people. I regularly encounter organizations, both secular and religious, that point to the education and development of women as the answer for many global ills.

Women, from young girls to the elderly, need to know they are valued and that they are not this world's afterthought. It is when we lift women up and honor women and girls for being who God created them to be that we will see many of our social ills start to recede. And I'm not talking about women's "liberation." I'm talking about general respect and value for all persons. Females are repressed and disadvantaged in so many countries that there has to be a more balanced approach. The world knows it and is pursuing a better balance with fervor. That's not to say that the Church should follow the world. It is to say, however, that *all* humans are created in God's image, and with a sense of justice and compassion we should be the example and not just idle bystanders.

So what does this have to do with little girls in our world today? When people do not have a God-centered view of the value of life, those deemed less important become disposable!

China's one-child law is a case in point. Boys are more highly valued in the Chinese culture, so if a family can only have one child, most prefer to have a boy, regardless of the consequences. Through the ultrasonic technology of prenatal sex selection, women may choose to abort a baby girl or bring the pregnancy to term but then abandon the baby girl so that they can have another child—this time, they hope, a boy.[22]

Across the globe, boys are given more privilege, more attention, and a better education than their female counterparts. In some cultures girls are not allowed to attend school after they start menstruating unless the school has proper toilet facilities, which many schools in underdeveloped countries cannot afford. Girls are also given more responsibility in the homes and are required to take part in the domestic workload in addition to their education, or in place of it.[23]

The ultimate gender inequity, which is all too common in the Hindu religion, especially in some areas of India, is female infanticide. A 1995 study of 1,250 mostly Hindu families in the Indian state of Tamil Nadu indicates that 249 families (20 percent) agreed that they had disposed of an unwanted girl child (which includes both abortion and infant murder).[24] This is a brutal picture of the devaluation of human beings, and it doesn't stop there!

Where Killing Baby Girls Is "No Big Sin"

Lakshmi already had one daughter, so when she gave birth to a second girl, she killed her. For three days of her second child's short life, Lakshmi admits, she refused to nurse her. To silence the infant's famished cries, the impoverished village woman squeezed the milky sap from an oleander shrub, mixed it with castor oil, and forced the poisonous potion down the newborn's throat. The baby bled from the nose, then died soon afterward. Female neighbors buried her in a small hole near Lakshmi's square thatched hut of sunbaked mud. They sympathized with Lakshmi, and in the same circumstances, some would probably have done what she did. For despite the risk of execution by hanging and about sixteen months of a much-ballyhooed government scheme to assist families with daughters in some hamlets of Tamil Nadu, murdering girls is still sometimes believed to be a wiser course than raising them. "A daughter is always a liabilities. How can I bring up a second?" Lakshmi, 28, answered firmly when asked by a visitor how she could have taken her own child's life eight years ago. "Instead of her suffering the way I do, I thought it was better to get rid of her."[25]

Issues of gender inequality contribute significantly to the global orphan crisis and has to be taken seriously and addressed with intention. Global leaders are already recognizing the devastation caused by gender inequity and are developing goals and programs to solve the problems. But to make significant and lasting change, the Church needs to follow Jesus' example of valuing all people equally and rise to meet the challenges, too.

Orphaned by Abandonment

Children are sold or given away every day in our world. Families in severe poverty might feel they don't have enough resources to feed a child, so they give or sell the child to a wealthier family with hope that the wealthy household will at least feed the child. A parent or parents might give away a child because the child is sick or has a physical or mental disability the family is not equipped to handle. In some countries it is a badge of honor to have many children, even if parents choose not to parent. However, very seldom does selling a child make the child's or the parent's life better, and it usually makes it very much worse.

The practice of selling children into slavery, is, unfortunately, common in Haiti. Due to the general culture, extreme poverty, and Haiti's high unemployment rate (higher than 80 percent)[26] the practice of selling children has put between 150,000–500,000 children currently in bondage in domestic servitude (slavery) called "restavèks."[27] "The term *restavèk* comes from the French and Creole meaning "to stay with." Restavèk are generally children of poor rural families who are sent to stay with and work as unpaid domestic servants for less poor, urban families. Parents send a child away with the hope that in return for the child's labor, the host family will provide the child with food and shelter and send the child to school."[28] This practice has become part of the slave trade, and intermediary traders have filled the gap between parents and slave owners taking their cut along the way.

Children as young as five years old are forced to work twelve to fourteen hours a day in complete and unquestionable service to their masters. This not only includes physical labor but can also include sexual acts as well.[29] Generally the children are not treated as family but are seen as servants only and denied any rights for themselves and any personal property or education. It is common to beat restavèks if they do not perform the duties required. This practice is so ingrained in the culture that even pastors have restavèks, and one ministry gives seminars to pastors in Haiti to try to enlighten them as to God's response to the practice.[30]

Abandonment: Children Having Children

Unplanned pregnancy is common among young girls and especially so in underdeveloped countries. With a lack of education, early sexual activity, unprotected sex, and so many young women being raped or forced into the sex slave trade, young girls find themselves pregnant and often are not prepared to care for the baby. More than 15 million girls ages fifteen to nineteen give birth each year,[31] which doesn't account for the girls who aborted their babies before birth.

Young women who choose to care for their children often forfeit their own childhoods, forced to become caregivers well before they are mature enough to handle the role. Although in some countries a welfare system provides support, this, too, can be a crutch creating an unhealthy cycle of dependency. The young girl with family support has the best chance of success, but the path is nonetheless difficult. In 2003 there were 42 million abortions worldwide, with 35 million of those performed in developing or underdeveloped countries.[32] The Church is poised to engage strategically in the lives of teens who are pregnant, who choose to give birth then relinquish their children, and for those who make the brave choice to parent. In every case there are tremendous opportunities for the Church to walk alongside and support these young women. As we put our judgment and biases aside we can show the watching world that God is pro-LIFE, for a person's whole life, not just pro-birth (meaning only till a baby is born).

Abandonment: Parental Deficiencies and Mental Illness

Substantial parental deficiencies and mental illness come in many forms from mild but manageable to completely debilitating. Although parental deficiencies and mental illness are global issues, in emerging countries other, more consuming issues supersede these issues. In developed countries, however, the cultural norm is such that a person can hide slight mental illness and some deficiencies, but if substantial they stand out from the norm. In developed countries, for example, children who consistently miss school or who show up without a lunch and in dirty clothes are soon identified. School authorities have mandated responsibilities to address the well-being of their students and might proceed down an investigatory road that could result in child welfare workers becoming involved and eventually lead to the child being removed from the home.

> Deficient parents hurt their children more by omission than by commission. Frequently, chronic mental illness or a disabling physical illness contributes to parental inadequacy. Children tend to take on adult responsibilities from a young age in these families. Parental emotional needs tend to take precedence, and children are often asked to be their parents' caretakers. Children are robbed of their own childhood, and they learn to ignore their own needs and feelings. Because these children are simply unable to play an adult role and take care of their parents, they often feel inadequate and guilty. These feelings continue into adulthood.[33]

I heard a story of one woman with mental health issues having more than eight children, not any of whom stayed with her for more than a few years. Each child was eventually taken away from the mother because she didn't have the capacity to care for the child. Repeat unplanned pregnancies are more common than we would like to think and strikes at the heart of our moral and ethical consciences. While there are no easy answers or solutions, the reality is that hundreds of thousands of young girls have children every year and many of those precious babies end up in the care of a family member, neglected, abandoned, or worse.

With mental illness and with the topic of Drug and Alcohol abuse that we will talk about next, the parents can be functional at times and at other times be completely dysfunctional. Children who grow up in difficult environments learn early in life that their needs are not the priority and adapt as best they can. As the children grow older they become the caregivers of their parents and have to deal with shame, unpredictability, and constant disappointment. As one child describes it: "I was like a miniature adult. I cooked and cleaned and made sure my little brothers got off to school. My Mom was always depressed and stayed in bed—she was in the hospital a lot. I guess I never really was a kid. Now, I work hard to get *A*'s, take on lots of responsibility, put on this competent front. Inside I still feel really empty."[34]

Abandonment: Drug and Alcohol Abuse

Drug and alcohol abuse affects children and increases the risk of the children becoming orphaned. In fact, in the Ukraine, "only 10% of the orphaned children are due to the death of the parents. The rest are social orphans—due to alcoholism, abandonment, or imprisonment of parents."[35]

One missionary who has started several children's homes in Bolivia says that many of the children who come to them are due to the mother or father being alcohol and drug addicted. Since the parents are unable to care for the children, the children are left to fend for themselves or are left at an orphanage by a parent, relative, or by the government. The government has so many children who need temporary or permanent housing that any openings at children's homes are filled immediately. To complicate the issue, sometimes the government takes the children away from a substance-addicted parent but then tells the parent where the child is located, making it difficult for the caregivers to protect the child. In one devastating case in Africa, an angry father came to the orphanage and took the child by force. The father killed the child and then committed suicide. Both the child's and the father's bodies were found in the bush several days later.[36] Without parental rehabilitation, the child's safety is at risk and reunification is not optimal.

Abandonment: Child Abuse

Child abuse comes in many forms and is found in every corner of the world. Although it would be nice to say that in developed countries child abuse is not as pervasive as in other cultures, this has unfortunately not been found to be the case. In fact, one study found that "violent physical and harsh psychological discipline focused on children 2 to 14 was quite common across all the countries included [in the survey]. While overall rates of violent discipline are high (39 to 95 percent of children 2 to 14 are reported to receive violent discipline) they do not appear to be unusual compared to those found using similar methods in high-income countries."[37]

Another study included in a United Nation's report in 2006 reveals a "shocking picture of physical, sexual and psychological violence being perpetrated against children on a daily basis."[38] The article by the BBC News explains:

> The first UN study of global violence against children says such abuse is often socially approved or even legal. It concludes that violence against under-18s occurs in every country, every society and every social group . . . The study suggests that between 80–93% percent of children suffer physical punishment in their homes, although many of them do not speak of it due to stigma, shame and lack of faith in legal systems.[39]

For our purposes, child abuse is:

- The inappropriate or manipulative use of verbal, emotional, and physical force or control
- Any sexually exploitive or inappropriate physical contact
- Forcing a child to participate in or to even view abusive or sexually inappropriate behaviors

- Failure to act where there is imminent risk of serious harm
- Abandoning a child not capable of caring for or protecting himself or herself

Studies have shown that single-parent families have a higher incidence of child physical abuse than two-parent families. The Canadian Children's Rights Council states that the majority of physical child abuse is by the mother, who is usually the primary caregiver, and that "father-deprivation is a more reliable predictor of criminal activity than race, environment or poverty."[40]

Child abuse results in orphaned children in several ways, the most notably a child being taken away from the parents because of verified instances of child abuse in the home. In many developed countries, children can be taken from the home and placed in foster homes to protect the well-being of the child. With reunion being the goal in many cases, children might be returned to the parent or parents at some point depending on the parent's rehabilitation. In cases of severe child abuse, the caregivers might be charged and incarcerated. Reunification might or might not be possible depending on the potential danger to the child. If reunification is not an option, parental rights could be severed, potentially freeing a foster child for adoption.

Abandonment: Disabled Children

In many parts of the world, children who are "imperfect" are considered disposable. In some cultures, having a physical or mental disability is a death sentence. In emerging or least developed countries parents who have compassion for their children might not have the medical resources needed to care for a disabled child. Orphanages, hospitals, and mental institutions around the world are full of "emotionally" orphaned children who are abandoned by their parents; many of whom were put there, not to receive better care, but just to be put away out of sight. One organization states,

Disabled children are always at great risk of discrimination and are particularly vulnerable when there is a shortage of resources. An estimated 97 percent of disabled children in developing countries are denied even the most rudimentary rehabilitation services . . . Disabled children suffer more violence and abuse than other children—they are imprisoned in institutions, cupboards and sheds and, all too often, starved to death. Even in the wealthy and "enlightened" developed countries, the birth of a disabled child is almost invariably viewed as a "tragedy."[41]

In 1999 a Charter for a New Millennium was adopted in London stating: "During the last century in most countries, disabled children were often overlooked, excluded, hidden away or exiled to institutions. In the twenty-first century, we envision 'a world where equal opportunities for disabled people becomes a natural consequence of enlightened policies and legislation supporting full inclusion to and access to all parts of society.'"[42]

The root of the issue gets back to the same issue as gender equity, which is the perceived value of a human life. When any population is marginalized, it drags the entire culture down, and it is only a matter of time until another population in that culture suffers the same fate.

Abandonment: Escape from the Home

Children who have grown up in an abusive or neglectful home have many difficult issues to contend with on a daily basis. Sometimes when the child is old enough to take care of himself and can't see the point of staying, he runs away. This is the case in many situations where a child who lives on the street has parents but for many reasons feels that life is better on the street than with his parent or parents. As an emotional orphan, the plight of the child becomes surviving any way he can. Unfortunately, the dangers on the street are real and often final.

Abandonment: Separated by Rebellion

Sometimes a child's rebellion becomes an issue that drives the child out of the home. Although technically these children are not considered "orphaned," they can have the emotional feeling of being an orphaned child. Sometimes the separation comes by the choice of the child and other times by the choice of the parent, the end result is the same: a child on her own, before she is ready. The challenges of living without parental support can be more difficult than children ever imagined.

When a child rebels, most parents hope they will one day be restored to a right relationship with that child. Life for a prodigal child can be heartbreaking and difficult as well. Being the relational creatures we are, conflict is never easy. But hope always remains for these emotional orphans, especially when God is a part of the equation.

Abandonment: Incarceration

The United States has the highest number of incarcerated people in the world. More than 2.7 million children live with one parent, usually the father, in prison. One in every twenty-eight children in the United States has a parent in prison.[43]

> The chances of seeing a parent go to prison have never been greater, especially for poor black Americans, and new research is documenting the long-term harm to the children they leave behind. Recent studies indicate that having an incarcerated parent doubles the chance that a child will be at least temporarily homeless and measurably increases the likelihood of physically aggressive behavior, social isolation, depression and problems in school—all portending dimmer prospects in adulthood.[44]

Children with a parent in prison usually struggle more in school and have more difficulties growing up. In addition to parental loss, these children generally have to deal with feelings of anger, isolation, and resentment over the stigma of having a parent in prison. Children with a parent in prison are more likely to get involved in delinquent behaviors such as drug use, gangs, and criminal activities. Economically, a family with an incarceration suffers the loss of approximately 22 percent less income, thus decreasing the family's resources.[45]

"Federal data indicates that one eighth of all children in homes investigated by child welfare authorities have a parent who was recently arrested. A smaller but significant percentage of currently incarcerated parents report having a child in foster care."[46] Having a parent in prison and a child in foster care is called a "dual-system" family and "both child welfare and law enforcement leave an indelible mark on the parents and children."[47] Over time, reunion is sometimes possible, but depending on the age of the child, the child might not even recognize his or her parent once the parent is released from prison, which results in difficult adjustments and emotional issues. In some cases, the child might be placed with a relative who is given custody. Other times the child is placed in foster care, and occasionally the parent's rights are terminated and the child is freed for adoption. It is a very dynamic system with many people involved, and solutions are not always clear.

Where Compassion May Lead

As we have unfolded this chapter together, we've see the many ways a child can become orphaned—physically, emotionally, and socially. Many variations exist, but in every circumstance a child being separated from a parent is emotional and tragic.

In the next chapter we are going to dig a little deeper into the dangers children face when they become orphaned. The impact of losing a parent affects every area of a child's life, but that doesn't have to be the end of the story. With support, love, and positive action, an orphaned child can still move toward a happy and fulfilling life. It is up to those of us who are moved by compassion for these children to ignite our creativity and develop the strategies that will make a difference in the lives of orphaned children. Let's keep pressing forward to find solutions to one of our world's greatest ills, the global orphan crisis.

QUESTIONS TO PONDER

1. Before reading this chapter, what did you think was the most significant cause of children becoming orphans?

2. What surprising information did you discover in this chapter?

3. How might knowing this information help you as you are thinking of meeting the needs of orphaned children?

4. Giving away or selling a child seems like an unbelievable act to most of us. How do you think that a parent can justify this act? Do you consider this a cultural, economic, or biblical issue?

5. If you were talking to a friend about the plight of the orphaned child, what nugget from this chapter would you want to communicate?

ACTION POINT

Pick one of the topics we touched on in this chapter and do a little more research. For example, you might try to find out more about how poverty relates to a child becoming orphaned. Then, come up with some possible solutions or ideas that might help the children who have become orphaned because of the issue.

This little girl lives in the city dump of Phnom Penh, Cambodia—a dangerous, toxic wasteland. Children previously rescued from a similar dump brought these children sandwiches, gifts, and the Christmas story. *Brian Gray, photographer © Brian Gray*

3

The Dangers
Orphans Face

But you, O God, see the trouble of the afflicted;
you consider their grief and take it in hand.
The victim commits himself to you;
you are the helper of the fatherless.
Psalm 10:14

Brian grew up as the son of missionary parents working in Chad, Africa. I knew his parents before he was born. Brian's dad, Larry Gray, was my seventh-grade teacher. Years later, after my husband and I were married, Larry and Jan visited our church while they were in the process of raising funds to go to the mission field. This time we became friends, family, supporters, and partners in their ministry.

Growing up in Chad wasn't easy for the Gray children. Solidly placed at the bottom of the least developed countries list, Chad is one of the most physically inhospitable places in the world. With extreme heat, desert conditions, lack of resources, and governmental corruption and instability, the Grays' call to Chad was a difficult one. Several times the Grays were evacuated because of localized conflict or government takeovers. Once they became the target of a mob riot. Their home was overrun, and they lost every "thing" they owned, but God spared the family and the life of the household worker the mob was trying to kill.

Larry was once taken captive by rebels and forced at gunpoint to drive the rebels to another part of the country. All this, as horrendous as it is, pales in comparison to their most difficult experience: losing their youngest son to a medical condition that would have been easily treated in the States. This was the training ground where the Grays' son Brian learned the faithfulness of God, love for lost people, and a desire to make a difference in the world.

After graduating from a boarding school in Kenya, Brian came to live with Dave and me for a year. We helped him get a job, earn some money, and get his driver's license (that was my second ulcer; the first came from teaching his older sister to drive a few years earlier). He joined the military and served tours of duty in Japan and Guam before attending college in southern Illinois. Shortly after he finished school he left for China to teach English as a second language. It was there, in southeast Asia, that Brian felt at home.

For a holiday one year Brian went to Cambodia. What he found haunted him and changed his focus. He discovered a garbage dump that was home to many people, most disconcertingly, to orphaned children. Brian made it his personal mission to help these children find a better life. He partnered with a local children's center to house, educate, feed, and love these orphaned children. Moving to Cambodia longer term, Brian works with the Center for Children's Happiness and creatively assists in multiple ways, including raising awareness and funds, educational development, vocational training, positive exposure in the community and country, finding volunteers, throwing parties for the children, and ensuring the children's safety.

I have a feeling that Brian's life will never be conventional. Neither will the lives of the children he has touched. Their lives will be forever changed because an ordinary guy, with God's help, did something extraordinary.

The Vulnerable among Us

Orphaned and abandoned children are the most vulnerable among us. Children who have no one to protect them, care for them, or give them guidance can experience the worst our world can offer. In developed countries, children who have lost one or both parents often have a child welfare safety net. Although the system doesn't offer perfect solutions, generally orphaned children will have their basic needs met. Orphaned children in impoverished communities in emerging or least developed countries can find themselves in very different situations altogether. Children who should be in school looking forward to opportunities and a future spend their days scrounging for food and creatively trying to make money whatever way they can. They have little hope and sometimes no vision at all for their future. Without intervention of some kind, their chance of living a healthy and productive life diminishes greatly.

I must warn you: This is going to be a difficult chapter, focusing on the dark side of the world we live in. Some of the topics will make you angry and hurt your heart. Guaranteed, you will want to stop and deny that these atrocities are happening today in our world. However, as difficult as it is to read about these things, it is in understanding the dangers orphaned children face that will equip and motivate us to do something to change the lives of these children, and ultimately change our world. We have to see the truth so that we can understand the importance of God's call to care for the most vulnerable among us—orphaned and abandoned children.

Care at Its Best

In the best circumstances, if a child loses his or her parents, other adults already a part of the child's life step in and take on the responsibilities of parenting. I'm thankful to report that in many cases this does happen. Although no child can lose his or her parents without having some residual effects mentally, emotionally, physically. and spiritually, the trauma can be minimized and the child can move toward a full and productive life.

Child welfare through governmental, private, religious, and other nongovernmental organizations is another option exercised in many countries when orphaned children have no family members able to care for them. The topic of child welfare has become a global issue in recent decades.

An adequate child welfare system has become one of the measuring sticks used to assess a country's human capital rating and contributes to the country's global classification. Countries working to raise their status in the global economy are addressing and, in most cases, improving the child welfare infrastructure. Unfortunately in many of the least developed and most impoverished countries, child welfare is not high on their list of priorities. When the global community creates a significant outcry, a country may be forced to make improvements, but with a lack of resources the results can still be sorely inadequate.

In resource-poor countries other agencies try to step in to fill some of the gaps. These governmental, nongovernmental, and religious organizations deal with hundreds of thousands of children each year. Using the tools of adoption, foster care, group homes, children's homes, and other means, many children are given the support and care they need to grow and develop in a relatively normal environment. However, we know that "systems" are not perfect, and although created with good intentions, many of these systems are flawed and at times even dangerous. Be that as it may, child welfare must continue to be developed at every level of our society in general and in the Church in specific, if we have any hope of impacting the lives of orphaned children.

On January 1, 2007, seventeen years after the fall of Communism, Romania celebrated their acceptance into the coveted European Union.[1] The process was started years earlier and was bumpy at best, but in the end they met the EU requirements. Part of the reason for the long courtship was substandard child welfare and protection laws and practices in Romania. Laws had to be made and changes had to occur in the institutionalized child welfare system.

In the '90s Romania was widely criticized for its inhumane treatment of orphaned children. News reports showed neglected children in rows of cribs in dingy sterile rooms. It stung the moral conscience of viewers worldwide and caused Romania national embarrassment. The system needed reform, and acceptance into the EU was the motivation that Romania needed to finally improve their child welfare system.[2] Today, years later, Romania has made significant changes with child welfare and protection services, but continued reform is still needed to close antiquated facilities and replace them with more individualized childcare.

Lack of Basic Provisions

In resource-poor countries, not only are orphaned children in crisis, but layer upon layer of everyday challenges and crises complicate life in general. For a country like Somalia that has experienced a drought of epic proportion, feeding the country's entire population takes precedence over meeting the needs of a smaller population. Orphaned children are the most vulnerable and in turn will be the first casualties of such a widespread crisis.

In an already weakened country, a lack of resources combined with natural disasters becomes the perfect storm for the orphan crisis. Haiti, the most impoverished country in the Western Hemisphere, provides a textbook example. We already mentioned the earthquake of 2010, but that was just a small part of the greater problems plaguing that country.

The southern part of the island that Haiti shares with the Dominican Republic sits on a major fault line. On Tuesday, January 12, 2010, Haiti was struck by a 7.0 earthquake, with the epicenter just a few miles outside the capital of Port-au-Prince. However, the reality is that the day before the earthquake, Monday, January 11, 2010, the country was already in a state of disarray from political instability, government corruption, deforestation, poverty, lack of resources, and certain cultural attitudes. The earthquake took an already devastated country and magnified the intensity, resulting in approximately 316,000 dead,[3] 300,000 injured,[4] and 680,000 homeless.[5] Over the next months, cholera broke out, leaving another 6,600 people dead.[6] In June 2011 floods killed twenty-three people,[7] followed in November by hurricane Tomas, which caused massive coastal flooding. The world watched, was moved by the devastation, and pledged or sent more than 5.2 billion dollars in aid to the ravaged country.[8] The road to recovery continues to be long and difficult, but in the end, the question still remains, even with all the global aid and support, will the people of Haiti be any better off tomorrow than they were the day before the earthquake? The problems run deep, and there are no easy answers.

One of the major issues facing the least developed and emerging countries is the lack of basic provisions for the local population, and especially for orphaned children. We will look at several critical areas lacking in many countries that continue to affect the very foundation of the well-being of orphaned children. In a developed country we take many things for granted. In a resource-poor country, clean water, food, and adequate shelter are not a given, and it can be an everyday struggle to get even the basic needs met.

Lack of Available Water

Clean water is a rare commodity in many parts of the world. Those of us who live in developed countries don't think about it much, as we have easy access to clean water. However, the reality is that much of the world has difficulty obtaining this life-sustaining resource.

While traveling internationally I have stayed in places with no running water. It is amazing how difficult it is to adjust to limited water. The first thing I noticed was how much I missed having a shower and quick access to a tall glass of clean, refreshing water. We easily take such gifts for granted when we can just go to the sink and turn on the faucet. When you have to walk across a courtyard and carry a forty-five-pound, five-gallon bucket of water, it tends to make you conserve every drop. I could barely carry such a bucket a few steps, let alone across the yard. Without quick access to water, everything takes longer; even the simple act of washing dishes takes time and significant effort. To make the issue that much more difficult, even when you've done all the work to get the water where you want it to be, it isn't safe to drink or use for food preparation unless it is filtered or boiled. Unclean water is at minimum annoying and at its worst, deadly!

The statistics are astounding: "Roughly one-sixth of the world's population does not have access to safe drinking water. Some 6,000 children die every day from disease associated with lack of access to safe drinking water, inadequate sanitation and poor hygiene—equivalent to 20 jumbo jets crashing every day."[9]

Part of the problem is the inaccessibility of clean water: "The average distance that women in Africa and Asia walk to collect water is 3.7 miles."[10] This issue relates to children in general, and orphaned children in specific, because it is typically women and children who are given the task of being the carriers of the water. The task is so vital that it takes precedence over education and other critical tasks. An orphaned child's primary role becomes acquiring basic necessities, leaving him little opportunity to move forward in other areas of life.

Dirty water is also a major issue in global health care: "Half of the world's hospital beds are filled with people suffering from water related illnesses. In the past 10 years, diarrhea has killed more children than all the people lost to armed conflicts since World War II."[11] Clean water is not just an issue—it is a matter of life or death.

Lack of Quality Nutrition

Food is another necessity of life. Unfortunately our global access and distribution is not even close to being fair. Hunger is caused by food insecurity, which has a multitude of contributing factors—rising prices, poverty, war, natural disasters, disease, and falling agricultural productivity.[12] "Hunger is the world's number-one health risk. It kills more people every year than AIDS, malaria,` and tuberculosis combined. There are more hungry people in the world than the combined populations of USA, Canada and the European Union. One in seven people in the world will go to bed hungry tonight."[13]

There are two issues related to hunger: calories and nutrition. In some circumstances people have access to calories but not to nutrition. Because of this, children can suffer from severe vitamin deficiencies. Haiti's mud pies are an example of empty calories: "Today, when even a bowl of rice is an extravagant luxury, mud pies—known simply as *terre* in Creole—are increasingly becoming the only food many families can afford to [eat]."[14] These mud pies contain a yellowish soil containing calcium, and they do contain calories. Beyond that, they are devoid of nutrition and full of parasites and toxins. Mud pies might temporarily fill the belly and keep hunger at bay, but they are no cure for the underlying problem of malnutrition.

According to the Global Hunger Index of 2010, the areas of most concern are South Asia and sub-Saharan Africa. The most critical population is young children. "Undernutrition in the first two years of life threatens a child's life and can jeopardize physical, motor and cognitive development. For those who survive, having been undernourished during the first two years of life can cause irreversible, long-term damage. It is therefore of particular importance that we take concerted action to combat hunger, especially among young children."[15]

Lack of Adequate Shelter

Shelter becomes an enormous concern when a child is left orphaned and unable to take care of life's basic needs. Not only does shelter protect a child from the elements but also provides much-needed security from predators, both human and animal.

The loss of a father can be devastating to a family, this much we know. But, if you're like me, you perhaps have not thought about another critical issue that impacts widows and orphaned children: the loss of a family's home, land rights, and possibly income. In many parts of the world the rights of land and ownership are held only by a father and not by a mother. Even if the mother and children are still intact, unscrupulous people can force them off their land and out of their home. "In Uganda, for example, more than one in five widows and orphans lose all or part of their rightful inheritance through illegal property seizure. This injustice has ramifications far beyond the initial theft; for many families, property can literally be the difference between life and death—it is the source of shelter, and in many cases, livelihood and food."[16]

The loss of the family farm, home-based business, or cottage industry is just the tip of the iceberg. The most difficult losses are the safety, security, and continuity that a home brought to the family. When a widow and orphaned children are displaced, the financial, emotional, and physical burdens leave them to pick up the pieces as best they can. With few resources, this can be a near-impossible situation.

Finding Shelter Anywhere They Can:

At night, they emerge to steal, forage and earn money from prostitution; by day, they cuddle up to the giant hot water pipes that serve public buildings. These are the street children of Kharkiv, in eastern Ukraine, just 40 minutes from the border with Russia.

As many as 200,000 such unaccounted-for children have rough lives in a country where winter daytime temperatures can be minus 4 degrees Fahrenheit. They live in subterranean dens under the manholes that cover the maintenance points for the city's heating system, where conditions are cramped, unsanitary and dangerous—many are burnt by the scalding pipes. But it is their means of survival in a country beset by the problems of adaptation after independence from the Soviet Union in 1991.[17]

Lack of Money, Resources, Skills, and Education

Shelter, money, and resources are hard to obtain when a child loses one or both parents. In least developed countries, hardship is so widespread it is nearly impossible to break the cycle of poverty. Even in developed countries, if a child doesn't have some type of insurance or inheritance or some resources to get started, he or she is vulnerable to predators and scams. Some countries have scholarships and grants available for education, but young adults often start from a monetary and resource deficit, making it difficult to get ahead.

Skills and education come at a price. Some children can literally not afford the uniform that would allow them to attend school. In other countries shoes are required to attend schools. For those children without the money or resources to buy a simple pair of shoes, education is denied.

The poverty cycle continues: Without money a person can't afford critically needed education. Without an education a person can't find a job. Without a job a person has no way to earn income—and so on, and so on. The cycle has to be broken.

Lack of Opportunities

My friend Charlotte is an amazing networker (I actually call her a "relational animal"). Drop Charlotte on a desert island, and within a matter of days she will have found all the different tribal groups, gotten to know each of them, and assessed their strengths, had tea with the chiefs, and planned a party to bring everyone together. Shortly after, she would organize a workday, build a community center, and abracadabra, a new level of life and community is born. In short, when I need to find someone or something, Charlotte is my first call.

Unfortunately for orphaned children, they don't have a "Charlotte" in their life. When they need a job, they have to knock on every door. When they need to find housing, they have to ask, beg, borrow, look in a phone book, or search the Internet. They don't have the knowledge, experience, or connections we all need to move forward in our lives. They start from zero with only the skills they have received up to that point. Mind you, many orphaned children become highly creative as they learn to cope with their reality. However, the finer points of education and life skills that are passed along from adults during a child's formative years remain missing. It's a heartbreaking reality that when many orphaned children do find someone "willing" to help, that someone may have his own bank account's best interest in mind and not the orphaned child's.

Lack of Health Care and Disease Prevention

Orphaned children are at-risk for insufficient health care, which makes them susceptible to disease and infection. In developed countries child welfare protocols are often in place to care for the health needs of the child. In the United States, for example, when a child enters the foster care system, mandatory assessments address the physical, behavioral, and oral health of the child.[18] In Norway a social-democratic governmental health care model operates both locally and nationally with "about 35 per cent of the state's budget spent on health and social welfare system."[19] Children who are in "out-of-home care" have their medical needs covered through the country's local and national system, which includes preventative and comprehensive health care.

In emerging and least developed countries the health care protocols for orphaned children are not as predictable or routine. Many countries have no health care assistance at all, leaving the foster parent or care facility to acquire and fund treatment on their own. Even when there is a system in place, many children never come under the umbrella of care. These children are on their own and have limited resources, making disease prevention and health care minimal or nonexistent.

Of the major disease killers that have been identified, some of them have been eradicated in developed countries or are very rare. But a few—respiratory infections, HIV/AIDS, malaria, diarrhea, tuberculosis, and measles—cross all borders. In the case of such diseases, the availability of proper medical treatment can minimize the negative effects.

Respiratory infections range anywhere from the common cold to pneumonia and bronchitis and are responsible for more than 4 million deaths every year: "In all, these diseases account for nearly half or more of fatalities worldwide every year."[20] Of child deaths under age five, 20 percent are due to respiratory infections.[21]

Respiratory infections are generally highly contagious and especially so with children in close proximity at schools or residential care facilities. Adding to the challenge, undernourished children are more susceptible to infection, and recovery is much more difficult for them. Respiratory infections can be treated with antibiotics, but in resource-poor situations the infection is often left to run its course.

HIV/AIDS is another danger for many orphaned children.

Although the HIV/AIDS statistics can be mind-numbing and worth an encyclopedia-sized book in itself, bear with me as we look at a few of the extremely relevant facts.

More than 30 million people have died of HIV/AIDS since it was first recognized in 1981.[22] No wonder this disease has rocked our world. Sub-Saharan Africa is the hardest hit region in the world; it "has just over 10% of the world's population but is home to more than 60 percent of all people living with HIV.[23] "As of 2010, there are now an estimated 33.4 million people living with HIV, including 2.1 million children under the age of 15. . . . Nearly 18 million children have lost one/both parents to AIDS."[24]

Once one or both parents contract HIV/AIDS, the family starts the downhill slide resulting in increased economic hardships. In countries where medications are available, the progression of the disease can be slowed, but most people don't have geographic or economic access to the medication. Severely complicating the issue, when one parent acquires the disease, the likelihood of the disease spreading to the other parent skyrockets. Children often have to take over some of the household responsibilities just to keep the family surviving. With this tragic mix of poverty, disease, and lack of resources, the family's chance for successful recovery is minimal.

Another by-product of losing a parent or parents to HIV/AIDS is the stigma that follows. Overwhelmed in their own grief, children are likely to feel shamed and rejected by some in their community. Children left behind are often assumed to carry the disease as well. If indeed they do, there is even more discrimination, and sometimes these children are cut off from access to education, health care, and other resources.[25] I heard a story about a child in a least developed country who lost his parents to AIDS. Although relatives were willing to let him stay with them, they were afraid the orphaned child also had AIDS and would expose their family to the disease. To prevent exposure they only allowed the boy to live outside on the lawn or on the porch. This boy's plight is hardly an isolated incidence; it is probably more common than we can imagine.

So much more could be said about HIV/AIDS because it affects so many people, and specifically children, worldwide. Suffice it to say that it is a complicated and tragic issue that has gotten a lot of attention but still needs more solutions.

Malaria, a disease carried by mosquitoes, poses significant health problems in tropical areas of Africa, Asia, and Latin America. "Nearly 1 million people die each year because of malaria. Of these deaths, 80 percent are children under age 5 in sub-Saharan Africa."[26] Pregnant women are more susceptible to malaria, with malaria contributing to low birth weight.

Diarrhea is usually a symptom of an infection caused by food-borne parasites, contaminated water, and other environmental issues. Water contamination "causes 90 percent of the diarrheal cases among children."[27] Children's immune systems are less able to handle the effects of diarrhea, and the child can decline rapidly with diarrhea's ravaging effects. Millions of children live in areas with limited or no access to clean drinking water, making exposure to toxins and parasites inevitable.

Tuberculosis (TB) is a highly contagious disease spread by the bacillus germs propelled through sneezing and coughing by an infected carrier. Although nearly eradicated in some developed countries, TB is still prevalent in some parts of the world such as Southeast Asia and sub-Saharan Africa. It is estimated that, globally, "1.4 million people died from TB in 2010."[28]

Although there have been medications for the treatment of TB for about fifty years now, strains of TB have now been identified that are proving to be drug-resistant. Another failure of treatment occurs because people are only partially treating the condition or do not complete their medication. Drug-resistant TB is still treatable with chemotherapy, but it is much more costly and much more severe. TB mixed with other diseases such as HIV/AIDS makes a lethal combination that is proving even more problematic; it remains to be seen what the long-term effects will be.

Measles, a viral infection of the respiratory system, is highly contagious, spread through aerosol transmission. Measles typically includes a high fever, respiratory distress, flu-like symptoms, and a rash. Since 1963 vaccination has made the disease much less evident in developed countries. However, "measles has been a major killer of children in developing countries (causing an estimated 750,000 deaths as recently as 2000), primarily because of underutilization of the vaccine."[29] The majority of deaths attributed to the measles (as many as 90 percent) is in children under five years of age in the Eastern Mediterranean and Africa.[30]

The lack of basic provisions in the lives of orphaned children continues to make them a highly vulnerable population in our world. To complicate the life of orphaned children even further, there are other, more devious and evil ways they are harmed, and these atrocities are at the hands of fellow humans.

Lack of Protection: Violations of Children's Rights

Children need protecting. Parents, extended family, and the local community are essential elements of a child's overall protection. Break down any or all of these components, and the worst can happen. Children with no protective adults in their lives are left vulnerable to the elements, predators, and other evils.

Human Trafficking

During the early years of a child's life, adults are supposed to provide a suitable environment for growth. Adults are bigger, wiser, and stronger; they should love and protect defenseless children, giving them the time they need to understand the world and their place in it.

Yet instead of reaching out to help orphaned or abandoned children in their vulnerability, many adults take advantage of them. Either well-meaning but misguided, or just pure evil, their assertion of power and control over children subverts the children's normal development, forcing them to resort to coping mechanisms and basic survival instincts. Adults become the enemy—not trustworthy, not safe. Adults can be horrible and despicable. Brutality knows no bounds. Things most well-adjusted humans don't even contemplate become the norm with defenseless children taking the brunt of adult cruelty.

> Child sex slavery is one of the most hideous crimes possible. Diving into the stories of young children who have lost their childhoods to brothels, pimps, and johns is beyond heartbreaking. The more you learn, the more unsettled your spirit will become. The learning resources here are designed to unsettle your spirit and empower your actions. You will know the work of the enemy and it will leave a stain on your spirit. Move from here to act on behalf of these children. You are their hope for prevention, for rescue, and for restoration.[31]

There are 12 million to 27 million people enslaved in our world today.[32] *Trafficking* and *slavery* are terms used to describe making people do something against their will through force, coercion, or deception. Sometimes people are enslaved in their own countries; sometimes they are taken across borders into others. People in general, and children specifically, are abducted, given, or sold to the slave owner who then forces them to be a laborer, prostitute, or child mercenary, among other things.

In the last decade, the issue of child trafficking has received worldwide attention and concern. Yet after researching subjects, writing papers, passing resolutions, and holding conferences, the numbers of child victims continue to rise. "Approximately 80 percent of human trafficking victims are women and girls, and up to 50 percent are minors. The total market value of illicit human trafficking is estimated to be in excess of $32 billion. Sex trafficking is an engine of the global AIDS epidemic."[33]

It is impossible to estimate what percentage of children who are trafficked are orphaned children, but it is safe to say that being orphaned leaves the child more vulnerable and appealing to traffickers, especially in the least developed countries. Even within the protection of family, a child's parent or guardian might think sending the child away to work at a factory or market is a good option—when it's actually the ruse of clever traffickers. That story is told countless times with all kinds of variations, but the outcome is always the same: A child is victimized and will forever be scarred.

Children's rights are violated all around the world. As I've researched, it would seem as if I'd seen it all, but then my studies would reveal another deplorable atrocity. I've found that the more I look for them, the more I find. There seems no end to the despicable atrocities that harm the vulnerable. This picture of humanity's sinfulness shouts the truth that without the love of Christ there would be no redemption. But our Father redeems and transforms, and for that fact alone, we still find hope.

Child Pornography

We live in an amazing technological age, and we all enjoy the tools that have been created. However, technology is a double-edged sword and can be used for good as well as for tremendous evil. Child pornography is one such by-product of technology. Today any deviant with a camera and access to the Internet can broadcast child pornography worldwide.

Child pornography is an international phenomenon. Most of the data that exists regarding the extent and nature of the problem has focused on North America and Northern Europe— regions which have played a key role in the production, distribution and consumption of child pornography. "The U.S. market for child pornography is widely thought to be the most lucrative in the world."[34]

Although the statistics are wildly dynamic and ever increasing, in 2006 it is estimated that pornography revenue was $97 billion dollars, $13 billion in the United States alone. The United States, by far, is the largest producer of pornography while China brings in the largest single country revenue at $27 billion.[35]

Most Western countries consider child pornography a criminal offence. Global organizations, such as the United Nations and the European Commission, are working toward globalizing the laws so that progress can be made in the arrest and convictions of criminals, regardless of location.

Child pornography does not stop with photographs but extends to physical abuse through molestation, sexual intercourse, physical abuse, and mental and emotional damage. And where do the children come from? Although older children may participate under their own volition, any child, of any age, involved in child pornography is considered violated and abused because children are generally not mature enough to make that choice. They have been forced or coerced. Even in developed countries children can be abducted to participate in this criminal activity, and any adult involved is considered a criminal pedophile.

Sex Slave Trade

Wicked adults target the young as sexual prey.

A female cousin had taken Neth [a very young girl in northwestern Cambodia] from her village, telling the family that Neth would be selling fruit in Poipet [another village]. Once in Poipet, Neth was sold to a brothel and closely guarded. After a doctor confirmed that she was a virgin, the brothel auctioned her virginity to a Thai casino manager, who locked her up in a hotel room for several days and slept with her three times (he later died of AIDS). Now Neth was confined to the guesthouse and was young enough and light-skinned enough to rent for top rates.[36]

Virgin girls bring top dollars. In addition to virgins being the cream of the proverbial sex crop, a widespread myth suggests that having sex with a virgin can cure AIDS. Girls as young as four years old are abducted and sold to brothel owners who then sell their virginity to the highest bidder. The girls, after they are "ruined," are turned into sex-slave machines, beaten and tortured if they resist or try to escape. Often given debilitating drugs to dull their senses and decrease their resistance, they are forced to have sex multiple times a day. AIDS and other communicable diseases spread rapidly in the sex-slave trade. Without medical treatment these young girls are destined to short and painful lives.

Created more than a decade ago, the Palermo Protocol prohibits the use of children in the commercial sex trade under U.S. law and legislation in countries around the world. This makes the acts of sex trafficking an illegal offence and "no cultural or socioeconomic rationalizations [can] prevent the rescue of children from sexual servitude."[37]

Unfortunately due to governmental corruption, lack of resources, and the absence of positive pressure from the global community, many countries still fail to prosecute those involved with sex trafficking, which keeps the trafficking engine turning. The International Justice Mission, active in this arena since 1997, finds that without prosecutions the violations continue unabated.[38]

So that male readers don't feel the guilt of this crime by gender association alone, women, amazingly, must own a significant portion of the sex-slave trade guilt as well. Both men and women are involved in abducting, selling, torturing, and brokering young women for sex. Women act as "aunts" to the recently stolen victims, giving them false reassurance that everything will be all right. Often as brutal as their male counterparts, female brothel owners and managers can drug and beat girls into submission, demonstrating that they are also in the commodities game. The unfortunate children are just the commodities they deal in.

Bacha Bazi

Although young women are more often the victims of sexual trafficking, in some cultures, particularly in Middle Eastern countries, Bacha Bazi (or dancing boys) is another form of abusive entertainment.[39] Men of means and power congregate in dingy rooms filled with smoke and flowing with alcohol as they watch young boys dressed in feminine clothing dance provocatively. The boys, usually tricked, abducted, or sold into slavery, are young enough that they have smooth, beardless skin and boyish features. Dancing is the gateway to other predictable sexual activities desired by the watching men. Some of the boys are treated richly and can actually experience a rise in their social status for a time.

With the onset of puberty and facial hair, these young boys are discarded, shamed, and disgraced, to navigate in a world where they will never belong. The abusers, often wanting to spare their betrothed or wife their deviant sexual needs, find other boys to use. They pray to their god for forgiveness on their holy day, then go back to abusing young boys whenever they feel the desire to do so.

Rape as a Form of Terrorism

Rape is pervasive in many parts of the world, and in war-torn countries rape becomes not only about sexual domination but becomes a tool of war.

Mass rapes have been reported at stunning levels in recent conflicts. Half of the women in Sierra Leone endured sexual violence or the threat of it during the upheavals in that country, and a United Nations report claims that 90 percent of girls and women over the age of three were sexually abused in parts of Liberia during civil war. Even in places like Pakistan, where there is no genocide or all-out war, honor rapes arise from an obsession with virginity and form the authorities' indifference to injustices suffered by the poor and uneducated . . . "When I [a prominent gynecologist] treat rape victims, I tell the girls not to go to the police," Dr. Syed added. "Because if a girl goes to the police, the police will rape her."[40]

In their book *Half the Sky: Turning Oppression into Opportunity for Women Worldwide*, authors Kristof and WuDunn state that the worst place in the world for terrorism rapes is eastern Congo in Africa. As a means of war, "the most cost-effective way to terrorize civilian populations is to conduct rapes of stunning brutality."[41] I won't go on to describe what the book says about these brutal rapes, but *Half the Sky* is an amazing piece of literature that has brought to light what needed to be recognized. Terrorism rape is a despicable evil in its most inhuman form.

Child Soldiers

A form of human trafficking seldom talked about is the use of children as soldiers. In war-torn countries government forces, paramilitary organizations, and rebel groups run short of workers. Through abduction, coercion, and force, they make children part of their ranks. "Armies in more than thirty countries use children as soldiers."[42] Male children are taken as soldiers, laborers, cooks, guards, servants, and sex objects. Young girls are forced to be slaves, provide sex, or marry their captors. Sometimes young boys are even forced to kill their own families as their first act of brutality. From this type of violence there is no recovery. Only God's grace and forgiveness can make a person whole again.

Forced Child Labor

People are designed to work. Work brings income and feelings of accomplishment, and working contributes to an overall healthy society. In the Western world we have become accustomed to seeing adults do the heaving lifting, so that children can focus on their education until they are officially adults, around eighteen to twenty-two years old. In some cases children work to acquire money for auto insurance or other ancillary expenses, but in general, children are not responsible to provide the family's "daily bread." However, in much of the world children have to become part of the family workforce to literally put food on the table. This is where it gets complicated.

Education is vital to a child's overall development. We like to see children given the opportunity to be as educated as opportunity affords. However, when a child is part of the family workforce, education suffers. Then there is the issue of "sweat shops"—environments with inhumane working conditions.

Years ago quite a backlash stirred when Hollywood stars promoted clothing lines created in emerging countries by child labor in sweat shops. It just doesn't look good for "notables" to have children making their merchandise. But children at work remains a challenging problem because many children, far from choosing to work, needed to work because their families depended on that child working for their very survival. The issue is really not children working as much as it is the conditions in which they have to work, or if the child is forced to work by coercion, exploitation, manipulation, or abduction—that is, whether the child has been enslaved.

Recent studies show the majority of human trafficking in the world takes the form of forced labor. The International Labour Organization estimates that for every trafficking victim subjected to forced prostitution, nine people are forced to work. Also known as involuntary servitude, forced labor may result when unscrupulous employers exploit workers made more vulnerable by high rates of unemployment, poverty, crime, discrimination, corruption, political conflict, or cultural acceptance of the practice. Immigrants are particularly vulnerable, but individuals also may be forced into labor in their own countries. Female victims of forced or bonded labor, especially women and girls in domestic servitude, are often sexually exploited as well.[43]

Child Abuse

Degrees of child abuse are pervasive in all countries of the world at every socioeconomic level. Without parental protection, orphaned children are especially vulnerable to child abuse. That is not to say that parents always protect children as they should; in many situations the home can be a dangerous place for a child (especially in the case of drug and alcohol addicted parents). However, in general, the bond between the parent and child theoretically should provide more protection for the child.

Children who are orphaned find themselves in many high-risk situations that make child abuse more likely. Living on the street or in a child-headed household, children are vulnerable to outside forces. Even in foster care, children's homes, or orphanages, children are not protected from abuse. We have all heard stories of a child being physically and sexually abused or neglected while in protective care. In fact, abuse can also come from an older child also in protective care, who dominates or bullies a younger, more vulnerable child.

Agencies around the world struggle to find the best approach to the issue of child neglect and abuse. Children need protecting. Some propose more legislation, more research, more oversight, and more education. The bottom line is that abusers, perpetrators, and pedophiles need to be caught and prosecuted, and abused children need to be cared for and rehabilitated.

Self-Destructive Behaviors

The great deception is when an adult, someone who should be trustworthy, deceives a child and takes advantage of that child. But sometimes a child can cause his own destruction. In such cases, the child needs protection from himself, from his own self-destructive behaviors.

Sometimes orphaned children don't need any help to sabotage themselves. Self-destructive behaviors start when individuals don't know how to cope with trauma, stress, and difficult changes in a healthy way and resort to punishing themselves instead. An orphaned child who has dealt with tremendous difficulties can easily fall prey to inappropriate behavior patterns that might temporarily relieve some of the stress but quickly become self-destructive patterns.

Self-medicating is a destructive behavior that dulls the senses, usually as an attempt to hide the pain. Many destructive behaviors become this kind of "self-medication": drug and alcohol abuse, sexual promiscuity, physically harming oneself, crime, violence, and gang involvement. All of these behaviors have longer-term effects. While some can be recovered from, others leave permanent scars. Some lead to death.

Cutting is one such behavior. While the cutter is physically harming himself, endorphins are released that dull emotional pain. But once a child is dependent on the practice, it can get out-of-hand leaving scars that last a lifetime.

Unfortunately, for many orphaned children there is no easy fix. They are caught in a web of self-deception that makes it nearly impossible to see the truth of their behavior and to break the cycle. They get caught in destructive patterns, and in some cases the abused becomes the abuser. I heard a story recently about a trial where a trafficker was being charged for his crimes. While he deserved to be put away for the rest of his life for the abuses he caused to young women, it was also devastating to hear the pathetic abuses he had experienced himself that led into self-destructive behavior.

Institutionalization and Impairment

Another significant danger orphaned children face is the effects of institutionalization. Children without regular opportunities for growth, learning, and physical development can become debilitated for a lifetime. Without a personalized development plan and caring people to love these children, their outlook is dismal.

Many studies have shown that children in institutionalized settings frequently lack quality nutrition, adequate disease prevention protocols, and needed medical treatment.[44] The results are developmental delays and higher susceptibility to illness. In recent years concerted efforts have improved residential care and changed that stereotype, but much still needs to be done. A major shift to a more family-based, community-based, or foster care approach has been widespread, but because of the large numbers of orphaned and abandoned children in our world, it is unlikely that institutionalized care will be eliminated altogether. We will discuss this at length in future chapters.

Aging Out

Aging out is a common term used in the temporary child custody world. For the child who never becomes permanently adopted or placed, his or her days in the system are limited. When that child turns sixteen (or eighteen, or whatever the "magic" number is in his or her particular country), he or she "ages out" of the system and is released from the foster home, children's home, or orphanage. Often these kids are released with nothing! They leave with no training, no money, no resources, no connections, no family—nothing! Can you imagine that? What would you do if that happened to you? Where would you go? The world is a big place, and a young adult without resources can easily become overwhelmed, defeated, and hopeless. Unfortunately, in many parts of the world that hopeless feeling can result in choices that give way to devastating results.

Here are some alarming "aging out" statistics:

- The global orphan spends an average of ten years in an orphanage or foster home.[45]
- Every day 38,493 children age out of the system; that is one child every 2.2 seconds.[46]

- In Ukraine and Russia 10–15 percent of children who age out of an orphanage commit suicide before age 18.[47]
- One study showed that of the 15,000 orphaned children who age out of Russia's child welfare system annually, "5,000 were employed, 6,000 were homeless, and 3,000 were in prison within three years."[48]
- 60 percent of the girls who age out in the Ukraine and Russia enter into prostitution and
- 70 percent of the boys become hardened criminals.[49]

For children who age out of the system, there is no safety net! In recent years developed countries have begun addressing these issues and providing some of the necessary tools for successful reintegrating previously institutionalized children into society. In Norway, children in the child welfare system are free to be released at age eighteen but have the option of voluntarily staying until age twenty-three, to give more time to mature, to get educated, and to be prepared for adulthood.[50] Unfortunately, in emerging countries, and certainly the least developed countries, children age out of the system at younger ages and are ill-equipped for life.

Pray, Provide, and Protect

The dangers orphans face because of lack of provisions and lack of protection are extensive and real. This chapter has only scratched the surface of these issues and could be expanded exponentially. Orphaned children are precious gifts from God and deserve our prayer, care, and concern. Now that you know a few of the dangers orphans face, you can be a part of the solution. Orphaned children need protection, advocacy, support, and assistance. Keep reading. Soon you will capture a vision of many opportunities for your involvement in these critical areas. Pray about how God can use your talents, gifts, and willing heart to make a difference in the life of an orphaned child. We can't all do everything, but we can all do something. May God continue to bring thoughts to your mind and tug on your heart to help you to be part of the solution to the global orphan crisis.

QUESTIONS TO PONDER

1. This chapter is a difficult one. Has anything especially challenged you as you read about the dangers orphans face?

2. Which dangers to orphaned children had you never considered before?

3. Can you imagine how you might have felt in any of the situations described?

4. What particular issue sparked your interest so that you wanted more information in order to understand the issue more fully?

5. Can you think of a practical way to help with any of the situations listed in this chapter?

ACTION POINT

This week, pick one of the dangers faced by orphans that really struck you, or pick a topic that wasn't even mentioned that you know a bit about, and do a little research on your own. Condense your findings and be ready to share for a few minutes with your group about the information you found. Be thinking of possible solutions and how you might make a difference in the life of an orphaned child, especially in the area of your own research.

In the United States the orphan crisis is most widely manifested in children of single parent families. Anya Yirenkyi and her mom, Chere, live happily in Silver Springs, Maryland, with a strong team around them. *Chere Williams, photographer © Chere Williams*

4

The Orphan Crisis in Developed Countries

> Do not oppress the widow or the
> fatherless, the foreigner or the poor.
> Do not plot evil against each other.
>
> Zechariah 7:10

A Single Mom's Story by Chere Williams

A fifteen-year-old girl in a cream-colored dress with gold buttons sat nervously in a doctor's office in a small Pennsylvania town, her mother at her side. The doctor entered with a grim look on his face and placed a handful of papers in front of the young girl. They were adoption papers; the girl was pregnant. The doctor handed her the pen to sign away the growing baby in her belly to another family. The girl's mother didn't urge her to sign the papers but told her it was her baby and her choice. Much to the doctor's chagrin, the girl never signed the papers. Instead, she and her mother marched out of the office and into an ice cream parlor at a popular department store to share a banana split. That young lady was my mother. On April 17, 1972, I was born to an unwed, fifteen-year-old girl, into a

family that embraced and surrounded me with extraordinary love.

My childhood was very happy. I was blissfully unaware
of all the struggles my mother endured. She shielded me
from the ugliness of people who looked down on her because of her age and marital status, and because she was
Caucasian and had me by an African-American man. I was
oblivious to her money woes, her heartbreak over my biological father's lack of participation and support, and the
stress she must have suffered raising a child when she
was only a child herself. I saw a mother who worked hard,
held her head up high, strived to do better, and fiercely
protected me. My mother was, and is, my hero. I didn't
care that she was a single mom. She was my mom, my
anchor, and the love of my life.

Fast-forward to February 16, 2006: A beautiful baby girl
with a head full of hair was born at George Washington Hospital in Washington, D.C. I gave birth to my daughter, and
my mother was right there with me along with the next
most significant person in my life, my grandmother. The
same woman who stood by that young girl thirty-four years
before was now standing beside my hospital bed as I experienced my own miracle of life. I had great expectations
for my baby girl, none of which included me being a single
mom. But, on a sunny crisp day in November, 2007, I found
myself unloading a U-Haul and moving into a two-bedroom
apartment with my twenty-month-old daughter. That year
wasn't my finest. I separated from my daughter's father,
lost my beloved grandmother to Alzheimer's the day after
Christmas, and was an emotional disaster. I had become

what I dreaded, a statistic—a single mom. I wasn't fifteen; I was thirty-four, but I was still scared out of my wits! This wasn't how I envisioned starting off motherhood!

In hindsight, it isn't a big surprise that the relationship with my daughter's father failed. We fell in love at lightning-bolt speed and neglected to nurture our relationship or give it the time it required to evolve into a mature and stable partnership. We went from enjoying a carefree relationship to starting a family unprepared and with an idealized perception of parenthood. Yet, I still hadn't anticipated I'd be a single mom.

During my first year of single motherhood I faced a number of challenges that rocked me to my core. The hopelessness and isolation I felt were paralyzing. I was four hours away from my family and had very few friends. One day when I was having an emotional meltdown, I glanced over at my coffee table and noticed my grandmother's Bible sitting there. My grandmother was a Christian soldier. I never met anyone with the faith or love for Christ that she embodied. Her Bible was a part of who she was, and I desperately needed a part of her at that moment. I opened the Bible and through my tears began to read.

The floodgates broke open as I read the Scriptures. As I knelt in prayer I was hit with the realization that I wasn't a statistic: I was a child of God! God was my partner and had never forsaken me. His arms were open the whole time. I just had to run into them. The days following this newfound revelation were lighter but not easier. I was thirsty for God's teaching and began to pray and feast on the Word. I became God-reliant instead of self-reliant. I viewed motherhood in terms of what being a mother meant to me and not in terms of my marital status. I rested in the joy my daughter brought me. If I hoped to reap the rewards of being a mother, I had to consciously change my perception about single motherhood. I viewed my circumstances, though not ideal, as an opportunity to strengthen my relationship with my daughter, with God, and eventually with other single parents.

Single moms can emerge from brokenness and merge into wholeness if their faith is rooted in the Lord. When the bills are overdue, the child support check isn't coming in, and the walls are crumbling down around you, know that God is going to take your hand and lead you through the storms.

The Global Community

There are more than 7 billion people around the globe, spread out among 196 countries around the world. Although we are all inhabitants of the same planet, we are far from equal in our resources, wealth, privilege, and quality of life. We differ greatly depending on what nation and culture we live in, whether we live in a city or in the country, our families of origin, and many other factors. As you already know, there is an enormous disparity between the haves and the have-nots.

The next three chapters may offer more detail than you necessarily wanted and you may be tempted just to jump to the solutions section of the book. But hang in there! As we peel back some of the layers, we will better understand the scope of the issues at play in various countries and how these issues impact the global orphan crisis. A better picture of the relevant issues will lead to clearer understanding of where service opportunities exist.

As we dive into the deep end of the pond, a sampling of the massive available information will focus on key indicators that will help us to sort and categorize different areas of the world. We'll begin with the Human Development Index. Other key indicators will be unemployment rates, relative poverty by percent of population, economic ranking, and estimated number of orphaned children.

For ease of clarity, the nations of the world can be divided into three categories: *developed countries* (DC), *emerging countries* (EC), and *least developed countries* (LDC). In this chapter we will focus on the orphan crisis in a developed country (DC), which you are probably most familiar with. But you may be surprised by the orphan crisis within our DC borders.

The Human Development Index

The human development index (HDI) is a measurement that rates a country's life expectancy, education, health care, child welfare, and other issues related to a human level of services and general satisfaction. The scale goes from .2 being the lowest level, to a .9 being a very high level of development. A high HDI doesn't necessarily indicate that the people of a country are the happiest. It also doesn't mean that people whose country has a high HDI rating are superior or more "evolved" than people in other countries. A high HDI may indicate progress in certain areas of development and education, but it's still just a small piece within the context of a total package. A higher HDI carries along with it privilege and responsibility but never superiority.

The HDI from November 2, 2011[1] rates forty-seven countries as "very highly" developed, and forty-seven more as "highly" developed. As of November 2, 2011, there were forty-seven countries considered "developed countries." Of those top forty-seven countries, all have an HDI number higher than .788, and the top ten are all more than .904. In contrast, the least developed countries have HDIs under .344, the lowest being the Congo at .280. Below are the top ten countries, their HDI levels, and a few other telling statistics.[2]

HDI Country Ranking	Country	HDI number	Unemployment rate–Nov. 2011 %	CIA poverty numbers by percent of population	Gross Domestic Product (GDP) per Capita–CIA World factbook	Orphaned Children Estimates
# 1 (9 out of past 11 years)	Norway	.943	3.4	1.8	$ 54,600.	35,000
# 2	Australia	.943	5.3	11	$ 41,000.	80,000
# 3	Netherlands	.910	4.2	10.5	$ 40,300.	82,000
# 4	United States	.910	7.9	15.1	$ 47,200.	2,100,000
# 5	New Zealand	.908	6.6	n/a	$ 27,700.	36,000
# 6	Canada	.908	7.2	9.4	$ 39,400.	45,000
# 7	Ireland	.908	14.5	5.5	$ 37,300.	39,000
# 8	Liechtenstein	.905	1.5	n/a	$ 141,100.	n/a
# 9	Germany	.905	5.8	15.5	$ 35,700.	380,000
# 10	Sweden	.904	7.7	n/a	$ 39,100.	63,000

HDI statistics for DCs provide a snapshot of where each of the countries rank globally, as well as identifying areas where various countries excel and where they need improvement. As we talk about developed countries here and about emerging countries and least developed countries in the following chapters, these same statistics will play out in very different ways.

Life expectancy is actually factored into the HDI. This individual factor is a strong indicator of the general quality of life, health care, disease prevention, available nutrition, and other factors that affect an individual. Japan has the highest life expectancy rate at 83.4 years, and all of the top ten HDI countries have lifespans higher than 78 years.[3] In contrast, Swaziland has the lowest lifespan at only 31.88 years.[4] That's a significant difference of 46.2 years. In a developed country, we consider a person who is thirty-one as still young, with a full life to live. When a person dies at age thirty-one, we are devastated and think that his life was cut short. In Swaziland, those living much older than their thirties would be considered unusual. These measurements confirm that while we might live on the same planet, we certainly don't all share the same experiences, even in life and death.

The unemployment rate shows the general health of the country and economy.[5] In DCs you will see very low unemployment, but for least developed countries, unemployment soars to unbelievable numbers. It is hard to understand how a country can have 80 percent unemployment and still continue to function.

When creating the HDI, the United Nations assesses each nation's poverty level. There are two ways to consider and compare these poverty statistics. One is the absolute poverty line. They choose an amount, like $2.00 in U.S. currency, and show that nearly half the world lives on less than $2.00 per day, which is a staggering statistic.[6] The second is a relative poverty line, which indicates how many people live under the poverty line comparing people only to those in their own country. The relative poverty statistics serve our purposes, so that each country can be judged within the context of what is normal for that particular country. Obviously, it is easier to live on a small amount of money in some countries than in other countries where it would be impossible to do so. Relative poverty statistics provide great insight for understanding life within that country.

Gross Domestic Product (GDP) is a measurement of the market value of all final goods and services produced with a particular country. It is used as an economic indicator, a snapshot in time of the country's economic health. GDP per capita looks at the total market value of a country divided by the number of people in that country. If income were evenly distributed among all the people of the country, this statistic shows how much money each person in the country would earn. This income number helps to provide an accurate comparison between countries. The GDP per capita is not to be confused with the average or median income of a country's inhabitants, which can look very different due to the unequal distribution of wealth.

For our purposes, the number of orphaned children is the most compelling statistic of all. In many cases you will find that the larger the country, the greater the number of orphaned children. But in addition, certain stand-out countries have a staggeringly high number of orphaned children, such as India with 31 million children (see the chart on page 116 in chapter 5). The numbers of orphaned children, relative to the population in a country, tend to increase the lower you move down the human development index (HDI).[7]

Developed Countries' Strengths

The greatest strength of a DC can be summed up in one word: resources. With the availability of resources comes opportunity, advancement, and the ability to actually change one's own status. It is a privilege to live in a country where a person can be born into a family of limited economic means, but with hard work, ingenuity, and a little divine intervention, that person can have the availability to improve his or her life. We have all heard rags-to-riches stories about people who grew up "on the wrong side of the tracks," but who worked hard, studied hard, and eventually became millionaires. In a DC these types of stories are not fairy tales but literally happen every day. The United States holds the record for the most millionaires in any single country, with more than 8.6 million millionaires.[8]

In addition to the family of origin, most DCs have resources that come in the form of a "fairy-godmother" government. In some countries, the government's pockets are very deep. Many DCs have social programs that take care of health care, welfare, public assistance, job training programs, Medicare, senior meals, children's meals, student grants, unemployment, veterans benefits, subsidized housing, study grants, and more.

One of these fairy-godmother government benefits in many DCs is a child welfare system. While the system is not perfect and the staff is often overworked and underpaid, it is still an effective system to some degree, helping to assist children in critical need.

The Church is another definite benefit when living in a DC. While some DC countries are considered post-Christian, many still have a large number of churches involved in benevolent activities. In the United States 78 percent of the population considers themselves "Christian,"[9] and there are roughly 331,000 Christian churches.[10] In fact, there are so many churches that, if every church took seriously their involvement in the orphan care solution, we could empty the foster care backlog and find placements for all waiting children. Unfortunately, that is not the case. For the most part, the Church has stepped aside and let the government shoulder the child welfare burden. While there is a need for both to be engaged in the process, the mandate from God is for the Church to care for the orphaned and fatherless, not necessarily for the government to do it. It is certainly much more convenient for us to let the government tackle the job, and, of course, our tax dollars support that the country's welfare system, but what is missing in our current governmental program is the heart of a Heavenly Father.

The "P" Word Explained

Poverty is an interesting word and means something very different when comparing poverty in a DC and a least developed country (LDC), which gets back to the "relative poverty" discussion. The United States has approximately 15 percent of its population living in poverty.[11] A person is considered in poverty when individually he or she makes less than $11,702, or when a family of four makes less than $22,314.[12] To truly define the difference between poverty in a DC and poverty in a LCD, additional words are added to the word *poverty*. *Severe* is one of those words and is used to describe the bottom billion people who live on less than $1.00 a day. Around the globe, one person in seven makes less than $365 a year. That's a big difference! So poverty in a DC is significant and needs to be addressed and not minimized, but it is very different from the severe poverty that the bottom billion people face in many parts of the world. Another form of poverty in a DC is not monetary in nature but has economic results. This is the poverty of mind that results in inability to make choices or to change one's circumstances.

I have to be honest here. It is really difficult to look at the poverty statistics in a DC and compare them to the severe poverty of an LDC. I'm much more sympathetic to those who are living in abject poverty and facing starvation on a daily basis than those who have access to resources and are considered food-secure. In a DC, poverty is a difficult thing for sure, but with so much access to resources there are few people who are food-insecure and fear starving to death because of a lack of food. Shelters, food pantries, churches, and other benevolent resources ensure that people in DCs are not at risk of starvation. In the case of an LDC there are no safety nets and no backup plans.

The Developed Country Jungle: Distractions and Perspectives

All developed countries have one thing in common: distractions. DCs have a lot to offer, and it is nearly impossible to avoid being swept into the current of activities. Each day we are bombarded with activities to choose from. We have family and church obligations, school, and work. We even have to schedule time for fun to make sure it happens. You have likely lamented over the insanity of it all, just as I have. While each of us has to find a pace that works, we also have to ask ourselves, Are we sacrificing what is best for what is busy? We are so busy that sometimes we miss the needs of the hurting, the poor, the oppressed, and, yes, the orphaned. If the enemy can't get us to live a life of sin, his most effective tactic is to render us ineffective by making us busy.

In a DC, we also tend to lose perspective on what *needs* actually are. Instead of being content with what we have, we are always wanting more. Our focus becomes what we don't have rather than the blessings we do have. This makes for an egocentric society—self-focused rather than other-focused. A self-focus is more than a distraction that keeps our attention away from the needs of others; it often also results in our having to work hard to pay for all the stuff we have purchased or desire to purchase. When is enough enough?

For years my friend Marc was part owner of a successful building company. One day while praying, he felt God asking him what he wanted his life to look like in the future. Among other things such as good health and a happy family, Marc responded that although he had a nice house and two cars, it might be even better to have a nicer house and better, more useful vehicles. That way he could serve God even better. To that, he felt God say three simple words: "And then what?" So Marc turned up the volume, adding bigger and better things to his request. Again God's response was simply, "And then what?" Taken a bit aback, Marc added his wildest dreams, coming up with everything and anything that would satisfying his heart's desires. In the quietness of his heart, Marc felt the final challenge: "So you have it all—fame, power, all the money in the world, whatever you want. And then what?"

Marc recalls that discourse with God as a turning point in his life. Marc and his wife closed the business, sold their home, and moved to a different part of the state. For more than twenty years, Marc and Roberta have worked with Campus Crusade for Christ. Marc realized that things were never going to satisfy him and he already had everything he needed. He discovered that his deepest desire was not to have more but to be more like Christ and to give more of himself. His realization changed his life, and his family members' lives, and the lives of countless others.

All of us have to consider the deeper issues and decide when enough is enough.

Living in a developed country jungle highlights a few of the cultural issues that can divert our attention from what is most important. In future chapters, we'll cover many suggestions for ways to swim against the cultural tide and change some of the distractions that keep us from seeing the needs of orphaned children both in our own culture and around the world.

The Face of the Orphan Crisis in Developed Countries

Probably the most confusing aspect of the orphan crisis in a DC is defining the word *orphan*. Orphans are "over there" in that far-away country, not here in this country. And, as we have mentioned before, the definition of an orphaned child is one who has lost one parent, or both parents, which technically qualifies a child of a single-parent family to be an orphaned child. One of the characteristics of a DC is that we are "civilized," so we try to use more palatable terms in an effort to be less offensive—terms like *vulnerable child, at-risk child*, etc. While defining a child with one parent as "orphaned" might offend a single parent, to get an accurate picture of the crisis in a DC, we have to address the issues, hopefully without offending. In reality, regardless of the terminology, the point is that children in any country who are raised without two parents have disadvantages. And those challenges increase exponentially if the single-parent family is also economically disadvantaged.

Single-Parent Families

In 2007, 13.7 million single parents in the United States were responsible for raising 21.8 million children. In other words, 26 percent of all children under twenty-one in the United States in 2007 resided in single-parent families.[13] That means one quarter of the children in the United States were considered, to a lesser or greater degree, living as single orphans. Of the single parents, 84 percent of them were mothers, 45 percent were divorced, 34 percent were never married, and only 1.7 percent were widowed.[14]

The cause of becoming a single-parent family has changed over the years. In the 1950s it was most often the death of a spouse that left a child with only one parent. Today the main cause is divorce.

In the United States, half of all marriages end in divorce. That means one out of every two children will live in a single-parent family at some point before they reach age eighteen.[15] Globally, divorce is affecting most DCs. The countries with the highest divorce rates are Belarus, Russia, Sweden, Lativia, and Ukraine.[16] In the United States the top five states for divorces are Kentucky, Alabama, Alaska, Arkansas, and Oklahoma.[17]

A growing contingent of women are intentionally choosing to have babies or to adopt as a single person. In general, these women have a higher economic standing and more support in their lives, which helps considerably.[18] Unplanned pregnancy is another area that has grown in recent years and, depending on the circumstances, could be a blessing or could be devastating.[19]

Culturally, it is now much more acceptable to be a single parent than in the past, and resources for single parents are much more available in a DC. Living in a single-parent family is difficult, but both single parents and children seem to fare best when they have a strong web of connections, a true support network. A single mom with two children and few relationships and connections are bound to experience more difficulties when anything goes awry than the single mom with family close by, neighbors, and other significant relationships. The mother with few connections has no backup to make everyday life a bit easier, while the mother with a safety net has someone to call when she has an emergency at work.

Some of the stated risks for the children of single parents are significant, particularly in lower-income families:

- Lower levels of educational achievement
- Twice as likely to drop out of school
- More likely to become teen parents
- More conflict with their parent (s)
- Less supervised by adults
- More frequently abuse drugs and alcohol
- More high-risk sexual behavior
- More likely to join a gang
- Twice as likely to go to jail
- Four times as likely to need help for emotional and behavioral problems
- More likely to participate in violent crime
- More likely to commit suicide
- Twice as likely to get divorced in adulthood[20]

While these issues are considerable, developing supportive relationships and setting goals and strategies can make a big difference. Supporting single parents may be the most beneficial way that we as the Church can address the orphan crisis in our own DC. With more than one-fourth of all children in the United States being in a single-parent family, the opportunities are endless. Parenting is hard work, and doing it all alone adds extra challenges. Following are two inspiring programs that continue to serve single parents.

Alpine Chapel in Lake Zurich, Illinois, has a ministry for single moms. The ministry is designed to encourage and mentor single moms while creating opportunities for connections and relationships. It is a great way to minister to children through parental development and encouragement.

Teen Mother Choices (TMC) is a ministry that has helped teenage mothers in the United States for more than two decades. Teen mothers who choose to parent their children find their lives especially challenging. TMC, utilizing the local church, stands together with these young moms. Through mentoring and training, the program empowers these women to get their parenting off to a solid start.

Perhaps you are a single parent and you are resonating with what we have been talking about. If you are struggling, I encourage you to do something as well. If you need help or support, pick up the phone and talk to someone. Create intentional relationships that will help support you and your children. Don't be afraid to ask for help. You can't do it all on your own. None of us were meant to. That's why we are part of a bigger picture: the body of Christ.

Trafficked Children

We tend to think that because we live in a developed country we don't have any of the same ills as emerging or least developed countries. Unfortunately, that is not always the case. Regardless of how we whitewash it, we have to face the alarming news that children *are* trafficked in developed countries.

The sex-slave trade is growing in the United States and can be found in every state, though it may take a different shape from the way trafficking happens in ECs or LDCs. It is definitely part of our new reality. I recently heard an interview with a teen who had been coerced at a local suburban mall to go "work" for a guy. She was promised a new car and other enticing benefits. She went under her own volition, so no one was the wiser. Unfortunately for her, he was a convincing liar and was part of a sex trafficking ring. By the time she realized what had happened, she was unable to escape. Within hours she became a sex slave and was sold to the highest bidder. But her abductor happened to have been under surveillance. Within forty-eight hours he was arrested and jailed, and the girl was sent home. She was one of the fortunate ones.

Other developed countries have experienced a surge in trafficking as well. Although it is hard to find statistics, Canada's sex-slave population is on the rise as well. Girls and women are brought into the country with promises. Once in Canada, the women's passports are taken away and they are forced into slavery.

Canada has enacted a provision for trafficked persons that, if a person is of age, she is not deported once she is rescued out of the sex-slave trade. She is given a Temporary Resident Permit, which includes health care. She is also fed, sheltered, and given an opportunity to apply for Canadian citizenship.[21] That's quite a benefit, and it serves the victim rather than further complicating an already difficult situation.

The sex-slave industry is already the third largest criminal industry in the world after illegal arms and drug sales, and it is not going away anytime soon.[22] In fact, in the United States in 2005 there were estimated more than 300,000 child victims and around 15,000 who were brought into the United States.[23] This is an atrocity that continues to grow, leaving a wake of devastation.

Child Pornography

Child pornography is an enormous industry in developing countries in general, and its production is a huge industry in the United States. Vulnerable children are the industry's special prey. We need to be vigilant to protect all of our country's children, but special cautions need to be given to the vulnerable.

Gangs

Gangs offer connection and camaraderie. For kids who need to feel a part of something bigger than themselves, a gang can provide pseudo-parenting, feeling of belonging, money, power, and in a way, direction. Children who are economically impoverished are especially vulnerable.

Street Children

Children who are emotionally and physically detached from family are easy targets for evil. Children end up on the street for several reasons, including by their own choices or because of things done to them.

Regardless of the reason, these kids are orphaned, emotionally and physically, and are in danger.

Emotionally Abandoned Children

Children need attention and care. But when parents are distracted, encumbered, and struggling to keep food on the table, children can end up a low priority. If parents are also unstable or abusing substances, the mix becomes a recipe for emotional abandonment.

Although there are no statistics demonstrating how many children have been emotionally abandoned, there is evidence all around: petty theft, gangs, children home alone, runaways, etc. Not all these problems are the result of emotional abandonment, but certainly emotional abandonment contributes to these difficult issues.

Children in Foster Care

On any given day there are around 500,000 children in foster care in the United States.[24] About 130,000 are available for adoption.[25] While we know the foster care system is not perfect, it is an imperfect solution to a difficult problem. Soon we will look at the specifics of foster care and how we might help. For now, it's most important to remember that for children in transitional care, the Church can be a place of safety and support.

Immigrants

Children of parents who have recently immigrated to the United States, legally or illegally, are considered at-risk. Whichever side of the immigration fence you stand on, these families are in our country, and many are poor and need help.

Not long ago I visited an impoverished area in Knoxville, Tennessee. Clayton Wood is the president of Allies for Orphans and is the director of the SOAR mentorship program.[26] He gave me a tour of the neighborhood surrounding his ministry, pointing out the highlights.

"This family is from Guatemala," he'd say. Then he'd point next door: "This house is where a drug dealer lives." Rounding the block, he told me, "A grandma raising several of her grandchildren lives here, and this house has a mom and several kids. The mom is unemployed." And there were many more. One of many local drug dealers lived on the same block as the school, just across the street from a church and next door to the public playground. It was a sobering tour. If we ignore the obvious problems now, we will end up helping to clean up the mess later. A better solution is to get involved in the community, as Clayton is doing. The SOAR program offers mentoring, tutoring, and safe afternoon activities for the vulnerable children in the community. Addressing these needs early in children's lives gives them a better chance for success later in life.

Response to the Orphan Crisis in Developed Countries

So what do we do? The orphan crisis is truly in our own backyard. Although the orphan crisis may not be as easily definable in a DC as in an LDC, the crisis merits our attention and action.

Three steps you can take may make a difference in the life of a child in a DC. All are manageable, and all will make positive contributions to the crisis. Although we will talk about many more ideas later in the book, here are three to get you started:

1. *See the problem.* You have to slow down enough to take notice. You will be amazed by what you see. Notice the single-parent families in your neighborhood and at your church. If you have children, listen to their stories and take note when you hear of children who are struggling, who lack supervision, or who might be from a single-parent family with few resources. Pray that God will show you what He wants you to see.

2. *Start right where you are.* You don't need to look far. Just look in your neighborhood, your town, and your area. You might undertake an Internet search for local mentoring programs, or find a family living lo-

cally who has foster children and offer to bring a meal.

3. *Start small, and focus on needs.* My grandmother used to sing me a cute little song: "One step at a time, only one step at a time. Take that one step carefully, take that one step prayerfully. This is the way to victory: one step at a time." That's what I'm talking about. Just take one step at a time. Identify a need, and then meet it. It's not rocket science. All you have to do is be observant, see the need, then be willing to do something about it.

In a developed country the door swings both ways; we receive tremendous benefits and live with great distractions. We have to be willing to minimize the distractions, see the needs of orphaned and vulnerable children, and then do something. You can't change the world by yourself, but you can change one little piece of it right where you live.

In the next chapter we will look at the global orphan crisis in emerging countries. Countries in a time of tremendous change can overlook orphaned and vulnerable children. We will explore what the crisis looks like and how we can be a part of the solution.

QUESTIONS TO PONDER

1. Before reading this chapter, did you realize that the United States and other DCs had an orphan crisis?

2. On a larger societal level, what do you think are the benefits of living in a developed country?

3. What are the biggest drawbacks?

4. How do you react to the definition of children in a single-parent family as "orphaned"?

5. Did reading this chapter spark any ideas that might lead to solutions to the orphan crisis in a developed country?

ACTION POINT:
DISCOVER TRAFFICKING IN
YOUR OWN BACKYARD

It's easy to think that trafficking takes place in other countries and not ours. Use the Internet to find out more about how trafficking is affecting your state. See what the problem looks like, what resources are available for victims, and if there has been any success in prosecuting perpetrators. Are you surprised at what you found? Discuss your findings with the group next week.

Young Marielena's has hope because of the persistence and love of a woman who sees a future for her even when Marielena can't see it herself. *Diane Lynn Elliot, photographer © Diane Lynn Elliot*

5

The Orphan Crisis in Emerging Countries

Do not deprive the foreigner or the
fatherless of justice, or take the cloak
of the widow as a pledge.
Deuteronomy 24:17

Marielena is only sixteen years old and lives in Peru. She is not your typical teenager. Marielena has an eighteen-month-old baby girl named Mercedes, but her daughter cannot live with her. Marielena is used to hardship: She lost her own mother when she was three years old. Unfortunately, it seems that she stopped progressing mentally around the time of her mother's death, perhaps as a side effect from the trauma.

After her mom died, Marielena endured other horrific experiences that further scarred her. She was raped, possibly by her father, her uncle, or a boy in the neighborhood. It is impossible to determine because she can't even tell you herself. We do know that her father had a medical problem that caused him to stay in bed a lot of the time and Marielena had to go out to do errands. While she was out in the streets, people took advantage of her vulnerability. One awful, unthinkable incident left her pregnant, and nine months later Mercedes entered this world.

Christen Morrow is a new friend of mine who lives in Lima, the capital city of Peru. Christen is an amazingly dedicated and—as I found out firsthand—quite fearless visionary leader. Through many circumstances that could only be credited to God, this southern California lady ended up serving in Lima with Young Life's Capernaum ministry to disabled youth. Several years into her ministry, she has become a part of the Peruvian culture, is newly married to a Peruvian man, and is tremendously networked in the ministry realm to both Christian and secular services working with disabled teenagers. It is through Christen that I was able to meet the shy and sweet Marielena.

Marielena now lives in a government-run girls orphanage in Peru along with 179 other girls ages fourteen to eighteen. Originally started by nuns 118 years ago, this orphanage has mostly been taken over by the government, with just a few nuns still in residence to direct the religious education. There are eight homes on the property where the girls live until they turn eighteen, when they are released. The residence is smaller than a city block and is barricaded from the world behind colorful concrete walls.

Entering the campus felt a little like entering a minimum-security facility with guards in black uniforms wearing military boots. After answering some questions and making several phone calls, the guard had us wait in the little guardhouse until a nicely dressed lady came to greet us. She became our escort for the rest of our tour.

Our escort was one of the orphanage's psychologists. After receiving Christen warmly, she greeted the rest of the team professionally. As our assigned host for our visit, she gave us a thirty-minute interview in her office. Eventually a house mother entered the room wearing a blue apron with the words *I love my job* printed on it. She brought Marielena along so we could spend some time with this precious young lady.

Marielena had long, curly black hair with bangs neatly swept up to the back and finished with a small braid. She was petite but physically mature for a sixteen-year-old. She greeted us with the typical Peruvian air kiss on both cheeks. We brought some pictures of Marielena's daughter, and she pulled the pictures close as if to draw her daughter near to her heart. During our conversation Christen asked Marielena if she had any dreams. Marielena said that she dreams of one day having a house and a bike and of living with her daughter, Mercedes. She says she has bad dreams, too.

The harsh reality is that it doesn't matter what Marielena dreams. Without help from someone of influence who cares about her future, her dreams will never come true. She will become just another sad statistic while her daughter relives the cycle of poverty she has been born into. Fortunately, someone has dreams for this teen mom and is looking out for her even though Marielena is completely unaware.

Christen has a heart for Marielena and is working to get her into a program that will teach her a marketable skill and could become a long-term family for her. Christen's friend Doris, who is caring for Mercedes, has a dream for Mercedes as well. Doris wants to raise her to be educated, well-behaved, well-adjusted, and able to understand several languages, which in itself is a marketable skill in Peru. Perhaps one day Marielena's dreams can come true. But it won't happen without enormous prayer and the relentless pursuit of these two compassionate, vigilant women who have chosen to be God's hands and feet in a broken world that so desperately needs His love.

The Emerging Country (EC) of Peru

After flying nine hours with a long layover in Houston, we finally arrived in Lima, Peru. Our excitement ebbed away as the clock ticked closer to midnight and we were stuck in the immigrations and customs lines for more than an hour. Finally, we got the little green light that told us we could leave the customs area. We bolted for the sliding doors leading to the reception area. As we rolled our luggage cart full of bags and a shop vacuum through the doors, we were elated—exhausted, but elated. Once we passed through the doors, we were shocked to see hundreds and hundreds of various shades of brown Peruvian faces standing behind small rope barriers smiling, waving, and holding signs in Spanish. But the crowd was not actually there to celebrate our arrival! It was close to Christmas, and whole families came to the airport to see their loved ones arrive. In the back of the crowd, I saw a tall gringa with strawberry blond hair waving pale arms frantically. I knew we had found our host, Christen.

Corrie, my twenty-something niece, and Morgan, a Moody college student helping me with projects related to the book, were my traveling companions. Christen was our tour guide, interpreter, ministry expert, and host. Her husband, Christian, became our driver, local culture expert, big brother to the girls, and chef of local fare (except when Corrie, an actual chef, joined in the local cuisine and cooked a harmless guinea pig for supper one evening).

The next six days were a blur of children's homes, orphanages, interviews with ministry leaders, and administrators. We snapped more than 4,000 photographs, attended Christmas programs, and used every spare moment to take in the local sights and culture. Peru is a fascinating place, even more so because this emerging country (EC) is so different from the developed country (DC) we had just come from.

Once we hit the streets we were confronted with the bumper-to-bumper traffic and crazy driving habits. In general, people drive faster and with much less order than in the U.S. In addition, because of the lax emission controls, pollution billows from the older cars and trucks. In Peru, many cars look like demolition derby cars with dings and scratches all over. It was not very reassuring. On the other hand, in the week we were there we saw only one minor accident. Somehow the crazy road and driving system works for them, but you need nerves of steel to actually drive there.

On most of the buildings, both residential and commercial, there are gates, bars, and walls—and even sometimes electric wire or razor wire. Security was much more evident than we would have seen in a DC; it was obvious there were significant issues regarding burglary and theft. I was reprimanded several times to keep my camera out of sight, especially when riding in the car. Each new Peruvian friend we picked up regaled me with a theft story about having someone smash through the car glass to grab a purse or camera. Although I couldn't wrap my mind around the idea of a snatch and grab because I have never personally experienced anything like that, I heeded their words, hid my camera under a sweater, and took more care to observe my surroundings.

Living behind gates and walls is also a foreign concept. Having always had a yard and green space around my house, I missed the openness and the feeling of freedom. While we make sure to keep our house locked when we're gone, we have the freedom of working in the yard with the garage door up without the fear of someone stealing from us. We also don't worry about leaving things in a locked car when we are at the local grocery store. Just having to keep safety foremost in my mind was a very different experience and not at all comfortable.

As one digs a little deeper, more subtle differences come to light. In the States, in general, family ties are good, but definitely not as strong as they once were. Families are busy, everyone goes in different directions, and independence is fiercely guarded, even within a family unit. There are limited expectations that the children will care for aging parents as many parents have saved for an independent retirement.

In Peru and in many emerging countries, family is the center of their world. Although in Peru the average workweek is about forty-eight hours a week or more, their one day off is spent with family. It is also common for family to live near each other or in the same family home or building. Grown male children often bring their new brides to their family home, where a new room or floor is added for the couple. In the several-story home where we stayed, Christian and Christen had their own apartment in the same building as Christian's grandmother and an uncle. Christian had lived in this building most of his life, which is not uncommon. There are significant expectations for Peruvian children to care for aging parents, financially and otherwise. Several people in their twenties and thirties whom we spoke to were already expected to support their parents and even grandparents financially.

Emerging countries generally desire to get into the global fast lane with the DCs, but ECs usually don't have the infrastructure or the economic resources to compete. In Peru's case, until the last fifteen years or so, they have been fighting in a civil war with a rebel faction called the Shining Path. Years ago rebels were more active in the cities, using guerrilla tactics to kill civilians as well as causing some problems in the jungles. Lately, they have been more active in the jungle areas and have joined forces with the drug cartel, which is very big into cocaine. This has forced an enormous migration, as the Peruvian people living in the jungles head for the seemingly safer areas of the cities. A city with an infrastructure meant to support approximately five million people now holds more than ten million, causing crowded conditions and bumper-to-bumper traffic. Because of the street congestion, it can take more than two hours to drive from one end of Lima to the other.

War and governmental disruption hold countries back from development. With governmental shifts and frequent leadership changes, the larger issues of globalization take a backseat. It is said that in Peru, the government and police are corrupt and look for handouts and bribes regularly. A problem that goes hand in hand with police corruption is the issue of theft. When a person is caught stealing, a well-timed bribe can turn an authority's attention another direction. The lack of justice and a reliable civil structure encourages lawlessness, which in turn causes corruption. A vicious cycle has to be broken in order for a society to progress.

Another small but notable issue related to infrastructure has to do with utilities. Electricity is fairly reliable in the cities. The water, however, is not as reliable and needs to be filtered, boiled, or bottled for safety. An inconvenience like that would be protested vehemently in a DC. Such issues affect not only the quality of life, but how much time it takes to function.

In Peru, as in many ECs, there is a high level of disparity between the haves and the have-nots. More than 34.8 percent of the people in Peru live under the national poverty line.[1] Although the unemployment rate as of November 2011 was 7.7 percent (while in the United States, in recession, it was 8.6 percent during that same time),[2] people in poverty generally have less education and are not able to find jobs to sustain their families. In the best of circumstances, they might make the minimum wage, which is roughly $4.00 per hour, though I'm not sure that the minimum wage is enforced. For the very poor who live outside Lima in squatter areas like Pachacútec, they have the distance disadvantage of having to bus into Lima to find work. With the transportation cost included, a best-case scenario is that they might make around $20 a day. That is barely enough to keep the bills paid and feed the family. There is no room for thinking about the future or for unexpected expenses like a medical bill. That is, of course, if they can even find jobs!

When income is so undependable and transitory, people develop the habit of spending money as soon as they have it. If a wage-earner received an unexpected bonus, he would tend to spend it quickly because who knows when money might be available again? This mindset is very difficult to break. The ability to think about or plan for the future is completely contrary to poverty thinking.

I once heard a story about a man in Haiti who had a mango tree. The mango tree produced fruit twice a year, and selling the fruit was the only source of income for his family. The money he made from each crop had to last six months until the next harvest was ready. At one point, between harvests, the family was out of money and in desperate need of food, so he decided to cut down the mango tree to sell the wood for firewood. When asked why he would cut down his only source of income, he replied that if his family starved before the next harvest, what difference would it make anyway? Although I can't imagine the agony of a father having to make that type of life-altering decision, the future for that family, unfortunately, looked even bleaker the day after that tree was cut down.

Because of the cycle-of-poverty mindset, another issue that surfaces directly impacts the global orphan crisis. When a family can't provide the necessary food for their children, they might be coerced into selling a child for money, or hiring that child out for, what they think, is legitimate work but ends up being a form of child trafficking. Either option is devastating to the child and breaks the family apart.

The double whammy in orphan care is when a family has a child they can't afford and that child also has a physical or mental disability. The reality for many parents of these special children is that they don't have the time, resources, or abilities to meet the child's needs. Such children end up in a facility, abandoned, or worse. In Peru, we were able to visit a government-run orphanage for children with neurological disabilities. The facility was very nice in terms of the local standards, with doctors, nurses, and staff to care for the children. Despite the good physical care these children receive, they still lack the love and care that fully functioning parents could provide. The one bright spot in this story is that, with Christen's help, churches are willing to get involved and make eternal investments in the lives of the children. I'll tell you more about this amazing program in the solutions section of this book.

In Lima, my friend Christen told me story after story of young children who were sexually abused, molested, and tortured. Perhaps because ECs and LDCs lack the infrastructure and resources employed to bring perpetrators to justice as they do in a DC, the overpowering of the weak and young for violent acts of incest, rape, and molestation is a pervasive issue. Violence against the vulnerable affects many more children than we would care to know. Christen's true stories were especially disturbing when the victims were orphaned, abandoned, and physically disabled children.

One young woman Christen works with is severely disabled. To Christen's horror, she had been repeatedly raped by her family and others, causing her to give birth twice during her teen years. Both of her children ended up in orphanages. Her mother was able to secure a low-paying job with an apartment included in the salary, and she and her daughter were able to escape the assaults. However, since the daughter was disabled and could not walk, her mother couldn't manage to get her up and down the stairs, leaving her stranded at home. The daughter was left in bed twenty-four hours a day, lying in her own excrement because they couldn't even afford diapers.

A local Peruvian woman, Julia, started a ministry through her local church for children with disabilities. Julia and her coworkers go into a home, help to solve the obvious problems, and take the children to another facility at least one day a week where they are given meals, baths, physical therapy, and love. Can you imagine the feelings of love and respect such care brings to these disabled children? What a tremendous gift of dignity a parent receives when she is finally able to care for her child in a more respectful and humane way. Nothing short of astounding, this ministry touches a child's life at the core and in the process points the way to the God who loves her like no other.

Emerging countries are under great pressure to experience economic growth. Sometimes that overarching goal leaves no room to care for the very people who make the progress possible. People are oppressed in an effort to boost the nation's international stature. For example,

> Slave labor in developing countries such as Brazil, China and India is fueling part of their huge economic growth, according to a State Department report. In Brazil there is a trafficking phenomenon with thousands of forced laborers found on plantations growing sugar cane for Brazil's booming production and export of the biofuel ethanol.[3]

The issue has no easy fix, but overall the globe is waking up to the problem. We hope new regulations and insights will continue to solve the issues.

Emerging Countries Globally

There are roughly ninety-three countries in the medium development category. With emerging countries the Human Development Index ranges from .783 in Uruguay to .522 in Bhutan.[4] We will take a hop, skip, and jump view through some of the notable countries in this category.[5]

HDI Country Ranking	Country	HDI number	Unemployment rate–Nov. 2011 %	CIA poverty numbers by percent of population	Gross Domestic Product (GDP) per Capita–CIA World Factbook	Orphaned Children Estimates
# 80	Peru	.725	7.7	34.8	$ 9,200.	550,000
# 98	Dominican Republic	.689	14.2	42.2	$ 8,900.	190,000
# 101	China	.687	4.1	2.8	$ 7,600.	Over 500,000
# 108	Bolivia	.663	6.0	30.3	$ 4,800.	320,000
# 111	Moldova	.649	9.1	26.3	$ 2,500.	14,000
# 113	Egypt	.644	9.4	20	$ 6,200.	170,000
# 121	Honduras	.625	27.8	65	$ 4,200.	150,000
# 123	South Africa	.619	25	50	$ 10,700.	3,400,000
# 134	India	.547	9.4	25	$ 3,500.	31,000,000
# 139	Cambodia	.523	1.68	31	$ 2,100.	630,000

Some of the notable countries that have been steadily progressing up the list are India and China. While it would take an extensive study to know what these two countries have been doing to fuel the growth, a few of the easy answers are *quality of education* (which positively affects the labor force), *science and technology growth*, and *increase in high-tech and general exports*. How long can they sustain this growth? China seems to have a better potential for continued growth and is actually considered the second largest world economy,[6] China does not yet have the economic power to overtake the United States, which is currently the global economic leader. After the United States and China, there is a significant economic distance before the next countries, Japan and India. What both China and India have going for them is momentum and drive in the new global economy.

China's overall numbers look very good but are actually suspect in some regards. Statistics are generated from within the country, and many outside organizations question the low number of orphaned children declared for a country the size of China. While we don't have any way to verify these suspicions, it is interesting to note that they are still ranked #101 on the Human Development Index, which for a country that otherwise looks good on paper is quite low.

The most notable finding is the enormous disparity between economic status and human development standing. In particular, India is ranked fourth in terms of GDP (size of their economy), but they are ranked #134 in terms of human capital, which is on the very low end of the EC status. Although India has progressed in economic development over the last several decades, there are still enormous problems evidenced by the fact that more than 25 percent of the people in the country remain in extreme poverty, with more than 31 million children considered orphaned.[7] Let me repeat that last part: There are more than *31 million* orphaned children in India alone. That is more than the populations of the states of Texas (25,145,561), Oklahoma (3,751,351), and New Mexico combined (2,059,179).[8] Granted, India has a higher number of people than any country in the world at 1.21 billion, but 31 million orphaned children make up more than 2.6 percent of the population, which doesn't include the potentially hundreds of thousands of street and trafficked children.

ECs are countries in transition, and we know transitions are never easy. ECs need strong leadership with intentionality and direction, or they may stay stuck in that middle ground—almost there, but not quite. In addition, ECs, especially ones ranked in the lower HDI levels, are just one disaster away from stepping back into the Stone Ages. While in Peru we experienced an earthquake of 4.8 magnitude, with an epicenter thirty miles off the coast of Lima. No significant damage resulted. Had the earthquake been a significant one, it could have sent millions of people and an entire country into chaos.

Orphan Crisis in Emerging Countries

So what does the orphan crisis look like in emerging countries? Several issues are common across most ECs, while other issues are unique to particular countries. A missionary from Cambodia describes a contributing factor to the orphan crisis in that country: "Twenty-seven years of civil war in Cambodia have left the country in a state of despair and decay. About one-third of the orphans in western Cambodia lost at least one of their parents to a land mine."[9] Although children orphaned by land mines may be unique to Cambodia, many other countries are recovering from war, natural disasters, and other troubles.

The following issues commonly contribute to the orphan crisis in most ECs. The first two seem to be the most prevalent, but the rest are in no particular order.

Poverty

Poverty is a major issue in ECs in relation to the orphan crisis. As you could see in the chart, 34.8 percent of Peru's total population are considered to be in poverty. Other countries with high poverty percentages are the Dominican Republic (42.2 percent), South Africa (50 percent), and Honduras (65 percent). This is a significant number of the population hindered by extreme poverty and struggling to provide basic care for themselves and their family, with limited ability to break the poverty cycle. Children are often abandoned primarily because their parents lack the resources to care for their children. In other cases, heads of families move to try to find work or abandon their families because they simply can't afford them.

I heard one very sad story about a little girl I met in Pachacútec, an impoverished area outside of Lima. When Vicky was only three years old, her mother sat her in front of a market with a sign around her neck that said, "Take me home. I'm to be given away." Fortunately, Vicky ended up at a small family-style children's home in Pachacútec, where she has been raised lovingly for the last five years. This story could have gone so many tragic ways, but God protected this little one, and marked her for something special. Vicky loves Jesus and is spiritually mature for her age. As she continues to grow in Christ, perhaps her testimony will bring others to know Him as well.

So why would a mother put a sign around her daughter's neck and walk away? Did she stand in the distance watching to make sure someone respectable picked up Vicky? Or did she just walk away, distraught but relieved of the burden of a hungry child? Perhaps she was running away from her past. Perhaps she felt she had no other choice. I can only imagine giving up her daughter was a difficult and painful decision. Such is poverty. There seems to be no hope, no way out. Breaking the cycle of poverty is nothing short of a miracle.

The other side of the poverty coin is that in ECs there is also the potential for great wealth. When I was in South Africa a few years ago, I was astonished at the disparity between the wealthy and the poor living in close proximity. I was going to visit a friend in a lovely, gated subdivision but had to drive by a long shanty town stretching for miles that literally went all the way up to the subdivision entrance. At the time, it puzzled me how people who lived in the lush subdivision could drive by the shanty town every day knowing there were starving people right at their gate. It seemed cruel. When I inquired about the situation, my friend said she and her neighbors didn't think anything much about it.

It was their reality, and they were used to it. At first I was a bit judgmental, but once I was really honest with myself, I realized I probably wouldn't have been much different. Just like my South African friend on the other side of the world, I, too, can get used to hearing about poverty and grow callused to God's heart and the needs of the world.

Many of the EC countries have a wide gap between rich and poor and have a considerably smaller middle class. It seems, however, that as a country progresses on the development scale, it tends to grow the middle class. In developed countries, like the United States, the middle class drives the country.

As Jesus says in Mark 14:7, the poor will always be with us. That doesn't give us permission to disregard the tragedy. Rather it should give us the incentive to be more like Christ and minister to the deep needs of an impoverished population. In the case of the orphaned child, helping to minister to the needs of a family in poverty can help to keep a child from becoming orphaned. For the child who has already felt the ill effects of poverty, providing the tools to break the cycle will be a worthwhile endeavor benefiting that child and future generations.

HIV/AIDS

In some countries, such as Peru, HIV/AIDS has not become a prevalent cause of children becoming orphans. In other countries, such as those in Africa, HIV/AIDS runs rampant, and the disease has devastated individuals and their families. South Africa is the emerging country poster child for orphans due to HIV/AIDS with more than 1.9 million children who are said to be single or double orphaned specifically as a result of AIDS.[10] Countries in Asia are also affected by HIV/AIDS, but unfortunately, in many cases, the data may not accurately portray what percentage of orphaned children is attributable to this illness. Many countries, like China, don't even report that information.

Regardless of statistics, we know that HIV/AIDS is a deadly virus that leaves destruction in its wake. In some ECs, information and education are in short supply, while sexual promiscuity is part of the cultural makeup. We know for sure that this battle is a difficult one, and the disease is spreading exponentially, leaving more orphaned children every day.

Missing Girls and Gender Inequity

Two emerging countries that are terrible offenders of gender inequity are China and India. Historical forces have been at work for centuries, but the invention of ultrasound technologies has taken the tragedy to a whole new level. "The destruction of baby girls is a product of three forces: the ancient preference for sons; a modern desire for smaller families; and ultrasound scanning and other technologies that identify the sex of a fetus."[11] In 2007 a report by the International Planned Parenthood Federation said there were about 7 million abortions a year in China and more than 70 percent of the aborted fetuses were female.[12] More recent surveys suggest the number is closer to 13 million per year.[13]

In 1979 China started the one-child policy that has exacerbated the abortion situation. Although concern has been expressed by some statisticians who complain that there are already significantly more males than females, the government vows to keep the policy until their original projected date of 2050.[14] China already has 25 million more eligible males than females of marrying age.[15]

Technically speaking, in both China and India, selective abortion based on gender is illegal. However, the empty threat doesn't seem to have any significant consequences. Interestingly, China offers a governmental financial incentive for a one-child family to have a daughter. However, regardless of the initiative, the certainty of missing girls still stands. A report found that "China and India together account for more than 85 million of the nearly 100 million 'missing' women estimated to have died from discriminatory treatment in health care, nutrition access or pure neglect or because they were never born in the first place."[16]

India's situation cold be considered even worse. Delhi's ratio is 866 girls under the age of seven for every thousand boys.[17] In the last thirty-plus years, the ratio of girl babies to boy babies has been falling.[18] And, in India, particularly among impoverished women, full-term daughters often die in early infancy, whether by neglect or by a parent's own hand.[19]

Gender discrimination exists in other ECs to a lesser degree. In many countries significant gender inequity exists in employment, general status, and value. In general, the higher a country ranks on the Human Development Index (HDI) list, the more balanced the gender equity seems to be.

Discrimination

Discrimination is a sickness found everywhere around the globe, whatever a country's status or ranking on the Human Development Index. Discrimination becomes destructive when contributing factors escalate discrimination, turning it into chronic strife, disorder, and ultimately war. The challenge for all governments, organizations, and people is to value each individual as God Himself values people. These values are not based on what a person deserves or has earned but based on the fact that we are all created in the image of God. As Christians we have the responsibility to be the leaders in this crusade to value all people in all circumstances as God values us.

Trafficking

Child labor and sex trafficking are also problems regardless of a country's status. In developed countries, though, more reliable resources exist to bring perpetrators to justice than in less-developed countries. Without the threat of some kind of justice to restrain it, trafficking crime will continue to expand. In addition to justice and compassion organizations relentlessly working to rescue trafficked children, it will take global pressure to cause governments in ECs and LDCs to fight injustice, end government corruption, and move toward reform.

Response to the Orphan Crisis in Emerging Countries

The orphan crisis in every nation calls out for a response. In emerging countries in particular, what's needed most is prevention, cooperation, and caution.

Prevention

Attempting to meet the needs of vulnerable and orphaned children begins *before* the desperate mother feels forced to leave her child at the market. By working with vulnerable children and families, many parents or guardians can be given the tools needed to prevent children from becoming orphaned.

Cooperation

Thousands of churches and governmental and nongovernmental organizations (NGOs) are already working to touch the lives of orphaned children. When Christen moved to Peru several years ago, she started developing a network of people and organizations already working with disabled and orphaned children. She quickly found where the organizations were coming up short and started networking with other individuals and churches to begin meeting those needs. Her approach sounds simple, but in fact these types of connections take years to develop and even more years to grow. With persistence and passion, Christen has developed an amazing network of passionate people who are reaching out to children in Lima and beyond. Here is where it gets fun! If a hundred Christens were willing to start taking a city captive for the sake of orphaned children, thousands and thousands of children and families would be helped. The power of one person to make a difference is astounding. Christen is living it. So can you.

We will talk more about methodology in the solutions section of the book, but remember that helping orphaned children is not done in a vacuum. Working with orphaned children, especially in emerging and least developed countries, has a ripple effect in the neighborhood, community, and city.

After Hurricane Gilbert ravaged Jamaica in the fall of 1988, Arlington Countryside Church put forth a valiant effort to gather food, clothing, and cash for a partner church that had been affected by the storm. Six weeks after the storm, a team of eight adults went to Jamaica to assist with the transport and distribution of the freight and gifts. As the team's leader, I could write a book about how *not* to lead a relief effort team with all the leadership mistakes I made on that trip. In fact, this was the one and only missions trip my husband accompanied me on, and I might have actually ruined him for missions because of it. When we returned, we didn't speak for a week! But now, after many, many years, the experience has become great fodder for a funny story.

The one good decision that came of the leadership misadventure was to give the distribution responsibilities to the elders of the local church. We were able to assist in the heavy lifting, but decisions regarding what families received was left up to the local leaders, who knew the needs. That made all the difference. Some people I would have guessed needed a lot of help really only needed a little. Others who looked just fine to me actually had lost all their belongings and needed significant assistance. The elders knew. We didn't. Without their wisdom and partnership, we would have surely made a mess of things.

When we enter a foreign country convinced that we know what is best for the orphaned children of that country, we lose a valuable learning opportunity. The missionaries and organizations that are most successful are learners first; then they develop partnerships that will work most effectively. Christen uses this methodology in her ministry in Peru, serving at a government-run orphanage with leaders and volunteers from the local church. Both groups will be there long after her involvement comes to an end. This thinking is key to developing lasting change.

Changes don't happen quickly. It takes time to learn what is already being done and to earn the respect needed to change the system from within. Because of the relationships that Christen has built over the years, she has earned the opportunity to help make the orphanage a better place for children. At one point Christen offered to bring in some child-welfare professionals to help with brainstorming and training at the government orphanage. Because of this help, the organization has made positive changes that serve the children even better. For example, rather than move the dorm moms to different houses every other week or so, they are keeping the caregivers with the children for longer periods of time. This little change will help children to bond to their caregivers more effectively, which in turn minimizes later attachment disorders. Little changes can make a big difference.

Caution

In developed countries, we tend to think we have all the answers and we are going to go over "there" and save children. I can't tell you how many people have said to me that they would love to go to _____ (fill in the location) and start an orphanage. Of course it is noble and kindhearted to desire to go to another country and help save children from the orphan crisis. However, traditional "orphanage" thinking has to change. We will cover this extensively in the second half of the book, but for now, hear me when I say that the world doesn't need another institutional "orphanage." What the world desperately needs is an orphan-care ministry with the cultural context and best practices integrated into the program and with local community and church involvement. We need long-term solutions, not just a Band-Aid approach to orphan care.

A great book about forging good relationships in different cultural settings is *When Helping Hurts* by Steve Corbett and Brian Fikkert.[20] It eloquently helps in determining the appropriate type of help needed. If only I'd had this book before my Jamaica disaster, it would have given clarity to my role and saved me from making cultural faux pas. This book will help you learn from your successes rather than by your mistakes.

All It Takes Is You

The global orphan crisis in emerging countries is heartbreaking and challenging, not only for our generation but for future generations. Emerging countries are burdened with conflict, transition, and pressure to grow, even while they are structurally ill-prepared to achieve their lofty goals.

There is a great need to minister to orphaned and abandoned children in emerging countries and to help prevent the problems that produce orphaned children. The opportunities are truly endless. The work is difficult and daunting and not for the faint at heart. Whether God calls you to serve in a front-line ministry or to support one that is already there, you can make a significant difference in the lives of orphaned and abandoned children. It is never too late to start. Today someone is praying that you will be brave enough to open your heart to what God has for you to do. All it takes is one—all it takes is you!

QUESTIONS TO PONDER

1. Emerging countries are a mix of contradictions. Have you ever been to an emerging country? What was it like for you?

2. What didn't you know about ECs before you started reading this chapter?

3. What challenges can you imagine coming to light for serving orphaned and abandoned children in an emerging country?

4. Do you currently know of or support someone working in an emerging country? What experiences make serving there a challenge for him or her?

5. How might we best make a difference in the lives of orphaned and vulnerable children in emerging countries?

ACTION POINT

Pretend you have been asked by your church to start an orphan-care ministry in Antananarivo. Where do you start? How do you come up with a plan? What should be included in the plan? Come up with at least five steps you think are necessary when considering starting a ministry to orphaned children in Antananarivo. (Hint: First you have to find out where it is!)

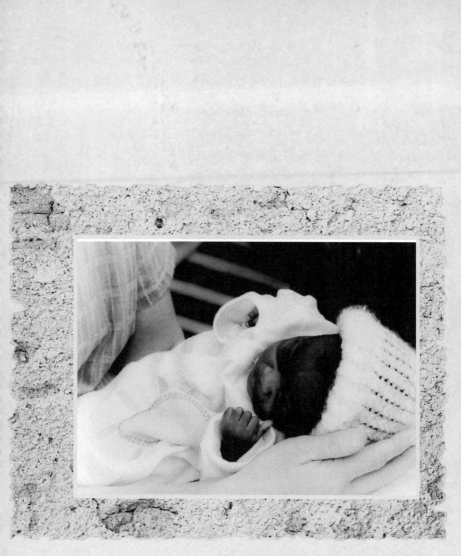

Baby Jennifer's parents have given her up for adoption because they are so poor they cannot afford to provide for her. Pray that God directs the hearts of a godly couple to find their way to this precious soul. *Diane Lynn Elliot, photographer © Diane Lynn Elliot*

6

The Orphan Crisis
in the Least
Developed Countries

He [the Lord] upholds the cause of the
oppressed and gives food to the hungry.
The Lord sets prisoners free, the Lord
gives sight to the blind, the Lord lifts
up those who are bowed down,
the Lord loves the righteous. The Lord
watches over the foreigner and sustains
the fatherless and the widow, but
he frustrates the ways of the wicked.
Psalm 146:7–9

We move on now to the world's least developed countries (LDCs), where, despite desperate conditions, the Lord is upholding the cause of the oppressed and feeding the hungry and lifting up those who are bowed down.

BLOG POST FROM PORT-AU-PRINCE, HAITI

Yesterday the team witnessed something I never wanted to see and hope I never see again.

Ruuska Village is a home for single mothers and orphaned children in Port-au-Prince, Haiti. Started by Barbara Walker more than twenty years ago, Ruuska Village has grown to more than a dozen buildings, with more than twenty full-time residents and many visitors. Over the years, Barbara has found adoptive homes for hundreds of children, two of whom were adopted by my friend and teammate Maggie Mohr.

For the last year I have had a strong feeling that I needed to go to Haiti to better understand this impoverished country. The orphan crisis here is severe, and I wanted to understand why. Through a friend of a friend, Maggie heard I was writing about the global orphan crisis and felt compelled to invite me to go with her to Haiti. I wasn't at all surprised to receive an invitation from a perfect stranger. That's how God has been working in my life lately—through strange and wonderful connections. I immediately agreed. Tonight, several months later, I'm sitting in a guest house in Haiti with Maggie (my new friend), Debbie (her good friend), Susan (a friend from church), Clayton Wood (a ministry partner), and Lucien (our new Haitian brother and fearless guide).

Three days into our trip we have toured three orphanages and four Homes of Hope, fallen in love with dozens of orphaned or abandoned children, had our hearts broken, inhaled more exhaust fumes than I ever thought humanly possible, been encouraged by dedicated ministry volunteers and child care workers, and ended up with more questions than answers.

Yesterday morning started out in an ordinary way with breakfast and waiting around the village until Lucien arrived to take us to visit several orphanages. On my way from the kitchen to my room (in two separate buildings), I walked by an alcove that had a forty-something Haitian couple holding an adorable little girl with beautiful brown skin and curly dark hair. The child was dressed in little, white pajamas and a pink, knitted hat. She was so tiny and beautiful. I didn't know who the people were, so I smiled but didn't stop. Several minutes later I walked by again, and Maggie was holding baby Jennifer, cooing over her and hugging her. I quickly snapped a picture, smiled at the couple again, and walked on. A few minutes later, off to the side, teammate Susan told me this couple was relinquishing their baby for adoption. Then it hit me: This birth mom and dad were actually there at the Village to give up their precious baby girl to a perfect stranger for the rest of her life. Why would they do that? I had been writing about this very thing for the last year, never thinking that I would actually meet the parents who would feel compelled to give up their perfect little girl.

Haiti is a difficult place to live. Infrastructure is minimal and chaotic. The government has been notorious for instability and corruption. Natural disasters set the country back again and again. Deforestation and poor resource management have caused scarcity, and the poverty is palpable. A true testimony of the country's condition is the Haitian Presidential Palace still in ruins two years after the devastating earthquake. Miles of tent cities surround the downtown area and serve as a continual reminder of the pervasive, unrelenting poverty. Billions of dollars have been poured into this country, yet it is still, by far, the poorest country in the Western Hemisphere.

Then, on a micro level, there is baby Jennifer. Her parents are poor. They already have four children ages eleven to eighteen. Her daddy has a job but doesn't make enough money to support yet another baby. He didn't want his wife to get pregnant again, but she did. So they feel the only option is to relinquish the baby for adoption and hope her adoptive parents can provide a better life for her than they can. I wish I had a nice tidy conclusion for this story. I wish the parents didn't feel driven to this decision. I wish I could understand, but I don't. God does. He created Jennifer in her mother's womb. God loves her more than we can comprehend and has a plan for her life.

I feel so helpless. I can't make this go away or make it better. But I can do one thing: pray for baby Jennifer. I pray even as I type, this very moment, that somewhere in the world God is prompting the heart of a godly husband and wife to expand their family through the miracle of adoption and that, somehow, maybe through some unexplained connection, they find baby Jennifer.

A least developed country (LDC) is a country with the lowest rating on the Human Development Index (HDI), exhibiting low socioeconomic and economic development. Since the HDI index was initiated, only three countries have managed to graduate out of this category and into the emerging country (EC) status. While it is exceedingly complicated to understand why these countries are relegated to this position, some of the contributing factors are government instability, conflict, corruption, lack of natural resources, being landlocked, lack of education, inadequate infrastructure, and pervasive diseases. In many cases these countries have also been subjected to natural disasters that have plummeted them back into the pre-industrial age. With globalization being the mantra of the day, the LDCs can't compete and are left in the dust of countries that can.

On a human development level, life is difficult in an LDC. Things that are taken for granted in a developed country (DC) are limited or nonexistent. Unless you live on or near a farm, when you drive down the roads near your home, you probably don't have the fear that a goat, chicken, cow, or crowds of people might step out in front of you (which we experienced as we grazed a baby goat scurrying across a busy road). Because of exhaust emissions requirements in a developed country, you don't pull up behind a cloud of black smoke coming out of a truck overflowing with goods, people, and animals. You also likely don't have to worry about mammoth potholes that could swallow your car, ruin your shocks, and bruise your head when you bang it on the inside car door jam (I say that from personal experience). And, it is unlikely in a DC that you have ever seen a lady on the back of a motorcycle carrying a dozen chickens by their feet, or a guy carrying a piece of plywood. In an LDC all these things are common, and the unpredictability and seemingly chaotic existence is at first unsettling. In developed countries, we have social constructs that keep things predictable and within certain expectations. And while LDCs also have social constructs, life in an LCD is generally just more chaotic and unpredictable.

A vivid picture that sticks in my mind from Haiti is driving at night. In my world, driving at night is a fairly easy, unsurprising occurrence. I have to look out for the occasional deer that might cross the road, but driving is generally a safe and leisurely experience along well-illuminated streets with traffic lights helping drivers flow easily in orderly patterns. The first night we drove in Port-au-Prince was truly terrifying for me. It was pitch dark in the middle of the city, with no streetlights, minimal stoplights (which were ignored anyway), and very few lights in the surrounding buildings. The only illumination for the road were the faint headlights of oncoming traffic dimly breaking through the dust-saturated air or the occasional barrel along the side of the road burning trash or cooking a chicken. People and animals were everywhere. From one moment to the next we didn't know if someone or something would run out in front of the car. The roads were an unpredictable mix of asphalt, dirt, and gravel with huge potholes that tossed the passengers around like a mechanical bull. Horns, music, and voices were a constant distraction, and with no air-conditioning in the car, our windows were opened letting all the dust and exhaust fill our previously sheltered lungs. There were no lane markers, and the bigger vehicles ruled the roads. Vehicles wove in and out of traffic as if it would actually help them get to their destinations faster. It was scary. I heard it said that the way most missionaries die in Haiti is through vehicle accidents. I believe it!

Least developed countries (LDCs) have high infant mortality rates, low life expectancy numbers, inadequate medical care, limited education, high illiteracy rates, high percentages of poverty, and few resources. When a person in a DC gets an infection, he can easily run to the doctor to get a prescription. There is generally a pharmacy on the way home, and in a short time the patient has the tools needed to start getting better. Most people in a DC have a hospital nearby; my own area has dozens of them within a short distance. Our hospitals are staffed with professionals, resources are abundant, the hospital is clean, and ready to serve our needs. Not so in an LDC. Medical attention is rare or nonexistent. Births take place mostly at home, and if the mothers are very fortunate they might have the assistance of a midwife. Complications are frequent, and conditions easily dealt with in a developed country can be life-threatening in an LDC.

Economically, LDCs have limited resources and opportunities for export. While there might be resources available within the country, the means to get those resources into a global market is extremely difficult.

Many years ago an enormous oil reserve was discovered in the Doba area in the southern part of Chad, Africa. Exxon/Mobile and other companies secured the land and started a $4.2 billion project funded by the World Bank. Despite environmental opposition, the project was completed.[1] More than 650 miles of pipeline were built from southern Chad to Cameroon's Atlantic coast in the fishing town of Kribi. Promises were made, and everyone hoped the project would benefit the people of both Cameroon and Chad. But through much controversy, accusations of government corruption, and many mixed reviews, it is still unclear if this project has actually benefited the people of both these LDCs.[2]

Change for an LDC is complicated and arduous. The United Nations, World Bank, and other global organizations have outlined programs to help grow the LDCs, but ultimately it seems that for a country to graduate from the LDC list, the motivation and momentum have to come from within the country. No wonder only three countries have managed to graduate from the LDC list.

The following chart displays information about eleven countries from the lower end of the Least Developed Countries list.[3] The actual bottom ten are all located in Africa. Rather than just look at one continent, we will look at several different continents and the countries that are struggling the most in those areas.

HDI Country Ranking	Country	HDI number	Unemployment rate–Nov. 2011	CIA poverty numbers by percent of population	Gross Domestic Product (GDP) per Capita–CIA World Factbook	Orphaned Children Estimates
# 143	Kenya	.509	40%	19.7%	$ 1,600	2,600,000
# 146	Bangladesh	.500	5%	49.6%	$ 1,700	4,800,000
# 151	Madagascar	.480	5.9%	67.8%	$ 900	910,000
# 153	Papua New Guinea	.466	1.8%	35.8%	$ 2,500	260,000
# 154	Yemen	.462	35%	17.5%	$ 2,700	n/a
# 157	Nepal	.458	46%	25.2%	$ 1,200	650,000
# 158	Haiti	.454	40%	54.9%	$ 1,200	440,000
# 172	Afghanistan	.398	35%	36%	$ 900	2,000,000
# 173	Zimbabwe	.376	97%	68%	$ 500	1,400,000
# 183	Chad	.328	50%	61.9%	$ 1,600	670,000
# 187	Democratic Republic of Congo	.286	68%	59.2%	$ 300	220,000

The high unemployment rate in the majority of these countries is immediately apparent, with the highest being Zimbabwe at 97 percent unemployment. Zimbabwe also has the highest number of people in poverty, at 68 percent of the population. The Congo has the lowest GDP per capita at only $300 per person per year. Bangladesh has the most orphaned children, claiming more than 4.8 million orphaned children, not including street or trafficked children. As you can see there is an enormous disparity between the least developed countries and the developed and emerging countries.

Strengths of the Least Developed Countries

Strengths of LDCs are sometimes difficult to identify, but the biggest two must be resolve and relationships. Without the constant resolve of the people of the LDC countries there would be no hope. Pastor Jacques is one such person in Haiti. He was born in Haiti and educated in the States; then he relocated back to Haiti to minister. Pastor Jacques and his wife are a beacon of hope in their community. Before the earthquake, they had a nice church in Port-au-Prince and were serving their community. At the time of the earthquake Pastor Jacques was in one of the buildings outside the main auditorium. Pastor Jacques breathed a prayer in what he thought were his last moments. What happened next was nothing short of a miracle. The main auditorium slapped down leaving nothing but dust, rubble, and debris. But Pastor Jacques and his wife in the other building were completely unharmed. In the chaos and misery that followed, God sustained Pastor Jacques and his wife and solidified one thing in their minds. The "things" they had built with their hands were all taken away in an instant. What remained was their unwavering commitment to God and to the people of Haiti.

Pastor Jacques and his wife realized thousands of children had been instantly orphaned. Existing problems had become multiplied. They started helping children. Within a very short time, they secured some property and buildings to start taking in orphaned children. Now, two years later, they have created a home for more than twenty children. With new and focused vision, they hope to care for, educate, equip, and love these orphaned children to ensure a bright future for them.

Dixie Bickel is the co-founder and director of God's Littlest Angels. Using her nursing and administration skills, years ago Dixie started a ministry to care for orphaned and vulnerable children. Dixie now has a neonatal unit for critically ill infants staffed by Haitian nurses and volunteers. God's Littlest Angels has become a well-respected adoption agency in Colorado Springs, placing countless children in Christian homes in the United States.

When we sat down with Dixie, I was instantly drawn to her. Her comfortable warmth was just what we needed after a busy day. We toured the facilities, then began exploring deeper questions. Dixie's love was obvious—for the challenged children, as well as for her staff and for the people of Haiti. Although she is a blonde from central Illinois, Dixie ended up in Haiti, changing the lives of thousands. Dixie has a passion for the community and a calling to bring Jesus to those around her. She also has a passion to change the system, especially to end corruption in governmental adoption practices. Dixie and dozens of other child welfare providers are working one person at a time to make a difference. With her contacts in the new government and with much prayer, Dixie is making progress. She, like Pastor Jacques, is a light that shines brightly in Haiti.

I could tell you dozens more stories of people like Pastor Jacques and Dixie. They have the resolve to change the status quo—to make a difference, to continue working for changes and reform, to keep loving people to Jesus, one person at a time.

Relationships are important in LDCs. People need people to survive. People need to work together for the common good. In some communities it can be every person for himself. But, by and large, a bond unites people and gives them the hope that together they can survive. When in crisis mode, it is rare to plan ahead or to think of the future. But one day at a time, they depend on one another to make it through that day.

The Orphan Crisis in Least Developed Countries

We've explored what the orphan crisis looks like in developed and emerging countries. The challenges in LDCs will continue to open your heart to the problems of orphaned children around the world.

Relentless Poverty

Like quicksand, poverty draws people in and doesn't like to let go. People who are in poverty are desperate and do whatever it takes to provide for their families. Like the couple in Haiti who couldn't provide for their baby girl, people are forced to make decisions that no one should ever have to make. Seeing family and friends suffer and die is a part of their everyday existence, not a rare occurrence. It pains them as much as it would pain you or me. It is just more of a reality than in our world. In Haiti, more than 300,000 people died in the earthquake in 2010.[4] Those numbers are staggering in a small country. Everyone was affected by the loss. Everyone lost someone. Many people never found the bodies of their loved ones.

Hunger and food insecurity make up another part of the poverty equation. There are very few overweight people in Haiti, or in other LDCs for that matter. Although there is a small wealthy class and, in many countries, a small middle class, most people are on the lean side and don't have any reserve when it comes to body fat. One nurse describes the typical diet for poverty stricken people as "high volume, low quality" food consisting mainly of corn, rice, wheat, and beans.

But the most devastating side effect of poverty is the inability of parents to care for their children. How heartbreaking it must be to see your own child suffer from malnutrition! Many mothers give what little food they have to their children, and still it isn't enough. Forced into the decision between watching their children starve or giving them to an orphanage or children's home, mothers often choose the latter. We saw that reality played out over and over again as evidenced by the hundreds of children we witnessed in the orphanages and children's homes during our visit to Haiti.

We saw another young mom hand her baby boy over to adoptive parents from the States. The birth mom sat watching as they kissed the baby and videotaped their first encounter. For the most part, she appeared emotionless. But for that second when the new father reached down to take the little boy from her, she held her arms up to him with a slight smile, as if offering the man her most prized position. That child was her flesh and blood, her baby boy. I don't know if it was her first, fifth, or only son. I just know it took great courage to do what she did for her child. I have to wonder, however, if we can do more to help struggling mothers continue to parent their own children.

Street Children

With poverty come street children. In Port-au-Prince, there are estimated to be more than 10,000 street children.[5] Although there is really no way to know for sure, it is very likely that the earthquake increased those estimates considerably.

One night while driving through Port-au-Prince on our way to Ruuska Village, we stopped at an intersection. In Haiti, piles and piles of garbage line the streets; garbage collection is nonexistent. We were accustomed to seeing dogs, goats, and pigs sifting through the piles of garbage to find something to eat. They act as the garbage disposals of anything edible; whatever is left over is burned. It is a messy but fairly efficient system. However, we were not prepared to see a ten-year-old boy picking through the trash. My teammate Debbie and I saw the boy, and his image will be forever etched in our minds. A little boy shouldn't have to find his dinner from a heaping garbage pile already picked over by dogs and rodents.

Some street children are orphaned and have nowhere else to go. Others have a parent or parents but because of their poverty have to scavenge for food. Regardless of their parental status, these children are more than vulnerable and desperately need help or they will be destined to the same poverty their parents experience.

Limited Health Care and Pervasive Disease

Health care is a constant struggle in LDCs. Disease is pervasive, and AIDS is rampant. "According to the World Bank, Haiti spends no more than $8 per capita (per person) on health care annually and has only 2.5 physicians per every 10,000 people. It is no surprise, then, that HIV/AIDS has been a leading cause of death among Haitians for more than 20 years."[6] Before the earthquake the statistics were slowly starting to decline, but post-earthquake experts fear an increase in newly infected people. One person I interviewed while in Haiti felt there had been an increase in births since the earthquake. This would also be in line with the idea that there were more HIV/AIDS transmissions as well.

HIV/AIDS is a personal battle that hits every segment of society. Loving Shepherd is a ministry that serves not only healthy orphaned children, but children who have HIV/AIDS. We visited two homes that house a few dozen children who are HIV positive or have AIDS. With a medical clinic right on the property, these children are given the necessary treatments to keep them as healthy as possible for as long as possible. From the smiles on their faces and the joy that exudes from them, you would never have known they were ill except for the tray of medications each of the housemothers administered multiple times a day. Without constant supervision and medical treatment, these orphaned children wouldn't have a chance for survival. Fortunately, with support from a wonderful organization, they will have many educational and vocational opportunities in their future.

Lack of Education

In Haiti only about 15 percent of children are enrolled in public schools.[7] Under the new president, this is supposed to be improving.[8]

The rest of the children, if the parents can afford it, have to attend private schools, which can be expensive.[9] Unfortunately, Haiti is not an isolated case. Most LDCs struggle with an inability to educate all of the country's children. Without education the children are stuck in the never-ending cycle of poverty. Education is a tool that can help people find good jobs if they are available, which in turn increases their income and helps to break the cycle.

I met Junior outside the Baptist Haiti Mission in Petionville, just outside of Port-au-Prince. He was a street vender, hoping I would be interested in purchasing some of the brightly colored beads hanging on his forearm. I told him I would come see his booth just outside the mission after our tour. While I waited for the rest of the team still inside the museum, Junior and I were able to stand and talk for quite a while.

Junior was young, probably eighteen or twenty, and already had two children ages one and two. He had some education but wasn't able to finish because of the cost. He had dreams of becoming a physician but knew it was unlikely he could ever afford the education. He also liked the idea of becoming a judge because he thought justice was important and there should be more accountability. He wanted to save money so he could afford to send his children to school.

Junior had hopes and dreams. His English was good, he was pleasant, and he was obviously a hard worker. Junior's products appealed to the tourists, and his booth had a good location. Quite a few gifts from that booth ended up coming home with me. Education would have made the process easier for Junior, but Junior has dreams for breaking the cycle of poverty and, if he stays his course, a hope of making a better life for his children. Though culture and history are against him, we hope Junior's resolve will carry him forward.

Education is a key to breaking free from poverty. Without education the process is very difficult—not impossible, but difficult. Children who are afforded education have more opportunities.

Exploitation

In an LDC exploitation is a common occurrence. The stronger members of society take advantage of the weaker ones. Unscrupulous employers can demand more out of their employees because they know people desperately need work and if one employee leaves there are hundreds more willing to take the place. Child labor is not regulated, and any existing laws are often not upheld. Some children are sold or given to others in the hope that they will have better provisions, with their parents or guardians not knowing that, in most cases, they are abused and exploited.

Leadership Vacuum

One of the issues that came up over and over on our trip was the lack of adequate leadership in Haiti. This manifests itself in the government, the community, and most importantly, in the family. Even in the Church in an LDC, there is often an absence of men in leadership, thus creating an epidemic of fatherlessness. As Clayton Wood puts it, Haiti has a massive leadership vacuum. Unfortunately the best and the brightest men tend to leave Haiti to seek a better life in a more stable country. That's why it was so encouraging to meet Pastor Jacques and other godly men who are willing to stay and serve.

Chadasha is an organization that serves in Port-au-Prince and in other areas. We stayed in their guest house for a few days. They, along with many other ministries, are working to disciple and develop godly Christian men.[10] Through a yearlong discipleship program, Chadasha hopes to raise up twelve young Christian men to become leaders in their community. It is slow and painstaking work, but the rewards of their perseverance will be felt for generations.

Orphan Crisis Response

The appropriate response to orphaned children in an LDC has to be, simply, basics first. Of what benefit is an education if a child doesn't have any food for his belly? It is like giving a person a car but no gas to run it. The basics are nutritious food, clean water, safety, and a place to grow up. Ideally, the best place for a child to grow up is within the context of his or her family or with extended family in the same community. However, if there are no family members, then what? In Haiti, as in many countries, there are orphanages and children's homes. Although not the perfect setting, these provide the children with the basics they need to survive. The thriving comes when the basics are met as well as their educational, social, emotional, and spiritual needs.

For the missionary or aid worker living and working in an LDC, life is not easy. During our stay in Haiti, we met dozens of people, both from Haiti and other parts of the world, who are compassionate, caring, and committed. Two girls from Croatia volunteered their time serving at an orphanage for six months. The lady I sat next to on the plane, Lynn, was a nurse who had helped start a birthing center by the Dominican Republic border the week after the earthquake more than two years ago. Jan and his family moved to Haiti to run the Loving Shepherd Ministries, where they serve dozens of children and are working to build local businesses and start a sustainable farm. Greg and his wife, Michelle, moved from Tennessee the week after the earthquake and for months ran supply trucks from the Dominican border to Port-au-Prince. They helped set up two clinics, a pharmacy, and eventually a home for transitional children. Dixie Bickel and Barbara Walker have been working in orphan care for years and don't show signs of leaving anytime soon. And then there are the amazing adoptive parents we met who traveled hundreds of miles, spending tens of thousands of dollars to fly across the ocean to love perfect little strangers and adopt them into their families forever. What is it that makes these people get out of their comfortable, developed-country existence, travel across the globe, and dedicate a part or all of their lives to make a difference in the lives of strangers? There is only one word with the power to touch the hearts of all these people: Jesus!

Beacons of Hope

There are millions of orphaned, abandoned, and vulnerable children living around our globe. The cycle of poverty is pervasive. Resources are scarce. Change is difficult. Life is hard, and there are no easy fixes. The easiest thing for you to do right now is close this book, put it on a shelf, and get back to your life. But I really hope you choose not to do that. In this situation that could be considered hopeless, we have to believe that, because of Jesus, we can make a difference. I have seen it. Lights shine brightly all over this world and have become the beacons of hope for the world. John, my friend from Chadasha in Haiti, reminded me that right after the earthquake, if he looked at the bigness of the problem, he was already defeated. He had to narrow his focus and look at the person right in front of him, and work to help just one person at a time. Then the task became manageable. Therein lies the answer. We can't change the world if we see only the enormity of millions of orphaned children. The problem is too big, too overwhelming! But if we see just one little person—like the children I met, Jennifer, or Genevieve, or Kevin, or Davidson, or Rowan—we can make a difference, one child at a time.

BLOG FROM PORT-AU-PRINCE, HAITI

A cool morning breeze was gently blowing as Susan and I walked across the courtyard to the kitchen for breakfast. It was so refreshing after spending a warm night in a hot building with little ventilation and no electricity for a fan. It was that peaceful time in the morning when the light is just starting to illuminate the sky. Few were awake, so the typical noises of children playing, horns beeping, pounding construction workers, and the revival church service around the corner were all silenced. The only sound was the gentle tones of wind chimes as they played a soothing melodious harmony.

As the team finished our breakfast of malt-o-meal, powdered milk, and craisins, we took a few minutes for morning devotions and then were ready to start our daily visits to Haitian orphanages and children's homes. Though our time in Haiti had been extremely busy, this moment was unhurried.

As we loaded the car with our bags for the day's trip, I was enjoying the morning and not really thinking about the deep issues related to the orphan crisis. We had already hugged dozens of orphaned children, saw a mother relinquish her child, cried many tears, and heard sad stories. We'd been overwhelmed with feelings of tragedy and hopelessness. Haiti, in so many ways, is such a disaster. In the previous days, I had been searching for the bright light in all of the brokenness. But this morning, after I had cried out to God to make sense of it all, God gave me peace. It was in this moment, like the sun peaking over the morning mist, God showed me a glimmer of hope, unexpected and amazing.

Aaron and Ashley Nieuwsma and their three biological children have a calling: They feel God has called them to adopt two boys from Haiti. There haven't been lightning bolts or some huge moment, but just a thought, a feeling that God wants them to expand their family through the miracle of adoption. Wonderful things came together, and they were connected with certain people and ended up with us in Ruuska Village in the capital of Haiti to meet their two sons for the very first time. We were privileged to be a part of their story and with them the first time they met their son Anderson.

Certain moments in life should be accompanied by fanfare, balloons, or at least some indication that this is a once-in-a-lifetime moment! But this particular morning didn't seem like one of those mornings. It was just a quiet, peaceful morning, a typical day. But when Aaron bent over and picked up a little baby boy, it was anything but typical. Aaron took this precious three-month-old baby and drew him to his heart, caressed his head, kissed him on the forehead, and smiled. Soon he handed him to Ashley, and she too immediately snuggled and kissed him. The four of them were together for the very first time: baby Anderson, toddler Davidson, Mom, and Dad. It was the continuation of the family that the Nieuwsmas had already started.

Therein lays a small part of the hope of Haiti.

Davidson and Anderson found a loving family. There are 500,000 or so other children in Haiti, some who will never be adoptable but still need a home, support, mentoring or some other type of care.[11] What I saw that morning was the passionate calling of one couple to make a difference in the orphan crisis. There are dozens of other people from Haiti, Croatia, Argentina, the United States, and other developed countries who desire to adopt as their way of reducing the orphan crisis and expanding their families.

There is no one way to address the issue, but by working together for the sake of the cross, we will continue to make progress. Overwhelming—yes! Seemingly impossible—yes! But God, in His mercy and kindness, is turning the hearts of His people toward orphaned, fatherless, and vulnerable children. There is hope: people willing to do whatever it takes not only to give children physical sustenance but a spiritual foundation as well. No easy answers, no quick fix—only Jesus!

We leave Haiti today with mixed emotions. Some of us have managed to feed many bugs and have the bumps to show for it. In just six days we have been hot, sweaty, dirty, bitten, thirsty, hungry, exhausted, crammed into multiple vehicles, yelled at, thanked, seen the best and the worst of Haiti. We've been brokenhearted, encouraged, and blessed. Faithful

Christians truly stand out as a beacon in this dark world. The team has been a source of deep discussions, amazing refreshment, and continual humor to get through it all. We came, were touched, and can't wait until God calls us back again.

Prayer for the Children

Thank You, Jesus, that You are the answer. You love each of these orphaned children more than we can fathom. You created each child in his or her mother's womb, forming each in a way that pleases Your greater purpose. Help us to see these children. Help us to be compelled to want to do something. Help us to understand our role and give us the strength to make a difference in the life of a child. Help us to be fearless and tenacious. Help us not to be distracted by our material comforts, which can consume us. Help us to be willing to be Your hands and feet to children who need You so desperately. Lord, please give us clarity of vision and the willingness to commitment to Your will, no matter what the cost. Amen.

QUESTIONS TO PONDER

1. When you think of the needs of orphaned, abandoned, and vulnerable children in an LDC, what comes to mind? Can you identify needs beyond the physical ones?

2. Have you been to a least developed country? If so, share a story from your experience.

3. Would you consider going to an LDC? Why or why not?

4. If you were given a million dollars to spend on orphan care in an LDC, what might be the best way to spend it?

5. Who can you pray for today who will make a difference in the global orphan crisis? It can be an organization, a

ministry, a person, or any of the people you learned about in this chapter.

ACTION POINT

This might be a tough assignment, but it will be worth the effort. My friend Susan had been on a mission trip before, but never to a Least Developed Country. After I asked her to join the Haiti team, it took her a good month to think it through. One day, out of the blue, she called and said short and sweet, "I'd like to go with you." God was working in her heart, and she was willing to take the first step. What about you? Is God calling you to something? Are you willing to listen? Are you willing to step out of the known and follow Him into the unknown even when it looks scary? For you it might not be traveling on a mission trip, but instead, to adopt or sponsor a child or to support a missionary. What is God calling you to do, and are you willing to take that initial step of faith?

Your assignment this week is to pray that God will show you what step of faith that He wants you to take. It might be reaching out to someone in need or being willing to give more than you think you should. The task is not the big question here, but rather your willingness to do what God impresses on your heart. If nothing comes to mind yet, keep reading! There are exciting adventures ahead.

Part 2

Exploring Solutions to the Global Orphan Crisis

UNICEF estimates that there are more than 100 million street children globally. Life on the streets has profound consequences for the safety and future of orphaned children.

Bill Wegener. photographer © God Loves Kids

Bringing God's Kingdom to Earth: God's Plan for Spiritual Adoption

Religion that God our Father accepts as pure and faultless is this: to look after orphans and widows in their distress and to keep oneself from being polluted by the world.
James 1:27

Ruthie, Ruthie! Come here, Ruthie," Kamau called from his bed as Ruth walked by. Ruth tried to ignore Kamau. Even though his room was next to the entrance of the house, she tried to sneak quietly by so he wouldn't hear her. Kamau was blind, but he knew the sound of Ruth's steps. Day after day, he called to her and finally his persistence paid off. Ruth finally stepped into his room.

Ruth was the youngest child of a missionary family serving in Kenya, Africa. In 1991 the family moved from their home in Florida to Kenya, where they started missionary work. But one afternoon an experience changed the trajectory of what they thought their ministry would be.

Ruth's father and oldest brother went into town for supplies and a street-boy touched her brother's heart. Eventually the street-boy came home to live with the family. Not too long after, they invited another street-boy to join them—then another and another. Soon there were more than seventy-four boys in several dorms on the property. Eventually there would be more than a dozen children's homes started by Ruth's family, each meeting the special needs of orphaned children.

Kamau was about five years old when he came into Ruth's life. Kamau had AIDS and went blind when he was very young. After living in one of the dorms for a while, Kamau was so sick that Ruth's family brought him into their home to care for him. Ruth, being only twelve, was jealous of Kamau because he took so much of her mother's time. Deep down, Ruth knew she didn't want to get attached. She saw what happened with AIDS kids.

Once Ruth had responded to Kamau's persistent calls, her defenses started to come down and their friendship began.

"Ruthie, what are you eating?" Kamau said in his Kenyan accent. Ruth said that she was eating a carrot because it was good for her eyes. Being blind, Kamau thought that maybe it would help his eyes too, so he asked Ruth for a carrot as well. That became their special "thing." Each day Ruth would bring him a carrot, and they would talk, tell stories, laugh, and—even though Kamau couldn't see—watch wrestling on television. Before long, Kamau became a special brother to Ruth.

Before Christmas, Ruth's mom told her that Kamau wasn't doing well. She thought it might be good if they had Christmas early that year. Ruth gave Kamau some favorite music, and he was so excited to get the special gift from her.

On Christmas Eve Ruth's mom called her into Kamau's room. When she walked in the door Kamau looked right at Ruth and smiled at her as if he could see her face for the first time. He looked out the window with a smile on his face and quietly passed away. Ruth used to tell Kamau that one day, in heaven, he would be able to see. That day, when he looked out the window, it was almost as if he could actually see Jesus coming for him. Ruth's biggest fear had come true: She had given Kamau her heart, and now she had lost her brother. Although she was sad, she couldn't wish him back. No longer orphaned, he was with his Heavenly Father in paradise. His pain was gone. Kamau could see. He was whole for the first time in his short life.

Ironically, it was that orphaned boy named Kamau who brought God's Kingdom to earth in the life of a bitter missionary kid. Although most people couldn't see it, Ruth had struggled with a hard and angry heart. She had not chosen her life in Kenya, and she didn't like sharing her parents with so many other children. Kamau changed that. He was always so happy, and through his love and friendship Ruth's hard heart softened toward God and toward others. No longer was she a missionary kid just tagging along with her parent's ministry; it was her ministry now, too. She saw the least of these, an orphaned boy named Kamau, and through his love and kindness, Ruth's life was forever changed.[1]

God's View of Orphaned Children

In God's economy, every child is fearfully and wonderfully made. In God's economy, every child is loved and protected. Every child is cared for. Every child is fed. Each child has a name, a purpose, a higher calling. With God's help, each person can accomplish extraordinary things. Unfortunately, on this planet we don't live in God's economy—we live in man's economy and man's economy is unfair and harsh.

In the United States, there is a 22 percent chance a child will be terminated before the child takes his or her first breath.[2] In man's economy, some children are born to families that lovingly care for them, providing a life of stability and privilege, while others are born to parents who don't want them and turn their backs on them in infancy or during a crisis. Some children have wealthy means, abundant fresh food, and complete stability and protection. Other children are born to families who love them but are too poor to provide food or keep them warm and safe. In the worst situations, defenseless children are taken advantage of, abused, neglected, exploited, abandoned, orphaned, and left to die.

Children, the smallest, weakest members of our human family, often pay the greatest price for our fallen world's sins. Yet they are the lowest priority among big institutions in our world. We must begin today giving our children the time, attention, respect, and commitment they deserve and our God requires . . . Jesus saved His harshest words of warning for adults to protect little ones, since he knew this world would wage abuses against them if they are not treasured, nurtured, and respected.[3]

Children are created carefully and thoughtfully in the image of God, our Creator. Because of this, we should be compelled, as humans, to care for the neediest and the weakest among us.

Regardless of their circumstances, children need to be loved, to have a name, and to have their basic needs met. They need to be protected by adults and have the opportunities to become something special—despite their parents' economic status. No child should be left to die in a trash can, alone and helpless. No child should be treated with brutality. No child should have to endure the gnawing pain of an empty belly or sleep in a sewer or on a front porch.

Laying the Biblical Foundation

Looking at orphan care in the Bible provides a theological foundation of "why" this issue is so important to God. I need to be convinced of the relevance of an issue so that when things get tough, I know, deep down in my core, that a concept is essential, so I can hang on to my convictions through the difficult times. In order to see the biblical foundation for orphan care, we have to look way, way back all the way to the beginning: "In the beginning, God" (Genesis 1:1). God was, is, and is to come. God is the beginning, the end, and everything in between.

In our recorded history of God, humankind's first encounter with Him is that He *is*. Then Scripture shows us God's next role: Creator. In the beginning God created everything in all of the heavens and in the earth, with His crowning accomplishment being the creation of humankind in His own image. In God's eyes, it was all good! Fast-forwarding through the story, in God's infinite wisdom, He knew that humans would sin against Him, and the rest of the Bible tells the redemptive story of God creating a way for humans to one day be restored to a right relationship with Him—that is, redemption through "Adoption."

Adoption and adoption

I use the capital "A" when talking about God's overarching redemptive plan of Adoption (often called "vertical adoption," God to humankind). You are also familiar with adoption, humans adopting a human child ("horizontal adoption"). These two words are the same, and yet mean something very different.

When talking about God's plan for Adoption (capital A), we are always talking about the big picture of redemption through salvation. When we use the small a, we are always talking about the choice to imitate, in a small way, God's redemption plan by folding a child into a separate biological family. Through adoption, in every way, the child becomes part of the family with all the rights, privileges, responsibilities, and inheritance fundamental within the family structure.

I'm often asked if this is a book about adoption. I probably confuse people more by saying that although adoption (horizontal) is one of the solutions offered, the biblical context of orphan care is about Adoption (vertical), the big picture. Confusing? It will become clearer as we journey forward.

God's Plan for the Universe

Noted Bible teacher, author, and scholar John Piper has this to say about Adoption:

> Adoption is greater than the universe. I say greater than the universe, not greater than the world, because it was there before the universe, and it is above the universe, and it is the purpose of the universe. I'm getting all those ideas straight from the Bible, in particular Ephesians 1:3–6. Let me give you a taste of what drives me in this cause of adoption at the horizontal level, rooted in the Adoption at the vertical level of God Adopting us: "Blessed be the God and Father of our Lord Jesus Christ, who has blessed us in Christ with every spiritual blessing in the heavenly places, even as he chose us in him before the foundation of the world, that we should be holy and blameless before him. In love he predestined us for Adoption as sons through Jesus Christ, according to the purpose of his will, to the praise of his glorious grace, with which he has blessed us in the Beloved" (Ephesians 1:3–6 ESV).
>
> Before the foundation of the world where God chose us, Paul says we were destined for Adoption. Which means that just as he says in Romans 11:36, "from him, through him and to him" is Adoption before the foundation of the world. . . . Adoption was God's idea. He created the world so that there would be a space and a place and a dynamic and a people in which He could do this thing called Adoption (capitalization of *Adoption* added).[4]

The very foundation of our relationship with God is Adoption. As Piper notes, God created this universe as the stage for which he would eventually play out the redemption of all humanity through the death and resurrection of Jesus Christ.[5]

An illustration, God's Plan of Adoption, will help to unfold the biblical concept of Adoption and will shed light on the significance of orphan care.

We start with the overarching plan of Adoption through salvation, signified by the top of the diagram. God then creates the heavens and the earth. The Bible also talks about part of the heavens as God's heavenly kingdom, which is also part of the creation story but explained later in the Bible. Then we add God's human creation, and for ease of illustration, humans are illustrated in the fallen state—people separated from God, at the bottom of the diagram.

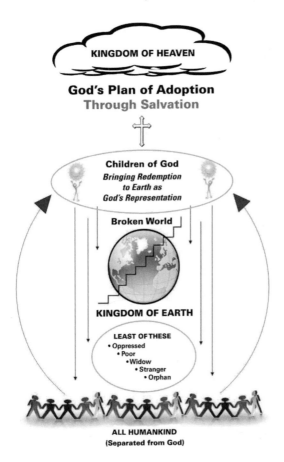

As you know, with the fall of humankind, both humans and the earth experienced brokenness and needed redemption. God sent His only Son as our substitute. By accepting Jesus' act of atonement, we are restored to a right relationship with our Heavenly Father, through the redemptive work of Adoption. The arrows indicate that in our world some of us accept His gift and are given a unique status as God's own children, His heirs and His representation on our planet.

As children of God, we are called into His service. Our service and good works don't redeem us! Redemption is only by faith alone: "He saved us, not because of righteous things we had done, but because of His mercy" (Titus 3:5). God calls us to be His hands and feet in His plan of redemption through Adoption. In other words, God calls us to be His coworkers to bring His light to a sinful world. After humans sinned, God could have scrapped the world and everyone in it and started over with people who were more cooperative. However, God, in His love for us, created us, redeemed us, and has a plan for our lives (Jeremiah 29:11). Part of that plan is for God's children to take part in the redemption story that will be told for all eternity. What a privilege that God invited us to be a part of His awesome plan for the universe.

As we look at the Adoption illustration we can see where the "least of these" come into the picture. God has a special place in His heart for those who are disadvantaged, oppressed, poor, widowed, and orphaned (sometimes called "fatherless"). God has a heart for the underdog and "is not willing that any of these little ones should perish" (Matthew 18:14). God's Son, Jesus, came into our world as a lowly child, grew to be a humble carpenter, and changed the world as a friend of sinners (Luke 7:34). We know that God loves every individual, regardless of that person's station in life, but over and over in the Bible God elevates the lowly and humbles the proud (Proverbs 3:34). As part of God's plan, He requests that we be His representation to all people, and in the case of those with the greatest need, we can serve as His voice and hands of help and healing.

On our illustration, we put a special place for the individuals who are most vulnerable and in need, including orphaned children ("the least of these" Matthew 25:40). By touching their lives through actions and words, we have the opportunity to show people the way back to God.

So where does adoption (little *a*) fit in? In the category of the least of these, God gives us specific instructions on how best to serve these individuals. Part of the solution to the orphan crisis is folding children into our human families through the act of adoption.

Out of the Overflow of What God Has Done

There are an estimated 4.3 million orphans in Ethiopia. The children are primarily orphaned due to poverty, and live in both government-run and privately established orphanages. There is much tragedy and sadness and a need for families to open their homes to these children. The home study we are filling out [for adoption] focuses on motivation, asking, "Why do you want to adopt?" We love Africa, we love the idea of having a beautiful, colorful family, and we love living an exciting story.

On a much deeper level, we see Adoption as a powerful illustration of the gospel. God Adopted us into His family through the ultimate sacrifice of His Son. This is key for us; we are rooting our motivation here. Obligation, duty, guilt, or emotion would never suffice. Out of the overflow of what God has done and continues to do for us comes our motivation for giving ourselves to a child in need (capitalization of *Adoption* added)[6]

Bringing God's Kingdom to Earth

Jesus said, "Let the little children come to me, and do not hinder them, for the kingdom of heaven belongs to such as these" (Matthew 19:14). Throughout the Bible, a main theme describes the Kingdom of God in heaven and the process through which God is bringing His kingdom to earth. While this certainly talks about our future in heaven, it also talks about the present, meaning that we, as Christ followers, are currently in the process of bringing this heavenly kingdom to earth even today (Matthew 6:9–10). We live in a fallen world, and as long as we are governed by evil forces, the Kingdom of God will not fully come to fruition until earth's final redemption. Nonetheless, we are commanded to pray earnestly for God's Kingdom here on earth and instructed to bring God's Kingdom to earth.

Pastor Darren Whitehead of Willow Creek Community Church teaches, "We have confused our comings and our goings. We have made the primary message of our faith that we are going. When the primary message of Jesus is that something else is coming: 'Your kingdom come, your will be done on earth as it is in heaven' (Matthew 6:9–10). Jesus' message is not only about us going to heaven. Jesus' message is all about heaven coming to us."[7]

Author, professor, and speaker Dallas Willard agrees with this observation: "The Christian life is not about getting into heaven when you die, it is about getting into heaven before you die."[8] So what does it look like to bring heaven to earth? How do we become an active participant of this process?

Every day we have opportunities to assist God in bringing His Kingdom to earth. Prayers have no boundaries, and through our fervent and earnest prayers, we can touch the lives of children, both near and far. By living intentional, missional lives, we can focus our heavenly efforts for earthly good. Through our voices, we can search out ways to find justice for those who cannot speak for themselves. God has given us this opportunity to show people through our compassion and love the way to Him through Christ Jesus. Making a difference in the life of an orphaned child is just one way not only to improve the quality of the child's life, both now and for eternity, but also to make a little part of God's Kingdom more visible to those around us here on earth.

As Christ followers, whether we accept it or not, we are God's representation at this time in history to a world that desperately needs to see and be touched by Jesus.

Christy's Story

For more than a year, Christy struggled to understand what it meant to be God's hands and feet to the poor in the poverty-stricken city of Mali, West Africa. She prayed God would use her to touch people's lives and to direct them toward Christ. She recalls one incident in particular that God used to show her how to trust Him as He opened the doors for her to help a family in crisis. In a tangible way, she became a human conduit, allowing God's love to flow through her.

Christy's friend Mamadou asked if she would go to a village to help a man named Balla who was very sick with AIDS and tuberculosis. When they arrived, she met Balla's father, an elderly man severely stricken with leprosy. As sick as he was himself, he didn't ask for help for himself but pleaded with Christy to take his son, Balla, to the hospital so he could get help. Christy and Mamadou started a long journey that ended with Balla's death. Returning to the village, they brought the sad news to Balla's orphaned young children and to his father. Shortly after, Christy helped the family to bury Balla. On her way home that day, Christy realized God had answered her prayer:

I don't know that I have ever heard the audible voice of God, but, if ever I have, it was in that next moment. As I drove away, alone and in the quiet, I heard the voice of God say to me: "That is what it means. That is what it means to be My hands. That is what it means to be My feet. It is when you are doing things you know you cannot do alone. It is there in those moments of human weakness that I transform you into My presence and use you as a source of hope and love to a people in desperate need. It is then that I say, 'Yes, you are My hands, you are My feet. You are My incarnation.' "9

Christy helped bring God's Kingdom to earth that day. She chose a difficult and painful path, which took willingness and sacrifice. She made an eternal difference to a grieving family. We can choose to bring God's Kingdom to earth a little bit every day, in the things we do and the steps of faith we take.

Another Day Coming

We have talked about the Kingdom of God at hand in the here and now. There is also another Kingdom God talks about, the future Kingdom. I sometimes find it difficult to imagine the future Kingdom because I'm consumed with the dailiness of my current life. Life is challenging, distracting, all-consuming, and I rarely actually take the time to think about what the future Kingdom of Heaven will be like.

During Jesus' brief time on earth, He talked frequently about the Kingdom of God, both in the present and the future. In one passage, He used a story that brings our understanding of both Kingdoms together. It shows our earthly actions have consequences both now and in the future.

When the Son of Man comes in his glory, and all the angels with him, he will sit on his throne in heavenly glory. All the nations will be gathered before him, and he will separate the people one from another as a shepherd separates the sheep from the goats. He will put the sheep on his right and the goats on his left.

Then the King will say to those on his right, "Come, you who are blessed by my Father; take your inheritance, the kingdom prepared for you since the creation of the world. For I was hungry and you gave me something to eat, I was thirsty and you gave me something to drink, I was a stranger and you invited me in, I needed clothes and you clothed me, I was sick and you looked after me, I was in prison and you came to visit me."

Then the righteous will answer him, "Lord, when did we see you hungry and feed you, or thirsty and give you something to drink? When did we see you a stranger and invite you in, or needing clothes and clothe you? When did we see you sick or in prison and go to visit you?"

The King will reply, "I tell you the truth, whatever you did for one of the least of these brothers of mine, you did for me." (Matthew 25:31–40)

To be clear, this passage is not saying we can earn our way to heaven through good works. Salvation is from Christ's death and resurrection, and it's by faith and trust in Him that we are Adopted as His children. However, when we experience live-saving grace from God, mentioned in the book of James, we realize that faith without works is dead (James 2:14–20). In other words, our outward actions are manifestations of what has already inwardly happened. Our acts of kindness and compassion are just external signs of that transformation.

Before the formation of the earth, God already planned His earthly and heavenly Kingdom. He already knew that during this time in history (between His resurrection and His second coming) His followers would be His physical representation, part of the earth's redemption in the greater salvation story. Then, after the challenges, difficulties, and blessings, we will meet together in the heavenly Kingdom to celebrate our triumph of good over evil.

On that day, as we stand before our King, the good Shepherd will divide us into two groups. We will forever be marked for Christ or selfishly for ourselves. The King will invite His followers to receive the inheritance He has created for us as our Adopted Heavenly Father.

Taking examples from our world today, the King's response might be something like this:

Even though you don't remember My face, you saw Me in the face of others. In fact, remember the single mom who was out of work and had a hard time keeping food on the table? She came to the food pantry when you were volunteering, and you brought her so much joy when you helped her choose groceries for her and her children. That mom—that was Me! Remember that steamy day in the park when you saw a man who looked so hot and thirsty? You gave him your water bottle. I was that man! Do you remember the college student from Chile who came to church one Sunday morning? You asked him out to lunch with your family. Me again! You saw a street girl in China shivering from the cold because she didn't have a coat, and you gave her yours. I was the little girl! Remember when you heard the church's prison ministry needed Christmas gifts? You heard my prompting, put some gifts together, and with your church you handed out the gifts and sang carols. I was there in that prison. You made Me smile.

My child, whenever you have given hope to the hopeless, help to those who couldn't help themselves, love where there was none and compassion where it was needed . . . whenever you did anything in My name, it was as if you were doing it just for Me.

When we are in God's heavenly Kingdom, we will not regret the things we once did out of love and compassion for others. I can't imagine at that moment thinking, "I wish I had watched more TV when I had the chance," or, "I wish I had worked more hours and made more money so I could have afforded a yellow Porsche." Not likely. Not that those things in themselves are bad; it's just that there is no comparison to engaging in activities that will result in Kingdom benefits.

Here, I must make a confession: I do watch too many movies. I waste too much time worrying about things I cannot change. I don't always respond to God's promptings. And when I do, sometimes I don't move as quickly as I should. I have wasted money impulsively on silly things rather than being careful to save money for causes that really matter. I have not always been intentional with my time, my abilities, and my heart. We all know the verse, "For where your treasure is, there your heart will be also" (Luke 12:34). Sometimes my treasure is where it shouldn't be. My heart gets so distracted, I forget to focus on my heavenly home. Earth is our temporary home. Eternity is forever. But we get that confused a lot, don't we?

What does this mean for us? What can we do differently? This has helped me in my life: Try to keep the end in view.

Keep the End in View

I'm a natural event planner. It's one of the many traits I didn't choose for myself; I think it was genetically programmed into my DNA. Seeing the budding signs of my organizational abilities, my high school principal asked me to organize a fund-raiser to raise money to help build a school gym. Somehow I came up with the crazy idea of a rock-a-thon—in rocking chairs. What can I say? I was young, creative, and our private Christian school didn't let us dance. All the high school kids asked people to pledge money, we booked the entertainment, moms made the food, and dads hauled the rocking chairs. For twenty-four long hours, we rocked our little hearts out, had lots of fun, and created some "war" stories we can now embellish for the kids in our lives.

I learned early on in my event-planning career that one of the tricks of the trade is to start with the end in sight. This happens by asking key questions: "What do you want to accomplish? What does the actual event look like? What is the measure of success for this event?" Once the end is in sight, the planner starts working backward with a timeline, laying out all the details and logistics to make sure those event goals are met. Let me tell you a little secret: There is no "simple" event. You can't short-cut preparation! Every event—even a small one—takes planning, hard work, and diligence.

Much more important than an event, are we trying to "short-cut" our Kingdom preparation, now and for the future? Perhaps, if we think of heaven with the end goal in sight, it would help us live here on earth a little differently—with no regrets, no need for do-overs—just full-speed ahead, keeping a laser focus on the goal. How would that change your everyday life? What would you do differently? Would anything look different to a watching world?

Sometimes I get so excited about our heavenly Kingdom! With no sorrows and no tears, we will bask in the light of our King. Here's the exciting bonus: In addition to all the loved ones we will be reunited with, we will finally meet the many "strangers" we touched along our journey. On that day, they won't be strangers anymore. We will be able to hear their whole stories, not just the parts where our lives intersected with theirs. We will be forever friends and can spend all eternity getting to know one another.

Not the End of the Story—Just the Beginning

As we have walked through this journey together, we have seen that God loves us so much that He put into action an Adoption plan even before the creation of the world. We have been given the amazing privilege to partner with Him to bring His kingdom to earth. In the next chapter we will uncover just how much God loves orphaned children and the biblical context that provides the blueprint for the solution to the plight of orphaned children.

QUESTIONS TO PONDER

1. Have you ever thought about your role in bringing God's Kingdom to earth? Is this a new concept for you or something that you have considered before?

2. What do you think the Kingdom of God will be like?

3. How do people help to bring God's Kingdom to earth?

4. What are the distractions in your life that make it difficult to focus on bringing God's Kingdom to earth?

5. Are there priorities in your life that need to change so you can focus on bringing God's Kingdom to earth? What might those changes look like?

ACTION POINT

Taking into consideration how God has made you—your uniqueness, your gifts and talents—what contributions might you make to helping bring God's Kingdom to earth?

Think about a good friend or spouse and assess what that friend's unique contributions are for helping bring God's Kingdom to earth. Encourage that friend by telling him or her what you see.

A Haitian pastor lovingly protects and guides orphaned children for God's greater purpose. *Diane Lynn Elliot, photographer © Diane Lynn Elliot*

8

Jesus Loves the Little Children

This is what the Lord says: Do what is just and right.
Rescue from the hand of his oppressor the one who
has been robbed. Do no wrong or violence to
the foreigner, the fatherless or the widow,
and do not shed innocent blood in this place.

Jeremiah 22:3

Early one morning I woke up from a deep sleep with stories of or-phaned children in my head. This was not too strange, since I had been immersing myself in the topic for more than a year. I prayed for my Compassion child, Mia, and also for two orphaned Russian children, Anna and Ivan. Then I started praying for those unnamed children I will never meet this side of heaven, who are suffering and in pain both here in my own country and halfway around the world. My heart was heavy as I prayed that God would give these children hope, even when it seems there is none. I prayed they would find love, joy, and protection. I prayed they would find God in their suffering. I prayed that, even though the children were abused, abandoned, and made to do unimaginable things, God would somehow redeem their situation and they would find peace in spite of their circumstances. I was completely overwhelmed.

In my sadness God reminded me of something very important: No matter how profound my grief, my emotions pale in comparison to God's pain, love, and compassion for these children. When no one else knows, God knows every child's name. He formed each child, knows each one intimately, hears every cry, and sees every tear. God loves each orphaned child and has claimed him or her as His very own. Not only that (as if that weren't enough), God, in His love and care for these children, has given us detailed instructions, laying out a plan of protection and deliverance for each child. And we have the privilege to be a part of this restoration.

It is such a relief to know God didn't leave our part of the equation up to chance. In His Word, God gives us specific instructions regarding how we are to support "His" kids. I had glanced over these Scriptures all my life, and although I had been touched by the words, I never really embraced the deeper meaning or contemplated putting the words into action. Only recently I began to uncover just how much God truly loves orphaned children and desperately wants us to be an active part of their story.

This is a dangerous chapter. Once you uncover the truth for yourself in the very Word of God, you will be moved as I was. These verses illuminate God's heart and the bigger purpose of His profound love for the orphaned child. Dive with me into the deep end of God's heart as we carefully uncover His master plan of redemption and restoration for orphaned and fatherless child.

God's Loving Plan for Orphaned Children

In addition to the more than 2,000 verses that talk about general compassion and justice in the Bible, there are forty-four verses in the New International Version of the Bible that specifically use the word *orphan* or *fatherless*. These words speak of the devastating loss of one or both parents and have significant ramifications.

The words *orphan* or *fatherless* are often paired with a select company of individuals: widows, foreigners among you, the poor, oppressed,

Levites, and prisoners. The number of times one of these populations is mentioned with the orphan or fatherless seems to be important to our further discussion. For example, the widow is paired with the orphan or fatherless more than three quarters of the time, foreigners about one third of the time, the poor and oppressed are mentioned a handful of times, the Levites four times, and prisoners just a few times. It is obvious that God demonstrates compassion for all disadvantaged and oppressed individuals and gives us specific ideas of how to help them.

It is no wonder that the orphan most often shares the biblical spotlight with widows. In reality, often the widow and orphan literally go hand in hand. Throughout human history, the patriarchal society has dominated our world. In biblical times, as well as in some countries today, women have limited legal rights, making life without a husband difficult if not impossible. Mix in a few children, and the widowed mother not only has a difficult time caring for herself but for her children also. In the Old Testament, God, in His ultimate wisdom, gives us specific directions on how to provide for the widow and orphan.

An interesting side note is that the New Testament includes additional instruction regarding taking care of widows. In Acts 6 the Grecian Jews were complaining that their widows were getting overlooked in the daily distribution of food (presumably other populations would be included in that distribution although no others are specifically mentioned). A new position of leadership to oversee not only the daily distribution of food but other ministry activities of the church as well was implemented. First Timothy 5 adds qualifiers and instructions regarding care for widows. Widows who have children or grandchildren should be taken care of by their family first, whenever possible: "But if a widow has children or grandchildren, these should learn first of all to put their religion into practice by caring for their own family and so repaying their parents and grandparents, for this is pleasing to God" (1 Timothy 5:4). Verses 5–16 gives some specific qualifications for the widow to meet in order for the church to become her provider.

Looking at the orphan crisis from a theological perspective offers some amazing insights both instructive in biblical times and relevant in our world today. Most notably, God does not give us passes when it comes to caring for the needs of the orphan. Over and over, God places this responsibility squarely on the shoulders of God's people; we are all expected to participate in some way, large or small, locally and globally. In fact, not only do some passages tell us what we must do, other verses tell us what we must *not* do in regard to orphans, widows, and other oppressed individuals. Sometimes even a blessing or warning is attached to the instruction.

Foundational Instructions: Laws of Moses

The book of Exodus opens with the oppression of the Israelites by the Egyptians. God raises up an unlikely man to become the deliverer of His people: Moses. After many trials and a lot of humbling, Moses leads God's people out of their Egyptian captivity right smack into an equally challenging desert existence. In this dry, barren desert, God meets Moses and unfolds His covenant of love that will protect and govern the Israelites. These words are recorded in the books of Exodus and Deuteronomy. This covenant comes in the form of the Ten Commandments and the subsequent instructions or laws.

Deuteronomy, called "the book of the heart," gives instruction in how to live intentionally as God's people in response to His love and mercy. There is concern with justice, especially toward the weaker members of the community, emphasis on intentional and joyful obedience of the heart as the proper response to God's grace and moves toward more responsibility for the individual.[1]

The instructions in Exodus and Deuteronomy show us that God has a bigger plan in mind for His people and lays out the guidelines that will protect them while creating a healthy functioning society. Within this context, God's plan for caring for orphans and other weaker members of the community is revealed.

Word Study in the Rest of the Old Testament

The rest of the Old Testament repeats and expands on the instructions God outlined to Moses regarding the care for the disadvantaged, each time with a slightly different viewpoint. For example, in the book of Job, many concepts of the law are brought up as Job struggles to understand why he is suffering so much. Job laments that he followed God's instructions regarding caring for the fatherless and yet he still going through such torment (Job 29:12). He also wonders how it is that evil people who don't look after the fatherless are not punished. This dialogue among his friends and with God shows how Job values God's laws and believes the importance of caring for the needs of the oppressed.

In Psalms, passages related to orphan care generally take a more contemplative and worshipful look at God and His love and mercy for orphans and other oppressed populations. We see that God is at work in the lives of the oppressed, in spite of the evil in our world. We are reassured that even when we don't see Him, God is still in control of our lives as well as in the lives of the oppressed.

The major and minor prophets of the Old Testament regularly refer to meeting the needs of orphans. In a roundabout way, many passages are related to the journey of the Israelites as they stray from God then are given mercy by God, in hope of their return to Him.

The book of Isaiah begins dramatically with Israel's rebellion. The Israelites have turned away from God. Although they are still going through the motions, their hearts are not in the right place. Isaiah immediately takes them to task: "Hear, O heavens! Listen, O earth! For the Lord has spoken: 'I reared children and brought them up, but they have rebelled against me'" (Isaiah 1:2). The Lord goes on to call His people a brood of evildoers, children given to corruption. The Lord confronts the people about their empty sacrifices and meaningless offerings (Isaiah 1:13).

Then, in Isaiah 1:16–17, God, out of mercy for His children, gives the Israelites the path back to salvation: "Wash and make yourselves clean. Take your evil deeds out of my sight! Stop doing wrong, learn to do right! Seek justice, encourage the oppressed. Defend the cause of the fatherless, plead the case of the widow."

The first few instructions are general in nature: Wash, stop, do right. Then God gets more precise: "Seek justice, encourage the oppressed. Defend the cause of the fatherless, plead the case of the widow." This fascinating passage not only instructs the Israelites to stop their bad behavior, but it also tells them to do right and specifically defines what right is. Doing right is defined as *seeking justice, encouraging the oppressed, defending the cause of the fatherless, and pleading the case of the widow.* How we attempt to execute these instructions is left to our creativity, but it is clear what the foundational mission entails.

Later in the chapter God reminds His people of the gravity and consequences of their decision: "If you are willing and obedient, you will eat the best from the land; but if you resist and rebel, you will be devoured by the sword. For the mouth of the Lord has spoken" (Isaiah 1:19–20).

Orphan Word Study in the New Testament

Only two passages in the New Testament talk about orphans, but what they lack in quantity is made up for in significance. Jesus has just told His followers that He is leaving soon (John 13). Then Jesus comforts His disciples, showing them the depth of His love by reassuring them that He is not leaving them as orphans but will be leaving the Holy Spirit. The Holy Spirit will be "with" them and in a miraculous way become a spiritual part of who they are (John 14). God truly understands the trauma associated with the loss of a parent. In the case of His followers, Jesus is quick to give comfort and reassurance; He understands their anguish.

The second passage including the word *orphan* in the New Testament is a widely quoted passage from James relating to the definition of "pure and faultless religion." The book of James is known as the "Proverbs of the New Testament" because it is full of many practical, bite-sized nuggets. The first part of chapter 1 talks about the reality of trials and temptations in our lives and how Christ followers should respond. The second part of the chapter discusses the challenge not only to listen to God's Word but to be "doers" of the Word. The last verse of Chapter 1 sums up the entire chapter with a powerful definition of pure and faultless religion: "to look after orphans and widows in their distress and to keep oneself from being polluted by the world" (James 1:27).

There are three notable aspects to this verse. First, the passage declares its intention to define God's expectation of what pure and faultless religion looks like in practice. Although we know that salvation is in Christ alone, our works are the outward manifestation of our devotion to Him. The second aspect contains the subject, *widows and orphans*, and the active verb phrase *to look after*. The phrase *to look after* could be taken rather casually. However, in this biblical context it means to care *actively* for someone who can't take care of him or herself, like a helpless child. So not only are we to be sensitive enough to see them and their need, but we are to strive to meet the needs intentionally and compassionately. The last section encourages us to keep ourselves from being influenced and ruined by the world.

> Altogether this is a biblical view, not just James's own thinking. Scripture says that God is committed to caring for the powerless and defenseless, including the poor, the alien, the fatherless and the widow. Since the needs of such people are on God's heart, he expects that same heart to be in us. Further, Jesus himself so identified himself with needy, oppressed people who when we care for one of his people in need, we do it unto him.[2]

So what does it look like to "keep oneself from being polluted by the world"? The apostle Paul addresses this important issue in the book of Romans: "Do not conform any longer to the pattern of this world, but be transformed by the renewing of your mind. Then you will be able to test and approve what God's will is—his good, pleasing and perfect will" (Romans 12:2). Sometime in the future, our eternal citizenship will be in heaven, but today we live in the earthly realm. Daily we are faced with the challenge of reconciling our current reality and our heavenly future. Because of the complications of sin, there will always be a tension between the two worlds, even as we are about the business of bringing heaven to earth. In a real sense, when we take the time to compassionately meet the needs of an orphaned child, we will experience less temptation to be overcome with the world's trappings. Taking care of those who can't take care of themselves changes us and keeps us grounded.

Orphan-care Basics

As we look at the blueprint for God's orphan-care plan, two primary directives need to be considered. The first is God's deep and profound love for orphaned children, widows, and the oppressed, which is the example for us to emulate. The second is God's plan for his people—the Israelites in the Old Testament and Christ followers in the New Testament.

God's Unique Relationship with Orphans

God loves every individual. However, God has a special relationship with marginalized individuals, often categorized as "the least of these"—the oppressed, the vulnerable, and specifically the orphaned child. Throughout the Bible, authors speak of God's love for orphans, some quoting God himself and others teaching additional biblical principles.

Two foundational teaching themes emerge. The themes of justice and mercy are front and center, and we play an important role in those endeavors. Another developing theme is that because of God's deep and enduring love for orphaned children, in some miraculous way He actually becomes part of orphaned children's lives in a unique way. The following verses show just a small picture of the Heavenly Father's love for the orphaned child.

Father to the Fatherless

When the psalmist David wrote, "A father to the fatherless, a defender of widows, is God in his holy dwelling" (Psalms 68:5), he was deeply grieved over some conflict with another individual. David laments the world's evil and the prevalence of enemies who do harm to us and to others. Despite the fact that David loves and prays for this person, he feels rejected by him. In his frustration, David calls God to arise and scatter his enemies, blowing them away like smoke in the wind. Then comes that small but significant word *but*, which turns David's focus away from his enemy and back to God: "But may the righteous be glad and rejoice before God; may they be happy and joyful. Sing to God, sing praise to his name, extol him who rides on the clouds . . . rejoice before him" (Psalm 68:3–4).

David realizes that, in spite of his troubles, God is still God. David praises God because of who He is. In spite of the established fact of evil in the world, the righteous are called to be joyful, rejoicing before the Lord. What a relief! It is overwhelming to see how evil this world can be. More disconcerting is to see the result of evil on the innocent and vulnerable. But still God calls the righteous to rejoice before God. From His vantage point, God can clearly see the temporary quality of the evil that bombards us. He knows that in the fullness of time He triumphs. It is a lot easier to endure difficulties if we are guaranteed that at the end of the game, our team wins.

This past year as I have traveled, researched, prayed, interviewed people, and thought more about orphaned children than ever before, I have struggled with the overwhelming enormity of the problem. This helpless feeling often resulted in a heavy heart. So the psalmist's lament and celebration acts like a salve to my soul. We can't deny the size and scope of the global orphan problem. To us, it is overwhelming. But God is not surprised. He specifically calls us to do something, yes, but he also calls us to have joy in our journey—to be happy and joyful, to exalt and praise God for who He is, our Father and our King. Although the work is hard and the battle fierce, we can still have joy. Our hope is in the Lord. Our happiness comes from Him now and forever. Praise God!

Defender and Provider

Deuteronomy 10:18 says, "He defends the cause of the fatherless and the widow, and loves the foreigner, giving him food and clothing." The Israelites are being called to "fear the Lord your God, to walk in all His ways, to love Him, to serve the Lord your God with all your heart and with all your soul, and to observe the Lord's commands and decrees" (Deuteronomy 10:12–13). The passage describes the wonders of God and His awesome ways, with Deuteronomy 10:18 mentioning one of the reasons God is so wondrous: God is the defender of the fatherless and the widow. He values their causes as His own.

Defending the cause of the fatherless, the widow, and the oppressed is high on God's priority list, and He gives instructions to His children who mirror His heart as well: "Learn to do right! Seek justice, encourage the oppressed. Defend the cause of the fatherless, plead the case of the widow" (Isaiah 1:17). Deuteronomy 10:18 goes on to tell how God gives the foreigner food and clothing, and presumably that instruction includes providing those benefits for the widow and orphan also mentioned in the verse. God knows what the disadvantaged need and makes provisions. God can and sometimes does provide the food and clothing in a miraculous way, but I suspect those essentials are more routinely given through the willing hands of God's children.

Watchful Helper and Encourager

In Psalm 10:14 the psalmist cries, "But you, O God, do and see the trouble and grief; you consider it to take it in hand. The victim commits himself to you; you are the helper of the fatherless." God is not missing anything. He is aware of the suffering of all His creation: "You hear, O Lord, the desire of the afflicted; you encourage them, and you listen to their cry, defending the fatherless and the oppressed, in order that man, who is of the earth, may terrify no more" (Psalm 10:17–18).

God hears the cry of the afflicted and knows their trouble. God takes their pain and grief to heart. He not only sees and hears, but He "understands" what the afflicted are going through. There is no place so dark that God cannot see. There are no tears so silent that God cannot hear. There is no pain so deep that God cannot feel. It only takes one reading of Psalm 139 to see God's overwhelming and incomprehensible love for each individual, and in spite of the fact that the oppressed have more difficulties than most, God is still always with them. The psalmist describes God's knowledge: "O Lord, you have searched me and you know me. You know when I sit and when I rise; you perceive my thoughts from afar. You discern my going out and my lying down; you are familiar with all my ways. Before a word is on my tongue, you know it completely, O Lord" (Psalm 139:1–4). And God is present everywhere: "Where can I go from your Spirit? Where can I flee from your presence? If I go up to the heavens, you are there; if I make my bed in the depths, you are there. If I rise on the wings of the dawn, if I settle on the far side of the sea, even there your hand will guide me, your right hand will hold me fast" (Psalm 139:7–10).

God sees, hears, and understands the cries of the oppressed, but God doesn't stop there. God also helps, encourages, and sustains the afflicted. We are not always aware of how God helps or privy to God's ultimate plan for each individual. But there is no doubt that God has a hand in the lives of the oppressed and afflicted who call out to Him in their suffering. Perhaps God is working by providing a way of escape or to change circumstances. Perhaps God is working spiritually, shaping the individual to be more like Him. We can't see much from an earthly, temporary perspective, but God has eternity in view.

Protector

God foils the plans of evildoers: "The Lord watches over the foreigner and sustains the fatherless and the widow, but he frustrates the ways of the wicked" (Psalm 146:9). Clearly, God is working both ends of the story to protect the vulnerable and to ensure that their lives unfold according to his bigger plan.

In a physical sense, God gives us opportunities to personally intervene, sharing His role of protector. Sometimes God calls us to be His helper and personal representative. We also need to be watchers/observers for God as well. We need to have eyes that actually can see a person in pain, ears willing to hear the cries, and hands willing to serve and comfort.

Judge of the Wicked

God's Word teaches, "Do not take advantage of a widow or an orphan. If you do and they cry out to me, I will certainly hear their cry. My anger will be aroused, and I will kill you with the sword; your wives will become widows and your children fatherless" (Exodus 22:22–24).

It is overwhelming to see the atrocities wrought by humans against the helpless, the oppressed, and orphaned children. While we can't fully understand why these evils occur, we know with certainty that in every case, in this age or in the next, God will be the judge of the wicked. God is the Father of the fatherless—and when you mess with God's children, it's not just serious; it is eternal. God will judge. God will bring retribution.

God is the perfect judge and will pay in full what is owed to each individual. It is reassuring to know that God is responsible for that part of the equation and it is not up to us to make those judgments. That being said, there are times when God will call us to physically intervene on a child's behalf, which we will talk more about later.

Giver of Blessings

God's people were instructed to share—in part, for their own blessing: "At the end of every three years, bring all the tithes of that year's produce and store it in your towns, so that the Levites (who have no allotment or inheritance of their own) and the foreigners, the fatherless and the widows who live in your towns may come and eat and be satisfied, and so that the Lord your God may bless you in all the work of your hands" (Deuteronomy 14:28–29).

God is a God of blessings—specifically, blessings related to the cause of the orphan. God wants to bless us because of our love for Him, because of the work of our hands, and because of our compassion and mercy extended to the oppressed and disadvantaged.

In this passage from Deuteronomy, God is calling the Israelites to joyfully give of their blessings to the widow, foreigners, and orphans. God also names the Levites, people set apart specifically for God's work, to benefit from the givers' benevolence. God does not ask the Israelites to give a small amount of sustenance to this unique group of recipients, but instructs them to give in abundance, until every individual is satisfied and completely, totally filled. Why? "So that God may bless you in all the work of your hands." God wants to bless our efforts, the work of our hands.

Did you happen to notice what this passage doesn't say? It doesn't say, "Hold tightly to what you earn and only give a tithe when you have enough." Nor does it say, "Give to others only after you have purchased everything on your personal or family 'wish list.'" It does say that we show our heart of worship to God by giving back to Him through our tithes and gifts. And God blesses the works of our hands, whether those works are large or small. And there is more!

Deuteronomy 16 lays out specific instructions regarding the Passover, the Feast of Weeks, and the Feast of Tabernacles. God truly knew how to plan a party: "Be joyful at your feast—you, your sons and daughters, your menservants and maidservants, and the Levites, the foreigners, the fatherless and the widows who live in your towns. For seven days celebrate the Feast to the Lord your God at the place the Lord will choose. For the Lord your God will bless you in all your harvest and in all the work of your hands, and your joy will be complete" (Deuteronomy 16:14–15). Now that's a party! Earlier in the same chapter, the Israelites receive an instruction about the Feast of Weeks: "Then celebrate the Feast of Weeks to the Lord your God by giving a freewill offering in proportion to the blessings the Lord your God has given you." The giving was part of the celebration.

The cycle of blessings described here is tremendous. God blesses us, we joyfully and thankfully give back to God as an act of worship, and in turn we are again blessed because of our giving. We get blessed both ways! Blessings come in many forms, not just financial. We experience blessings in many other ways, and we don't need to limit our thoughts and gifts to a monetary value. We are blessed with gifts and talents that can be given to God through acts of service. The person blessed with a compassionate heart will touch the lives of many through his or her kindness. The idea is that God gives us many different types of blessings and we can offer back to God all kinds of gifts. God knows our hearts and sees our intentions. God is not looking for a dollar amount as much as a heart and attitude of love to Him and to those in need.

Placing the Lonely in Families

It's wonderful that "God sets the lonely in families" (Psalm 68:6).

At seven years old, Ginny had an idyllic life. Growing up in a middle-class family in the United States, she was an only daughter. Ginny felt cared for and treasured. When Ginny turned eight, her whole world turned upside down. Her dad got sick, and within a year he had died. Ginny's hopes and dreams died with him. She and her mom tried to carry on the best they could. They moved to another part of the country, found a new church home, and eventually Ginny's mom was able to love again, get married, and add a little boy to the family. Though Ginny was supportive of her mom, she missed her father all the more.

When Ginny was fifteen, she and her mom were on vacation when her mom bit her tongue. It seemed a trivial incident, but when they returned home her mom still felt that something didn't feel right in her mouth. At the dentist, Ginny's mom's worst fears were confirmed: She had tongue cancer. After months of chemotherapy and a radical surgery leaving her unable to speak, there was nothing more that the doctors could do for her. She went into hospice on Good Friday and went home to be with the Lord that very day.

Ginny lost her father and her mother, and the side effect was that she also lost her childhood. Although she had a stepfather and a three-year-old brother, it wasn't the same. She felt abandoned, alone, and without the love of the biological parents she missed desperately.

It is at this critical point in a child's story that things can start spiraling out of control. And if it weren't for some important people in Ginny's life, Ginny's life may have started spinning. However, extended family, friends and their parents, and a dedicated youth worker surrounded her with support and love, walking with her through the next critical years of her life. People who embraced Ginny in the midst of her pain made all the difference. Emotionally, spiritually, and physically, they folded her into the church family and into their own families.

It has been more than five years since Ginny lost her mother. She is in college now and works with the youth in her church. With a beautiful smile on her face, she talks about taking kids from the youth group to summer camp for a week, and she laughs as she tells funny stories.

Ginny still struggles on certain days, like her parents' birthdays, but she doesn't wish them back. She remembers them being so much in love and holds on to the vision that they are together in heaven. As Ginny told her story, I knew that a huge factor in her recovering successfully from the devastation of losing both parents was the response of those around her. Ginny was enveloped with God's love in human form.

"God sets the lonely in families" (Psalm 68:6). God sees the needs of the widow, the orphan, and the oppressed (who could also be called "lonely"). Out of His love for them He surrounds them with families.

The lonely can be placed in families through corporate means—that is, through a group, like a church. A church family might purposely create a warm and inviting environment that welcomes the lonely into their church family. This happened for Ginny. Some churches go on to a deeper level of commitment to God's plans for the lonely, purposely creating a supportive and inviting environment for foster and adoptive parents.

The lonely also come into family relationships in a personal way. An individual family can assist in God's process of placing the lonely in families. Certainly adopting an orphaned child is a long-term solution to meet the physical and emotional needs of a lonely child. This is a solution that comes right out of the biblical concept of God's Adoption of humans.

Other families find that adoption isn't an option but still have the desire to be used as a temporary landing spot for an orphaned child, the widow, and the lonely. Over the years Dave and I have had such opportunities to open our home to people with a temporary need. Late one evening we got a call from a friend saying he knew a mom who was in trouble. The woman was trying to escape an abusive husband and take her young children back to her home country. The family needed a place to stay until they could get the money together to purchase plane tickets. We were able to offer a safe place to stay and some financial resources to the traumatized family. A short time later we were able to get them on a flight back home to family and friends who would help to ensure their safety. Even though our interaction was brief, it was a blessing to be part of this family's journey. We were able to meet the needs of a displaced family dramatically affected by evil. God temporarily placed them in our care, and we were able to give the lonely the shelter and the safety they needed.

Our Part of the Orphan-care Equation

While God certainly doesn't need our help to care for the orphans, God gives us the privilege of being part of their solution. The forty-four verses that mention orphans and fatherless children contain several overarching themes to point us in the right direction.

Practical Needs

As humans, our most basic needs are water, food, clothing, and shelter. It makes perfect sense that these areas are addressed when it comes to orphan care. While the Scriptures don't specifically use the words *water* or *shelter,* water and shelter obviously make up part of the "basic needs" package. Several passages talk about providing food and clothing (Deuteronomy 10:18), others talk about leaving part of the harvest behind so that the widows and orphans in the community can gather the remains of the harvest (Deuteronomy 24:19–21). The culture of that day was largely agrarian, but we can still apply the same principles into today's society. A software developer could assist the church's orphan-care ministry's computer needs. A meeting planner could host a strategic fund-raising event to help a prospective adoptive family raise funds for an adoption. Regardless of how we earn our income, God's plan for us will use all of our gifts, skills, and talents for His bigger plan of meeting the practical needs of an orphaned child in some way.

Emotional Support

Once the physical needs of the orphan are met, the emotional needs of the child come to the forefront. A child who has lost one or both parents is usually in an emotionally critical situation. Love, support, and encouragement can minimize the pain. God, in His wisdom, makes provision for the emotional support and encouragement of orphans.

Encouragement is a powerful tool in the life of an orphaned child. In Job 22:9, Job condemns those who "sent widows away empty-handed and broke the strength of the fatherless." "Breaking the strength of the fatherless" would be like breaking their spirit or taking away their hope. This passage instructs us to assist in giving a child hope through encouragement.

There is nothing like laughing to warm and encourage the heart. In Deuteronomy 14:29 and 16:11, God instructs the Israelites regarding their special celebrations. The Israelites are to include the fatherless, widows, household workers, and special guests in their celebrations just as they would include their biological children. This act of inclusion gives the widows and orphans a special place of honor and the opportunity to experience great joy and laughter. That itself is a precious gift to those who have experienced loss in their lives.

Justice

The most consistently mentioned topic regarding orphan care in the Bible is the topic of justice. Justice is a common theme throughout the Bible, especially in regard to the poor, disadvantaged, and oppressed.

> Justice had primarily to do with conduct in relation to others, especially with regard to the rights of others. It is [also] applied to business, where just weights and measures are demanded. In a larger sense justice is not only giving to others their rights, but involves the active duty of establishing their rights . . . To "seek justice" means to "relieve the oppressed, defend the fatherless, plead for the widow" (Isaiah 1:17; 11:4; Jeremiah 22:15–16; Psalm 82:2–4).[3]

Exodus 22:22 simply says, "Do not take advantage of a widow or an orphan." Straight to the point! Two verses later, a practical application describes lending money to those in need without making money in interest from the transactions. In fact, it even says that if you take a person's cloak as a pledge, it needs to be returned to him by sunset because it is the only covering that he has for his body. That sentiment is repeated in Deuteronomy 24:17, which talks about taking the cloak of a widow.

God's Word often reminds the Israelites why it is important to care about justice for the oppressed. The Israelites need only to look as far back as their past. Years earlier, when the Israelites were oppressed and held captive in Egypt, they experienced similar injustice. God took pity on them and delivered them from their captivity. That memory should serve as the catalyst for them to be compassionate and just with those in similarly desperate situations.

The subject of justice necessarily brings up ruling parties and governmental systems. The Bible speaks to those institutions in surprising ways. Psalm 146:3–4 says, "Do not put your trust in princes, in human beings, who cannot save. When their spirit departs, they return to the ground; on that very day their plans come to nothing." The rulers of our day, even if benevolent to the cause of orphaned children, are not the answer to the orphan crisis. They might be a part of the solution, but they are not the answer.

The Bible has a lot to say about the consequences of unjust lawmakers: "Woe to those who make unjust laws, to those who issue oppressive decrees, to deprive the poor of their rights and withhold justice from the oppressed of my people, making widows their prey and robbing the fatherless" (Isaiah 10:1–2). The passage goes on to say there is no place on earth that these people will be able to hide from God's judgment. The government and the leaders of a society, regardless of religious views or political orientations, are warned not to create unjust laws that oppress the poor. An extreme example of a law that oppresses the most vulnerable is the landmark 1973 *Roe v. Wade* decision by the United States Supreme Court, which gave women the right to "choose" to terminate a baby before birth. There is no more oppressed person than the one who resides in the womb of a woman choosing to abort her baby. Our government has issued the unjust law that deprives the oppressed child of the right to live. However, that is not the end of the story. God's judgment will reign supreme for all eternity, not the U.S. government's.

Through the prophet Jeremiah, God instructs us to rescue the oppressed from their oppressors—not an easy request: "This is what the Lord says: Do what is just and right. Rescue from the hand of his oppressor the one who has been robbed. Do no wrong or violence to the foreigners, the fatherless or the widow, and do not shed innocent blood in this place" (Jeremiah 22:3).

The idea of modern day slavery in the form of sex slaves is deplorable to God and should be to all of us. To fight this horrific atrocity against the innocent, God will call some of us to be active in the literal rescue of these oppressed individuals. They have no one else. With Christ on our side, we are their only hope. In this very dark place, God has called us to be a light that will lead children to safety. And the rescue won't end with initial removal from evildoers. Because of the extent of the child's emotional and physical damage resulting from the captivity, rehabilitation will be slow and measured one tear at a time. Thank the Lord that He has raised up outstanding individuals willing to put their lives on the line to save orphaned, abandoned, and at-risk children.

"God doesn't consider our caring response to the plight of the needs as optional or as a nice gesture. In fact, He sees a loving response to this group as a complete and pre-ordained human right—a legal right backed not by an earthly court, but by the very halls of heaven!" —a prospective adoptive mother.[4]

Ultimately Relevant

We have just started to scratch the surface of the forty-four Bible verses that instruct and teach us about orphans and the fatherless. For further study, all the verses are listed in the appendix of this book. God's Word is as relevant and useful today as when it was written thousands of years ago. I have found it fascinating and compelling to understand the heart of our God in relationship to the orphaned and fatherless children whom He loves.

As we journey forward we will start digging into the specific ideas related to these verses that will make us more effective ministers to orphaned and at-risk children.

QUESTIONS TO PONDER

1. Do you believe that Scriptures are significant to the cause of orphaned children?

2. Of the passages touched on in this chapter, which verses spoke to you? Why?

3. What was the most unexpected information that you learned from this chapter?

4. What difference does it make to have a better understanding about the biblical concept for orphan care?

5. What implications do mandates from God's Word have for your own life? for the life of your family? your church?

ACTION POINT

Option One

Choose one of the passages listed in the back of this book, and study it in depth with a focus on the cause of orphaned children. Let your study include:

- research on the book of the Bible where your passage is found, so you can understand the context, the writer, and the purpose of the book
- the surrounding verses to understand the context of the verse itself
- rereading the passage several times to see what insight God reveals to you about this passage answering the question: What difference does this passage make to you?

Option Two

Read Isaiah 58 one time every day for the next week and see what God shows you from this passage. Isaiah 58 addresses the conditions of our hearts in regard to compassion and justice. The Israelites were used to following the rules required by God, but over time they lost the heart and meaning behind them. In Isaiah 58 God sees that the Israelites are fasting as He required, but with bitterness in their hearts as evidenced by their incongruous actions.

This chapter challenges those of us who want to live what we believe. It is also amazingly encouraging as well. The passage assures us that, when we do follow God with our heart and actions, we will make a difference, not only in the lives of those who we touch with our actions of compassion and mercy but in the lives of those who surround us as well.

The summer of 1972 was a carefree time where games, fun, and laughter were the theme of every day for Diane's little brother, Brian Marquette. Here Brian plays with unabashed joy in Tamling Lake. *Beverly Marquette, photographer © Diane Lynn Elliot*

This Ugandan teen is able to attend a Christian high school, which will give him a chance to make a good living.

This young girl lives in Tharu village in southern Nepal. Her house, like most in the least developed countries, is very modest and made of mud.

In many countries young girls assume a large share of the household duties. This young girl smiles as she dutifully washes the dishes outside her humble house in southwestern India.

A steel rebar left over from a collapsed church provides a great vantage point for this curious, orphaned Rwandan boy to watch his classmates during a lesson.

Matthew A. James photographer, copyright © Matthew A. James

This young boy from the Paniya tribe in southwestern India knows firsthand about the global orphan crisis —without realizing that there are more than 31 million orphaned children in his country alone or that 25 percent of the people in his country live in abject poverty. He just knows he needs enough food to survive one day at a time.

In the last decade UNICEF changed the definition of an orphan to a child who has lost one or both parents, knowing that if one parent dies of AIDS the disease likely will affect the other parent as well. This young girl in Kampala, Uganda, has a much greater probability of becoming an orphan simply because she lives in sub-Saharan Africa.

Breaking the cycle of poverty is difficult when children caring for children is a common scenario. This little girl will probably forgo her own education because of her responsibilities for her younger sibling while the adult in their lives works to provide food.

This playful Rwandan boy looks as if he belongs in middle-class America stealing the heart of his preschool teacher. In reality, he is one of the privileged orphaned children who lives in a children's home. With training and encouragement, he may break the cycle of poverty he was born into.

These colorfully dressed Haitian girls enjoy a warm, sunny afternoon on their dorm room porch. Because of donors' sacrificial giving, these orphaned children are cared for, happy, and healthy. A donor's support dramatically improves the life of the orphaned child.

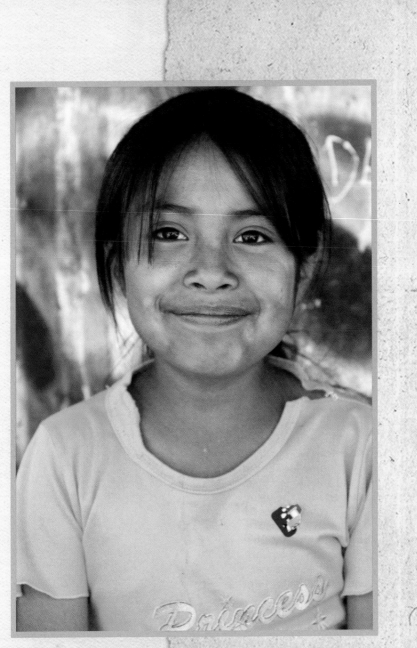

After-school ministries and Vacation Bible School make excellent prevention strategies to help meet the needs of vulnerable children like this princess from the Baja in Mexico.

Orphaned children come in every imaginable package. Ginny's tragedy turned to hope when her church family and friends in Sarasota, Florida, surrounded her with love and helped her deal with her parents' deaths. Ginny now works with youth at her church, giving back to others as so many gave to her during her time of need.

This young Central American woman lives in a home for abused and abandoned girls, rescued from the usual consequences of poverty, substance abuse, and tragedy. She is learning that God created her, loves her, and has a plan for her life. Compassionate Christ-followers help orphaned and abandoned children find their path in God's greater plan.

9

Moving Orphaned Children toward Permanence

I will not leave you as orphans; I will come to you.
John 14:18

I wanted the summer to last forever. Up-north days were filled with playing in the sand-bottomed lake, waterskiing, and cruising in the boat while listening to 4-track tapes playing songs from Herb Albert and the Tijuana Brass. Evenings were warm and breezy, busy with board games, puzzles, turtle ice cream sundaes, making cookies, camp-type pranks, and singing along with Elvis and Perry Como. There was nothing better than spending a lazy summer at our lake cottage in Eagle River, Wisconsin. We never counted the days or even looked at the calendar. One day ran into the next with no apparent beginning or ending. We marked the passage of time only by the growing pile of dirty clothes that forced us to go to the laundromat about once a week.

Family and friends came and went, and days were filled with giggles and fun. We played when we wanted, slept when we had to, and ate when food was put in front of us. Summer was great, and each day was better than the last.

The weather started to turn a little cooler, and the calendar appeared from the drawer to schedule our departure. A few of the trees started showing the colors of fall. Unfortunately, the season was changing; it was time to head back to the Chicago suburbs. We packed up the cabin, filled the station wagon with plastic garbage bags full of summer clothes, and felt sad as we drove out the long, gravel driveway for the last time.

Never once in the many summers we spent in Eagle River did I worry about . . . anything! Life was good. Life was simple. My parents loved me, and they had the resources to provide everything I needed. My two older brothers looked after me, and my two younger brothers looked up to me. And, as I look back now, I'm sure my childhood wasn't as idyllic as I remember, but I felt safe, cared for, and surrounded by family and friends who loved and nurtured me.

Plan A: Permanence

Family was God's idea. He created us to live in community, to need one another, to care for one another, and to raise children in a family environment. We would all agree that in a perfect world every child would grow up within the context of a loving family. Unfortunately, that doesn't always happen.

More than 153 million children do not have the reality of safety, comfort, provision, or a feeling of permanence. Millions of children do not have even the most basic of provisions: parents who can care and provide for them. Fortunately, the story doesn't end here. Each of us can play a role in helping a child to find some permanence in his or her life.

Permanence is defined as stability, consistency, and sturdiness. In the case of permanence in children's lives, a crucial aspect of permanence involves connectedness and community. To a young boy who has just lost one or both parents or a little girl who has just been sold to the highest bidder, *stability* is not a word that describes the turmoil they are experiencing. It probably feels more like a plane bumping along through turbulence with the accompanying sickening feeling that there will never be stability again. Finding permanence then becomes helping the child to find some type of stability so that eventually healing and growth can occur.

Permanence Explored

In the case of orphaned, abandoned, or vulnerable children, finding permanence means taking them from their current state of instability and moving them toward stability that will last throughout childhood. In child-centered care, there is a natural progression of options that makes the most sense. These options utilize the closest solutions first. For example, if possible, it is best to keep a child living at home with a parent. If it is a matter of economics, this is where child sponsorship is helpful for keeping a family together. If keeping a family together is not an option, the next best solution would be to keep the child in the care of a close relative. A subsequent step would be to keep a child in community-based or church-based care in an area that's already local and familiar, even if no relatives are available. As these options become available, kinship or foster care is sought outside the child's original area but within the same culture, if possible. Next would be residential care in either a small children's home or group home. The last option is the orphanage, or institutional care.

So where does adoption fit in? Adoption can be an option at any point along the continuum, once the parental or family rights have been relinquished or terminated. That isn't to say that adoption is the "last" choice! Adoption is a great permanent solution, and we know that children becoming part of a loving family is God's idea. We need more families who are willing to adopt. But the vast majority of orphaned children will never be adoptable, and we must make provision for them, considering this reality.

To understand the scope of the problem, let's unpack the permanence challenge a little bit. The latest number of single or doubled orphaned children is 153 million. This number doesn't account for children who are on the street or who are trafficked, which adds millions to the total. At a ridiculously conservative estimate, let's say there are approximately 175 million orphaned children in our world.

Globally it is estimated that there are roughly 260,000 official annual adoptions a year, with the United States accounting for nearly half of all the adoptions.[1] Doing the math can be tremendously discouraging, because 260,000 is less than a drop in the bucket of 175 million children. If we sought adoption as the solution to the global orphan crisis, we would need to mobilize millions more people to adopt. So let's think that through.

There are seven billion people in the world today, with approximately 2.1 billion people who consider themselves Christians.[2] If 8.5 percent of those were to adopt one child, that would eliminate the global orphan crisis, right? If it were only that simple! Unfortunately, the majority of the children who are considered orphaned (somewhere around 99 percent) will never actually be free for adoption. We find ourselves right back where we began.

If adoption, the best solution to the orphan crisis, only works for less than 1 percent of orphaned children, we have to change our thinking and expand our solutions to encompass the current reality. That brings us back to the logical progression of alternatives already mentioned. The first goal is to meet the children's needs as close to their families of origin as possible. Since every child's needs are unique, this is not a one-size-fits-all approach. Personalized solutions are time- and people-intensive, and that means hundreds of thousands of organizations and individuals helping orphans in diverse situations all over the world.

There is a tremendous organization called Charity Water that brings clean water to people all around the world. In only five years of existence, they have brought water to more than 2 million people—an amazing feat. But consider how different the two challenges are—bringing clean water to people compared to the complicated and painstaking work of caring for the needs of orphaned, abandoned, and vulnerable children. The progress is much easier to quantify for donors when it comes to wells. Charity Water can say to their donors, "We dug two wells today that serve two hundred people." A ministry rescuing children might be able to report, "We saved fifteen children off the streets today," but that's just the beginning of caring for the ongoing needs of those fifteen kids for food, water, counseling, safety, stability, education, and a permanent solution.

See the difference? Neither task is "easy," but changing the life of a child takes decades, not days. All to say, we need to take a long view of the solution. The needs are tremendous, the task is painstaking, and the results are eternal.

In Search of Permanence

VisionTrust, the international children's ministry operating out of Colorado Springs, defines their idea of what is most important in orphan care: "Our Mission is to develop orphaned and neglected children into mature Christians equipped to live in their own culture." They then explain how they accomplish the task: "We do this by enabling Christian nationals to meet the physical, educational, emotional and spiritual needs of the children."[3]

VisionTrust's mission is to take children from where they are, regardless of their challenges or circumstances, and lead them to full maturity as adults and spiritual maturity in Christ. They hope to provide the tools children need to live and work as a contributing member of their culture of origin. VisionTrust adds the element so crucial for true permanence: an eternal relationship with our Heavenly Father.

Because I adhere to a God-centered worldview, I believe the most important aspect of helping an orphaned child find a sense of permanence is introducing that child to the source of stability and connectedness, a relationship with the Heavenly Father.

During World War II, Corrie ten Boom's world was turned upside down when she was taken to the notorious Ravensbruck concentration camp. But there she found her own source of stability: the Solid Rock,

God the Father. Her home, her family, and all her comforts of stability were torn from her grasp, but her deep faith in God—in spite of her circumstances—held her firm.

The debate in the Church between the sometimes-conflicting issues of social service and evangelization has confused and frustrated Christ-followers for centuries. Christians have struggled with discerning what is *most* important—addressing deep social justice needs or bringing the good news of salvation through Christ. Increasingly, believers are accepting that these two can work in harmony. The truth is that both issues require intention. The Church can't be just a social service agency with the short-term view of experience in the here-and-now—not when we have the truth that leads to eternal life. But neither can the Church blindly expect people to be able to listen to the words of Christ while the distracting pain of hunger gnaws in their bellies. The two goals must coexist harmoniously, which is always a challenging balance.

Differing Philosophies of Orphan Care

There are many differing philosophies of orphan care and diverse methods used to implement them—and that's good because we actually need a wide variety of options to meet the ever-growing demand. Unfortunately, there will always be some options that are less than perfect. So we embrace a hope that we can continue to improve current systems while striving to create new ones that better meet the needs of orphaned children.

One of the buzzwords in orphan care today is *holistic approach*. What this means generally is that the organization or ministry is more child-focused, taking into consideration the whole person—spiritually, physically, and mentally. Many organizations prepare a care plan to assess the child's needs and how to meet them. This move to a more individualized assessment and program seems to be a positive one.

Prevention

Prevention is often overlooked as a category of orphan care. However, I have come to the conclusion that prevention is a vitally important part of the orphan-care package. When I saw parents signing over the rights to their babies, I knew we had to do more for families struggling to keep their children. We have to be able to reach them before they feel pressured to do something that will drastically affect them and their children forever.

Tirzah, a ministry dedicated to working with women all around the world, focuses part of their mission on helping widows and orphans. Tirzah is a global network of national movements organized and supported by indigenous volunteers. With more than 150,000 women in the network, work is being done all around the world. By supporting widows and orphans, Tirzah provides families a chance not only to survive but to recover. They support mothers and children, based on the need and available resources, generally with the goal of keeping the family intact.[4]

Child sponsorship is another way to support orphan prevention. VisionTrust encourages child sponsorships, and so does Compassion International. Some of the children available for sponsorship are orphaned and some have a parent or parents, but all are vulnerable—all the children and families are in desperate financial need. Sponsorship for one child is a small amount each month and is used specifically for the child based on the immediate needs. For example, a child might need a school uniform or a meal a day. Projects are established in a particular area, children and guardians apply for sponsorship, then the project director administers the donated funds to the families. This coming-alongside of a child with the specific type of care he or she needs can make a huge difference in keeping the family of origin together. Prevention strategies should be a critical part of any organization's orphan-care plan.

Adoption

Adoption is a wonderful option. In recent years, many developed countries have entered a new era of understanding and acceptance of building a family through adoption. In the United States, there is a growing movement among Christians to utilize the tool of adoption to bring permanence to orphaned children in this country and around the globe. Although much more can be said about adoption, we will just look at a few of the basics. For specific details regarding your country and state regulations, check with a local agency for accurate information.

Although the notion of adopting (or fostering) a child can seem exciting—even romantic—the reality is that adoption can be a difficult process and every child comes with baggage, some more extensive than others. We often think love can cure all ills. Love does make a world of difference, but much more will be required to successfully help a little person grow to full adulthood.

The process of adoption can be grueling, invasive, and heartbreaking. Then, once a placement is finalized, raising the child is even more challenging. People interested in adoption, foster care, or becoming a Safe Family need to consider their place in life, their abilities, their priorities, as well as their ability to cope with multiple challenges. While we desperately need more people to adopt orphaned children, adoption is not for everyone and adoptive parents need to find their deeper motivation solidly placed on a biblical foundation that will stand the test of time and not on romantic ideas of adoption.

Inter-country Adoption

Inter-country adoption has gained significant favor in recent years, and Hollywood has even made it fashionable to adopt a baby from another country. On the plus side, these adoptions bring many children out of countries that struggle with significant poverty and afford the children more opportunities. On the negative side, international adoptions are costly, difficult, time-consuming, and prone to fail before they come to completion. It can be a grueling process for adoptive parents, who have to set their hopes on the end goal in order to endure the ups and downs along the way.

Inter-country adoptions are difficult because there are no standard protocols from country to country. Organizations and governments involved in orphan care display tremendous differences in their philosophies and adoption implementation. Some organizations have well thought-out plans, others are passionately motivated but not well organized, and yet others are steeped in decades-old traditions and systems that might or might not work in our world today. When trying to manage an international adoption, every organization and every country has its own idiosyncrasies that make the confusing process even more challenging. Added to this challenge is the global resistance that has developed over the years.

UNICEF, a powerful player in the global orphan issue, discourages out-of-country adoptions.[5] Their philosophy has gained momentum and even made it difficult for some nations to participate in international adoptions. UNICEF's position stems from the desire to stop the flow of trafficked children, which is a noble goal. But an unfortunate byproduct is that the policy inadvertently closes the borders to *all* international adoption. There is no doubt that unscrupulous agencies have taken children and claimed they were orphaned—or coerced families to give up children. UNICEF theorizes that people from wealthy countries will pay substantial sums of money to adopt children from the least developed countries and that this practice will encourage the "sale" of children and a baby black market. Unfortunately, this cuts at not only the unscrupulous agencies but the legitimate ones as well and constricts the system, keeping many orphaned children from permanent families.[6]

A related global concern is that many countries open and close their borders to inter-country adoptions arbitrarily, causing untold frustration to all involved. This unpredictability can make it logistically difficult for adoption agencies and for potential adoptive parents, causing emotional upheaval and significant monetary setbacks. In some cases governmental corruption, disorganization, or pressure from UNICEF causes a nation to institute new protocols that take a substantial amount of time and money to implement. Regardless of the cause, inter-country adoptions are always difficult, and that isn't likely to improve.

Domestic Adoption

Domestic adoption is adopting a child from within your country of origin. Most developed countries have specific government organizations to deal with adoptions within their country as well as private adoption possibilities, which are conducted on a more individual basis and usually involve an attorney. It's interesting to note that adoption can be culturally taboo in some nations. In Haiti, for example, a woman who has processed literally hundreds of adoptions told me she has never placed an adopted child with Haitian parents within the country. Culturally, it is just not done. In other cultures when a child loses one or both parents, the family and community immediately and automatically take over the responsibility of the children, no questions asked. Although the child might never be "formally" adopted, that child is folded into another family and remains part of the community. It would make a fascinating study to discover why cultures differ so widely regarding orphan care; the results might even point toward more effective ways to administer orphan care overall.

Infant Adoption

Infant adoption is adopting children when they are very young. Many adoption agencies stipulate that the adopting couple must be within a certain age range to qualify to adopt an infant. For example, a public agency might use the combined ages of the husband and wife as a standard, saying that the total has to be no more than seventy-two years. Through private sources, age is not necessarily a limiting factor. Infant adoption through private sources or agencies can be quite costly, and unfortunately available infants are sometimes difficult to find or are not free for adoption for months or years. The great majority of children who are free for adoption and need families are generally older and special-needs children. One has to prayerfully consider the child's particular needs as well as the family's desire to bring a child into the family.

Special-Needs Adoption

Special-needs adoptions focus on children who are older and harder to place or who have some type of physical or mental disability. Unfortunately there are always far more children in this category than there are homes willing to accept them.

Special-needs is a category encompassing a wide range of situations, such as children with minor learning disorders that can improve over time or children with permanent physical disabilities like blindness. Every adopted child will require some additional attention, but many special-needs children will require a substantial commitment over the lifetime of the child. If an adoption is instituted through the state, subsidies are sometimes available for the child's needs. Some adoptive parents are particularly well suited for coming alongside a special-needs child and giving them the experiences and opportunities they otherwise wouldn't be afforded.

Adopting across Races

Adopting across races means that adoptive parents adopt a child from another race, either from their own country or through an intercountry adoption. Although developed countries have come a long way in accepting mixed-race adoptions, there are still issues the adoptive parents need to consider before adopting. Adoptive parents often consider what they are willing to do to honor an adopted child's race and heritage. One Anglo mom who adopted African-American children consciously chose to move from her very-white suburb to a location that was much more ethnically diverse, so that the children would have the ability to have friends from all different ethnic backgrounds.

Open or Closed Adoption

Open adoption and *closed adoption* are terms that describe the relationship of the birth parent or parents with the adoptive parent or parents. Years ago most adoptions were closed adoptions, and birth parents and adoptive parents never met or had any information about each other. Open adoptions have recently become more common. *Open* can mean different things for different agencies with varied limitations due to agency protocols. Open adoptions can be very inclusive to the point that a birth parent remains part of the everyday rhythm of the child's life with his or her adoptive family. There is no one way that is better than another, but it is certainly an issue an adoptive family has to consider before entering into a long-term relationship.

Foster to Adopt

The *foster-to-adopt* method places children who are likely to become free for adoption with foster families interested in officially adopting the children into their families. Anticipating the child's adoptability prevents the child from having to be moved from a foster family to a different adoptive family. Fewer placements are less disruptive for children and for the foster families. Although rewarding, this can be a very emotionally difficult way to adopt a child because, although there might be a high probability of success, there is no guarantee that the child will ever be free for adoption. A foster-to-adopt family has to feel called to minister to the needs of the child, whether or not they eventually receive their desired outcome: the adoption of the child.

Permanence through Expanded Care Options

Other care options, some of them not permanent or legally documented, allow for temporary or emergency placement. We will highlight a few of these here and expand in future chapters.

Familial Care

Familial care is the most common form of care outside of the biological parents. A child's extended family, if suitable for long-term care, is generally agreed to be the most reasonable placement in most cultures, including in developed countries. It is usually in the best interest of the child to stay as close to the family of origin as possible, if there are no dangers present. Keeping the environment familiar to the child reduces the number of difficult disruptions.

Community Home-Based Care

Community home-based care comes alongside families in order to help keep them together, so this is an excellent prevention solution. The World Health Organization defines home-based care as a situation where the guardian (a parent, parents, or extended family) has extenuating circumstances and needs in-home assistance of some sort.[7] For example, a parent may be sick or may be considered special-needs. Depending on the location, different types of assistance might be instituted and could range from once-a-month visits or daily childcare. The goal of in-home family support services is to prevent institutionalization of children and support the infrastructure of the family unit.

Foster Care

Foster care allows a family not related to a child to take over the daily care of a child. In many developed countries foster care is widely accepted, and years ago became the "new" answer to the old problems of child institutionalization. Foster care is now well into its adolescence and has been proven not to be the perfect solution once hoped but nonetheless is a solution for temporary assistance. There are many children who fall through the cracks of the system, and many foster parents who never should be licensed. However, even an imperfect system helps many children who have no other alternative.

Reunification is a term used to describe bringing the family of origin back together after a time of separation. Many circumstances can cause a child to be separated temporarily from his or her parents. Some parents need some time to work through issues such as drug addiction. Others find themselves incarcerated and unable to care for their children temporarily. Sometimes children are taken from parents because they are in danger. In many cases reunification is the ultimate goal. Many social workers claim it is in the best interest of the child to keep a family unit intact whenever possible, even if the situation is less than perfect. One child investigator stated that when there is a complaint against a parent, she tries to give that parent every opportunity to keep the child; investigators may be called back multiple times before they actually remove the child from the parent. Again, it's an imperfect system, and unfortunately many children get caught in the confusion.

Over the years some Christian adoption and foster care agencies have tried to improve on the foster care system. By recruiting, training, and giving adequate support to quality foster parents, they have been able to help give many children loving, stable environments. Unfortunately, in my state of Illinois, as in several other states, some agencies are no longer able to serve as licensing organizations. The state, through the Department of Child and Family Services (DCFS), had formerly subsidized foster care in both public and private agencies. A new law was instituted in 2011 stating that all agencies, regardless of their religious affiliation, have to accept and license people who are in same-sex relationships if they are to work with DCFS. Agencies unwilling to license people who do not meet their biblical criteria have chosen not to compromise their moral integrity and have forfeited their licenses to place children in foster care. It is a sad day when a quality private foster and adoption agency can no longer serve vulnerable children because a state agency dictates against their moral beliefs.

Conflict of Permanence and Protection

The most important aspect of permanence is connectedness and community, which often comes into conflict with child protection and safety. One of the biggest problems in the government-run foster care system in the United States is the lack of connectedness a child feels when moved through the system. The system, in a caring attempt to remove a child from an abusive situation, often has to move a child from the familiar to the unknown. So the loss of parents is compounded by the loss of extended family, friends, school, and everything familiar. No matter how wonderful the foster family may be, it can't replace the familiar feeling of "home" that the child has lost. Worse yet, when one placement doesn't work, the child is moved again and again! It is not uncommon for foster children to be bumped around the system, losing all sense of permanence and connectedness, resulting in what is clinically termed *Reactive Attachment Disorder*—a condition that can affect a child for the rest of his or her life.

Social worker Joanne Feldmeth looks at this phenomenon as a loss of belonging or "place" that has lasting effects:

> The sense of impermanence can permeate all of the physical aspects of these children's lives. Jumbo trash bags are called, cynically, "foster child luggage," because their belongings are often hastily scooped into them for a quick move. The loss of place extends to losing the physical talisman items of childhood—reminders of a place, like a special blanket or a treasured picture or toy. Lauren, a nineteen-year-old removed at age five because her father had molested all three girls in the home, still remembers that the policeman did not allow her to go back into the house to retrieve her beloved Cabbage Patch Doll. She went to bed that night in a strange new building without even the comfort of a familiar toy. "It was just the first of a lot of losses," she said.[8]

Foster care is likely to be a solution for temporary custody well into the future. Although the system isn't perfect, there are many dedicated and caring social workers, foster parents, and child advocates who try their best to serve children during tumultuous times.

Project 1.27

In the state of Colorado, the Project 1.27 movement has been sweeping the state and spreading beyond its borders. The organization name, Project 1.27, comes from the book of James, where pure religion is defined as caring for widows and orphans. "Project 1.27 is an adoption and foster parent program that trains and supports adoptive and fostering families so the family does not have to walk the journey alone! Project 1.27 also partners with local churches to assist these families through the process."[9] This wonderful solution seeks to assist adoption agencies, support the governmental foster system, and help both adoptive and foster families.

Project 1.27 takes some of the confusion and mystery out of foster care and adoption. In Colorado every county has different requirements for adoption licensing, making it an even more complex process than usual. Project 1.27 walks alongside couples and individuals, giving training and support all through the process of both adoption and foster care and works at times as an intercessor to the governmental bodies that are a part of the system.

Safe Families

Safe Families for Children (SFFC) was founded in 2002 by Lydia Home Association, a Chicago-based Christian social services agency, and is now established in many states in the U.S.[10] This unique program gives support to a troubled family before they reach a crisis mode. A child is voluntarily placed in a safe family's care for a short period of time, allowing the parent or parents time to sort out their issues. Safe Families is another method of prevention, as single moms benefit greatly from the much-needed support as they perhaps try to find a job or housing, etc. Safe Families works in partnership with churches and government agencies in the best interest of the child.

Residential Care

Residential care is a least-preferred solution to difficult situations. As mentioned, the best-case scenario is usually a healthy home as close as possible to the child's family of origin. That being said, when a child is in desperate circumstances, residential care might be the best solution, at least for the short term, until a more permanent solution can be established.

Residential care falls along a broad spectrum, with some of the homes or orphanages being a very good option and others completely detrimental to a child's health. The challenge with residential care is to provide the permanence and stability necessary for growth while giving consistent care and bonding with significant adults and other children.

Residential care covers a wide range of types of living situations and institutions. Because there is no standard terminology to categorize the types of services offered and how they are implemented, comparing programs can be confusing and there can be no assumptions about service protocols. For example, the term *children's home* can mean one thing in the Philippines and completely another in the bush of Uganda.

There are no broad-based "best practices" standards taught and accepted widely in the orphan-care world. Globally, some organizations are trying to establish standards for different aspects of orphan and child care, but these are not all-encompassing, and in many cases even the minimum standards are not met.

For our purposes, let's define *residential care* as caring for an orphaned or vulnerable child not related to the caregivers in a group setting. This can encompass any type of care ranging from a small family, home-type setting, holding eight to twelve children, to an institutionalized setting caring for dozens or hundreds of children. Residential care is not foster care, which is implemented in a singular family setting where a child is assigned to a specific family.

As mentioned, all residential care is not created equal. Institutionalization, a form of residential care in a large public or private setting, is utilized in many countries around the world. Having fallen out of favor about fifty years ago in developed countries, institutionalization is widely considered to pose significant health and developmental risks for children. Institutionalization employs the economy of scale, meaning that if there are a lot of children who need care, throw them all together to maximize the available resources. This archaic form of residential care utilizes an impersonal "herd" approach to childcare.

Beyond the big institutions, defining other forms of residential care gets murky. Many organizations and ministries come up with their own terminology to describe their unique brand of residential orphan care. In some cases the differences are a matter of semantics, but sometimes the methodology and intentionality of the care given can be substantially different even if called by the same name. This middle area of children's residential care may carry many different names, including *orphanage, children's village, boys' ranch, girls' villa, home of hope, baby home,* and *baby orphanage,* just to name a few.

New trends in residential orphan care have improved the overall care. One prevailing idea is that smaller is better. To better emulate a "family" feel, several organizations use smaller homes rather than one large facility. There might be a dozen homes in a village, each with one or more staff, that house eight to twelve children. One ministry is very particular to house a set of "parents" in an all-girl or an all-boy house with children of different ages, as it would be in a more traditional family. The idea is to create a family environment so children can be raised in a consistent, stable environment.

We have a long way to go before all orphan care is focused on family. Until then we will continue to push for increasing effectiveness and minimizing damage. Working within the system, not against it, might be the best course of action to support the children in residential care.

Where Do We Go from Here?

While permanence may remain a little elusive for many orphaned children, it is still the goal we should aim for. We have talked about many different methods of bringing about stability and permanence, with adoption at the top of the list. But adoption isn't enough. In order to meet the needs of the growing number of orphaned children, we have to utilize a fairly inclusive, multifaceted approach. Temporary care options include foster care and Safe Families. Residential care ranges from really good, child-centered options to not-so good institutions. Yet even with all the methods we have discussed in operation and functioning at their best, there are still millions of children falling through the cracks, unable to find any form of permanence.

With all the solutions that are already in place, there is still such so much more that needs to be done. So where do we go from here? One thing is for sure: We can't stop yet. We have to continue to break old paradigms, improve current systems, and encourage creative thinking that will spur on solutions not yet even considered. Join me as we move into the next chapter to sample a smorgasbord of ideas for serving orphaned children well into the future.

QUESTIONS TO PONDER

1. How would you describe permanence?

2. Did you experience permanence in your childhood? What were some of the contributing factors?

3. When considering the trauma and lack of stability that many children experience, what solutions do you think might bring about a sense of permanence in a child's life?

4. Adoption, foster care, and Safe Families are large investments people can make to help children find permanence. What are your thoughts about those options? Have you, or someone you know, ever considered those options for your family?

5. What are ways you, your family, and your church can assist those who foster and adopt?

ACTION POINT

Dave and I have been privileged to help several single moms over the years. Dave has been a big brother to a few children as well as a handyman for the moms when needed. I tried to be the fun aunt who babysat, took the kids on outings, and made craft projects with them. We also enjoyed spending time with the whole family in various settings and became good friends with the moms. Over the years we were able to build into the lives of these children and found it not only fulfilling in our lives but helpful to the stability and consistency of the families.

There are children in your church, neighborhood, and community who struggle with a sense of permanence in their lives. One population susceptible to issues of permanence are children of single parents. Consider ways you could reach out to a single parent, foster family, or adoptive family with encouragement and support. Keep in mind that, with issues of permanence already a problem, the child and family doesn't need one more person to disappoint them. Be realistic with your plan as you contemplate involvement.

After successfully raising three biological children to adulthood, Eileen and Jerry felt called away from the traditional retirement route to start "Family Part Two" with the miraculous adoption of five children. *Diane Lynn, Elliot photographer © Diane Lynn Elliot*

10

This and That: Improvements, Creativity, and the Global Church

**When you have finished setting aside a tenth of
all your produce in the third year, the year of
the tithe, you shall give it to the Levite, the foreigner,
the fatherless and the widow, so that they
may eat in your towns and be satisfied.**
Deuteronomy 26:12

Have you ever met someone who lives his or her life with reckless
abandon—not in a crazy, irresponsible way, but in a living-faith-
out-loud sort of way—a way that shows the kind of honest, simple faith
that God seems to honor? My nine-year-old niece, Kristen, is a little
like this. When she is happy, she sings. When she hears a sibling fall,
she runs to see what happened. When she is sad, you can see it all over
her face. When she hears that others are hurting, she draws them a picture or sends a card. When she is in charge of making lunch, she sets
out a buffet with decorated tent cards at every dish telling what the food
is (even though everyone already knows), such as "toast and peanut but-
ter." She lives her life out-loud with exuberance.

Eileen Mestas is that kind of lady.

I find it refreshing to see adults live their faith with abandon. Eileen,
who is in her early fifties, shows this kind of glad anticipation and enthusiasm. Everyone experiences troubles; even the Bible guarantees that

we will have troubles: "Consider it pure joy, my brothers, whenever you face trials of many kinds, because you know that the testing of your faith develops perseverance. Perseverance must finish its work so that you may be mature and complete, not lacking anything" (James 1:2–4). But the person who doesn't let her troubles define her or make her bitter but lets them spur her on to greatness is a person worth watching!

My sister-in-law Kerri had heard about Eileen Mestas, a sort of an adoption legend in Raleigh, North Carolina. So Kerri and I got in contact with her and arrived at her doorstep a few days later.

We were greeted warmly by the whole family—and I mean whole *second* family, which would include Eileen and her husband (Jerry) as well as their eighteen-year-old biological daughter (Eli), and five adopted children from about age four to seven. They were dressed in coordinating outfits ready for a family portrait. We quickly headed to the backyard for pictures before the little ones got into anything to mess up their clothes.

A little while later, Eileen, Kerri, and I went off to a quiet study to talk. For nearly three hours, Eileen told their story. She is a dynamic speaker, and she didn't hold anything back. We laughed, cried, were amazed, and saw God's touch in the lives of a family willing to walk in simple faith. Eileen has written a book, which will give you the whole story. But I can give you a few highlights.

Eileen's daughter Eli was the youngest of their four biological children. When she was in her early teens, Eileen was coming to the end of her years of homeschooling, as the kids were mostly grown. Eileen, as most mothers would be, was getting ready to slow down and start looking forward to her children getting married and starting families of their own. But Eli was convinced that her parents needed to adopt. She was relentless. Eventually Eileen and Jerry started praying about it. Long story short: Jerry lost his job because he did the "right" thing, the adoptions were expensive, they didn't have the money, and yet they became strongly convicted that they should adopt. God honored their faith in amazing ways. I saw five beautiful little faces to prove it! With Jerry in his late fifties and Eileen in her early fifties, they started Parenting Part II. Eli was right there, beaming as she lovingly fussed with all the children.

So why does God seem to live so boldly in some people's lives and not in others? Why do some people experience miracles nearly every day and others don't even believe in them? God doesn't change. God offers each of us the same opportunity to experience Him and all the benefits we should enjoy as His children. So the difference must be in us! Are we willing to trust? Are we willing to do what at times seems counterintuitive? Instead of only trusting our feelings, which can change with the weather, can we trust our God, who has all things under His control?

Eileen and her family inspire me, as they have so many others. They step out in faith, and God rewards their faithfulness. Even when they don't see the big picture, they willingly take little steps of faith. They believe that if God gives them a vision, He will also give them the strength to carry it through. They are willing, and they have received so much more than they ever imagined.

Eileen and her family prayed about God's leading related to their involvement in the orphan crisis, and God led them to adoption. I firmly believe each of us can do something to make a difference in the orphan crisis. It may be adoption, but God may also lead us in a thousand other directions as well. As we begin unfolding ideas for getting involved, I encourage you to pray about God's leading in your life as related to the orphan crisis. God is already on the move in the lives of orphaned children, and He is calling us all to join Him in this important endeavor. God loves each of us more than we can comprehend. He will give us the direction and power we need to make a difference in the lives of those who can't speak for themselves.

This and That

I have a friend with three adult children living in three different states. When she talks with them weekly on the phone, she likes to focus on what is going on in their lives rather than talking too much about her own and having to repeat herself three times. Then, sometime during the week, she sends out a group email called "This and That," a random compilation of the things happening in her life, keeping them all up to date at the same time.

This chapter is a "This and That" chapter. We have taken in the global orphan crisis, looking at it in various countries around the world and exploring some methods being used to meet the needs. Building on that foundation, we can turn the corner into "So what?" territory, to explore specific responses to the crisis. These ideas will provide a stepping-off point, letting you actively engage in creative problem-solving. This chapter and the two that follow hold dozens of ideas from which you can pick and choose as you and your church develop a plan to become part of the orphan solution.

Creative Solutions Needed

There are a lot of solutions in progress in orphan care today, but we need so many more! I propose that we learn from the past, improve what is currently in process, and creatively develop innovative ways to continue to serve the needs of orphaned children. Certainly not everything that can be done has already been implemented. There are new products, businesses, and ministry ideas created every day. How can we continue to create new ideas that will solve the obvious problems that currently exist?

Global Church Initiatives

There are more than 300,000 Christian churches in the United States alone.[1] Estimates also project that, globally, 2.1 billion people call themselves Christians.[2] More than 600 million people within that 2.1

billion call themselves evangelical Christians.[3] The body of Christ is already spread around the globe. Purely from an economy of scale mentality, it makes sense to work with that existing infrastructure of the global Church to meet the needs of the orphaned children around the world. Who better to meet the needs of a community's orphaned children than the local church already an intricate part of the community? This concept seems consistent with Paul's teachings about diversity and the unity of the body (1 Corinthians 12).

Yet, while the Church is spread out around the globe, the distribution of available resources is nowhere close to even. Many churches in emerging countries (ECs) or in least developed countries (LDCs) do not have the resources to support orphaned or vulnerable children in their communities, even though they might desire to tackle the problem. However, when partner churches from resourced countries work alongside to provide additional needed resources, they might be able more effectively to meet needs in their communities. If we are all the global Church of God and one part of the body lacks resources, doesn't it make sense that those abundant in resources should shoulder some of that burden? Together we can better magnify the ministry and mission of bringing God's Kingdom to earth.

No one knows the needs of a community better than those who live and serve in it. The Great Commission calls Christ-followers to go into all the world and teach the gospel, but Christians often mistakenly believe that missionaries are the only ones who should carry on such ministry. The more productive and progressive idea is not only to teach the gospel, but more importantly to equip the local body to spread the work and ministry of Christ in culturally appropriate and relevant ways. The patronizing, false idea of Westerners bearing the knowledge and imparting their wisdom to the ignorant is, at last, beginning to disappear. We know the indigenous body of Christ has wisdom and knowledge we can admire, respect, and rely on for kingdom work. If we serve together with humility, we can come alongside a local body to support them with resources, knowledge, finances, or ditch-digging—whatever they need most.

While churches partnering with churches is not a new concept in orphan care, it is tremendously underutilized. Existing and new ministries can do a better job of tapping into the global resources of the Church.

You and your church might begin by finding an orphan-care organization that is already facilitating these valuable partnerships with national Christians. There's no need for you to start from scratch and risk causing cultural harm. You need local ministry partners who are familiar with other cultures' practices and customs. These ministries can open doors for you and walk along with you as your ministry develops.

Improve What's Already There

Many years ago I worked as the administrator of a Christian elementary-middle school. As the board and I sought to grow the credibility and effectiveness of the school, I became familiar with the Association of Christian Schools International (ACSI). ACSI has a very aggressive accreditation process that serves to improve the quality of Christian education worldwide. One of my primary tasks became equipping the school to meet the ACSI accreditation goals, which was challenging but beneficial. With the ACSI rating a parent could know, with certainty, that if they moved their child from one ACSI-accredited school to another, the new school would hold to the same basic standards as the former school. This standard didn't take away the individuality and uniqueness of each school but established a common minimum standard for all schools holding the ACSI accreditation. The world of orphan care would benefit from a similar type of accreditation organization to define orphan-care best practices and set a minimum standard for faith-based orphan-care ministries.

The topic of best practices in orphan care comes up regularly when talking to ministry leaders, but as yet there is no standard protocol for best practices that I have found. I have heard horror stories of children's homes and orphanages causing more harm than good, or of organizations causing problems because of practices that are culturally insensitive. The standard practices of some institutions, despite their best intentions, cause long-term emotional issues for the children who live there. Even though I wish every orphan-care organization had the best interest of the child at heart, there are the occasional few who are in the "business" for the money. In Haiti, for example, unscrupulous people sometimes capitalized on the worldwide desire to help. They found out that if they took in some children and sent out a fund-raising letter, people would donate.[4] The establishment of best-practices standards would provide donors with a better idea of which organizations are reputable and which are designed to pad the directors' pockets. This may be an area where an enterprising orphan-care organization, or group of organizations, might seek to establish some minimum standard for orphan-care providers to follow. There might even someday be a training and certification program, like the ACSI certification program, that would raise the bar for all orphan-care providers.

Increase Communication and Connectedness among Orphan-care Providers

In many DCs competition is a part of the culture, both on a corporate and individual level. Oftentimes Christian ministries and churches aren't much different. Although we don't talk about it much, the competition phenomenon is not necessarily a good thing when it comes to the body of Christ. God's Word emphasizes connectedness and cooperation, not competition. While many church- and faith-based ministries prove better at cooperation than others, every group offers its own "brand" or style of ministry, and it's easy for workers to feel their chosen methods or approaches are superior to others.

Faith-based orphan-care organizations require more cooperation and communication and less competition in order to serve the millions of orphaned children in need of assistance. Orphan-care ministries don't have to emulate the cut-throat corporate culture. Our Heavenly CEO welcomes connectedness over competition. We can share ideas, support each other, and learn from each other, especially when one organization is doing a better job in a particular area of ministry. This kind of cooperation will improve the ministry effectiveness of everyone involved.

I enjoy seeing other people succeed, especially if it is someone I have encouraged or trained who surpasses what I had to teach and gets better at something than I am. I really enjoy working myself out of a job and have literally done that several times in my career. When I have supported the development of another person, it has always served to better the person and the organization as a whole. Freeing another person to succeed in one area allows me to give attention in another area, which stretches my development as well.

One ministry leader with a similar philosophy told me that his ministry was eager to partner with other organizations to reach orphaned and vulnerable children. The goal is not to create mega-conglomerates in orphan care but to create good working partnerships that will advance the cause.

One practical application is to find local churches and orphan-care ministries and start conversations about how to serve one another. Another is to join an organization like the Christian Alliance for Orphans and start to participate in the networking opportunities they provide.[5] It's not necessarily about re-inventing something but rather about learning the most effective methods from each other and supporting each other as we implement them.

Encourage Creative Solutions

I love creativity and admire people who exhibit their creativity in unique ways. When I was a young girl, I watched my mom and her best friend, Peggy, turn a table full of twigs, dead flowers, and rocks into beautiful pieces of art that graced the tables of special events or filled empty walls. Creativity inspires me, and I was captivated by a TV ad slogan that said, "Solve the obvious problems that others seem to ignore."[6] It seemed so simple and elegant—why didn't I think of that? The ever-growing demands of the global orphan crisis require all the creativity we can muster to "solve the obvious problems that others seem to be ignoring." There are ideas that no one has thought of yet that will be tomorrow's brilliant solution. Perhaps you will come up with the next amazing idea.

Blake Mycoskie, a young idealist, founded Toms Shoes in 2006.[7] This socially conscientious business donates one pair of shoes for every pair of shoes purchased, a "one for one" model. Amazing! We would have considered Mycoskie a hero if he'd started with a buy-six-donate-one model. But Mycoskie challenged old paradigms and did the impossible: He created a completely new, one-for-one entrepreneurial/philanthropic business model.

Toms actually started a movement that has pulled people in and engaged their hearts with a sense of purpose by providing shoes to children who can't afford them (including orphaned children). They defined the cause, made a good product, made wearing the shoes a statement, and thus made giving fashionable.

In an interview at Willow Creek Community Church,[8] Mycoskie shared a story about meeting a family on one of Toms' shoe drops. This family had three boys but could only afford one pair of shoes. Since shoes were a mandatory part of their school's dress code, only one child from this family could attend school at a time. For these children, having shoes meant more than just protecting their feet; having shoes enabled them to get an education. This story strengthened Mycoskie's passion and touched the hearts of Toms' customers, bringing even more supporters into the Toms fold.

When asked why Mycoskie chose to create a for-profit company rather than a nonprofit, he responded that it just made better sense. He could have used all his start-up capital to buy 40,000 pairs of shoes to give away, which would have been a good thing. Or he could use that same money to create an engine that would eventually provide millions of pairs of shoes in a self-sustaining manner, a more effective use of his investment. There's something to think about! Before you start a non-profit ministry, perhaps you need to visit the Toms business model and rethink the possible. Better yet, feel free to improve the business model and create the impossible yet again.

Philanthropic and entrepreneurial ventures have found new ways to coexist—ways that were not even considered in the not-too-distant past. Several nonprofit organizations are also starting for-profit organizations to fund their ministries. This concept of "business as missions" has been gaining momentum over the last decade or so, but still has the potential for tremendous growth.

Sustainable and Duplicable

When it comes to orphan-care ministries, two words that I often hear are *sustainable* and *duplicable*. Many ideas and organizations have great compassion and have positively impacted the global orphan crisis but are not sustainable and are not duplicable. Of course, not every ministry can be sustainable or duplicable, but to make real inroads in the orphan crisis we need methods that can be copied and sustained over time.

Sustainability is the ability for an initiative to stand the test of time. Some key indicators are effectiveness, length of time in ministry, and outcome. Measurable goals, although sometimes difficult to quantify, are important in orphan care. The length of time a ministry has been in operation can speak to the maturity of the organization. At VisionTrust, founder Ernie Taylor showed me pictures of children they had supported twenty years ago. In many cases Ernie could tell me about their education, where the young people were, and even what they were doing now. That was truly impressive.

Sustainability also speaks practically to the length of time an organization can sustain a ministry. If an organization makes a big financial push, pours a ton of money into a project, then disappears the next year, that organization's work is not sustainable. Deep-seated problems cry for long-term solutions. This brings us to finances.

Organizations that have stood the test of time also may have aging donors and need to bring new donors into partnership with them. I have seen churches close their doors because the congregation aged and died without bringing in any new life. Sustainability speaks of a holistic approach that continues the work and doesn't depend on any single donor or leader. Without a wide donor base or funding source, no matter how important the ministry, it is not sustainable.

During our recent years of economic challenges, nonprofits in the United States and other developed countries have experienced additional financial stresses. Fortunately, orphan-care ministries have fared much better than other nonprofits. But ministries of all kinds are seeking financial stability and sustainability. Some of them are finding a combination business-as-mission model can work for them (like the Toms' business model). Creatively addressing the financial needs of any organization is challenging, but sometimes those needs bring important change and sustainable innovation.

Duplicability can also further the effectiveness of many orphan-care solutions. While not every ministry can or should be duplicated due to their particular context or mission, certain models and concepts can be replicated. So the question becomes, What ideas can be duplicated, even if implemented in unique ways? Not every idea will work in every context, but we have to be willing to explore which ideas are worth duplicating and which aren't. This is cooperation and connectedness in action, as we learn from those already in the trenches, borrowing the best methods and applying them in fresh ways.

Improving the System from Within

Remember my friend Christen Morrow, the ministry leader in Lima? Her vision and ministry make up a specialized brand of compassion and creative thinking. Christen works with disabled children in government-run orphanages. Early in her ministry in Lima, Christen came to the conclusion that she couldn't possibly replace the care these children received, so instead of trying to criticize the system as an outsider, she created a way to work within the system to make it better from the inside.

Disabled orphaned children have been hit with a double whammy. Most of the children Christen serves will never be self-sufficient and will require some type of care for the rest of their lives. Taking a long-term view of ministry, Christen works to engage the local church to connect with these children and build relationships that will last long-term.

What organizations in your area serve orphaned children? What about government orphanages and children's homes in other parts of the world? Perhaps, rather than criticizing these organizations for what they are not doing well, you could start working to build trusted relationships that will start to improve the conditions within.

My friend Su and her husband, Woody, have been missionaries to Latin America for more than thirty years. I visited their leadership ministry in Costa Rica several years ago. In addition to being impressed with their training center, I was touched by Su's heart for the community where they live. Su makes it a weekly priority to go to a local retirement home and encourage the residents. Instead of criticizing what they do or don't do well in the facility, she has built a long-standing trust relationship with the director and residents. When Su does have a concern, she has the ear of the director. Su's current ministry is so demanding, she couldn't possibly take on the needs of the residents of that retirement home. But by faithfully investing in an organization already in existence, Su has made an incredible impact on the organization as a whole, while encouraging the residents with her weekly visits.

Economy of Scale

I learned the benefits of economy of scales in the meeting-planning industry and in education. For example, depending on the educational, social, and psychological needs of the children in a classroom, there is a maximum student per teacher ratio beyond which the classroom goals are sacrificed. If the teacher has too many children, then the classroom becomes counterproductive to the school's goals. It is also important to have enough students to keep the school doors opened and the bills paid. Scale has its economics.

Some residential and non-residential orphan-care programs use economy of scale as an important formula for ensuring that program goals are met without wasting precious resources. Depending on the scope of the program, one has to consider the most effective way to meet the needs of the individual in balance with the needs of the group. The more relational the goals, the higher adult-to-child ratio that is needed.

The bottom line in orphan care in balancing economy of scale is to be intentional with resources without sacrificing program and relational quality. There are always limiting factors to any ministry—and usually those are financial limitations, unfortunately. So caregivers are constantly seeking to do the most and best they can with the resources available. Wise stewardship is always a challenging balance, but one worth striving for.

Getting Personal about Motives

Before we finish this chapter, let's address the delicate issue of motives. We all have them. What's critically important is for us to examine and understand the source of our motives, acknowledge their reality, and if necessary take the appropriate steps to make adjustments.

My friend Brenda is a therapist. I have enjoyed our friendship because Brenda is willing to ask me the tough questions. Over coffee or breakfast we explore thoughts and ideas, motives, and more. We don't just report recent activities but are willing to really dig into the deeper issues far below the surface. When I have a tough issue to sort through, Brenda is willing to walk with me through the valley to get to the mountains on the other side. I appreciate Brenda because she helps me figure out what might really be motivating me.

When you seek to become involved in orphan care, your motives matter. At the very foundation, we hope the base motives are a love for God and a heart of compassion for children. But what comes after that?

This can get tricky, especially if our desire to serve grows because we are trying to fill a personal need at the expense of focusing on the needs of the children. Once in a while a couple will adopt children not so much for what they can offer those children, but so that they will forever have people around them to meet their relational needs. As in parenting, our highest goal has to be to equip orphaned children to grow up to full maturity and to contribute to the world in their own unique ways. In that way, we keep child-focused and put our own agenda aside for the good of the children.

A small team of adults visited a Mexican orphanage several years ago. The students at the Christian school where I worked had spent weeks putting together individual gifts for each of the children at the orphanage. We traveled over Thanksgiving break, and I was so excited thinking we would be able to be there when they opened some of the presents that we brought. I had a mental picture of wrapping paper flying and children squealing joyfully as they opened a pile of gifts. My motivation was to see the joy the children got from all the hard work my team and others had put into taking the gifts all the way to Mexico. That doesn't seem like such a bad motive, but I had not really considered what was best for the children. The director very wisely told us she was going to keep many of the gifts back for the future and only give the children a few gifts rather than the whole lot at once. As a wise "parent" she knew that to give the children all the gifts at once wasn't best for them. Although disappointed, I realized that the director knew much better than I did what was best for the children.

Sometimes we have to be willing to make the difficult decisions to put our agenda and motives aside for the best interest of the children. Our own passion for the work sometimes makes this difficult because we lose our objectivity. By keeping child-focused when caring for orphaned children, we can serve in a way that best represents our Heavenly Father.

The Lord can shape your motives as you jump in and seek to serve Him. As you move on to the next chapter, you will continue to stock your orphan-care toolbox with important tools and ideas.

QUESTIONS TO PONDER

1. How do you respond to the challenge of utilizing the global church to increase the effectiveness of orphan care around the world? What would be the benefits? What are the challenges?

2. Have you had any ideas or thoughts about improving the methods or practice of an existing orphan-care ministry? What would your strategy be? Do you have any examples from your personal experience?

3. What are your own experiences in solving problems creatively?

4. What do you think about using a business solution as an engine to fund ministry? Have you seen anything like that before? How did it work?

5. How does analyzing your motives apply to your efforts to care for the orphaned? What happens if your actions don't match your stated motives?

ACTION POINT

Write a paragraph about why it is important to you to be a part of the orphan-care movement. What motivates your heart? What are your fears? What would some of your goals be?

Claudia, a single mom of three children, remarkably manages to sponsor or correspond with seven orphaned and vulnerable children around the world. *Diane Lynn, Elliot photographer © Diane Lynn Elliot*

11

Making a Difference in an Everyday Way

When you are harvesting in your field and you
overlook a sheaf, do not go back to get it.
Leave it for the foreigner, the fatherless
and the widow, so that the Lord your God may
bless you in all the work of your hands.

Deuteronomy 24:19

Claudia was my tour guide at Compassion International's headquarters in Colorado Springs, Colorado, when I visited to learn about the work of the organization. Along with six Compassion leaders from Latin America, I experienced the history and vision of Compassion. I couldn't help but be touched by the story. Even more amazing was the sense of ownership and enthusiasm that Claudia had for the organization, the staff, and especially the children Compassion supports. Her energy was contagious.

Later, sitting down to a Mediterranean lunch of humus, pita bread, and salad, Claudia told me her own story. Claudia never planned on being a single mom; it just turned out that way. Having grown up in Germany, she left her family and friends and moved to the United States when she met the man of her dreams. After a time, her husband, a military man, went off to serve in Desert Storm. After his tour of duty he came back a different man. When Claudia's youngest was four years old, her husband walked out of the door and out of their lives. Claudia became a single mom of three young children.

A single mom in a foreign country with few resources and a small support system, Claudia found it very difficult to provide for her family. During those difficult years God became the father to the fatherless and the provider of every need for Claudia and her children. During that time God also softened Claudia's heart to the needs of single moms and their children, especially those in resource-poor countries.

One Sunday morning, Compassion International was setting up sponsor information to be displayed at Claudia's church. In the flurry of activity, someone asked Claudia to help organize the display. That day there was only one child sponsored, and the sponsor was Claudia. When she saw the picture of a little Bolivian girl named Nicole, she knew she had to sponsor her. With three children of her own and every reason not to spend money on another child, Claudia took the step of faith and started down a path that changed her life forever.

Eventually Claudia came to work for Compassion International and ended up sponsoring or corresponding with several more children. On a Compassion trip to Ecuador, Claudia met a three-year-old girl named Erica who needed a sponsor. Without hesitation she asked the leader of the trip if she could become Erica's sponsor. Now, besides caring for her own three biological children, Claudia sponsors seven Compassion children. She told me, "I just wish I could do more. I know God has to save them, but I'm a willing vessel and need to help."

I asked how she could afford to sponsor so many children while working on a ministry salary. She admits that it is challenging but she has chosen to live very frugally so she can put her resources where she feels God can best use them. Claudia is a joyful and humble woman who has experienced much adversity, but in spite of it, she is allowing God to use her to touch the world.

Shortly after I met Claudia, she was headed to Haiti to visit one of her Compassion children, a blessed little girl named Enderlove, whose life will never be the same because of the prayers, letters, financial support, hugs, and loving encouragement of a compassionate woman.

Sponsoring a child is just one of many ways you can touch the life of an orphaned child. Your efforts don't have to be huge or heroic; you just have to do something to make the life of an orphaned child a little easier. Some ventures will require specific skills or education. Others most anyone can do. Put them all together, and they will continue the wave of love from Christ followers to orphaned children worldwide. With prayer, these little acts of love will show orphaned children they matter to us and to God. Ultimately, through God's love and grace, children can come to know God in a personal and life-changing way.

As you are reading this chapter, you might find that certain ideas attract you—or spark other ideas. Don't wait until you get to the writing space at the back of this chapter to jot down your thoughts. Write them down as you go along. Feel free to post your ideas at globalorphancrisis.org, so you can share your thoughts with others as well.

As you're reading, the name of a friend or acquaintance may come to mind in conjunction with a suggestion or idea. Jot those names in your margins, too! You may be able to share what you're learning about the needs of orphans worldwide with those friends and encourage them to become involved.

Everyone Can Do This

This chapter is a "can-do" list for every person. I'm sure that by now you are convinced that there is a need—and that you are part of the solution. But perhaps you haven't figured out how or where to start, especially if picking up and moving yourself or your family to a remote village in Uganda is not possible in your current life situation. I get that! Here is the good news: God needs you as part of the orphan solution, even right from your current zip code. You will find manageable but crucially important options in this chapter. You might have to think outside the box or plan differently or make room in your schedule, but these options won't require a major life change.

Not long ago I met with a group of women who wanted to start an orphan ministry in their church. I was thrilled to encourage them in any way I could. I was encouraged by their willing hearts. I gave them some information about the crisis using statistics and stories, and they were more eager than ever to get started. At that time I had a handful of practical ideas, but not nearly enough to satisfy them. I decided that day that this book would contain dozens and dozens of ideas to help get people involved in solving the orphan crisis.

Some of these ideas might sound small and insignificant. Let me assure you: Anything and everything you do for an orphaned child is valuable. Big or small, any effort is significant. Some of the ideas might seem several steps removed from the orphaned child you long to personally hold and comfort. The reality is that, although some people do have the opportunity to hold babies and rock them to sleep at a children's home, many of us will make a difference at arm's length, perhaps even making the blanket the child is cuddled in. Rest assured: When you serve in any capacity, even as a support to those on the front line, your work indirectly impacts children and increases the reach of the childcare workers on the front lines.

My brother Brent is a flight nurse and an officer with the United States Air Force Aeromedical Evacuation unit. Although Brent and his medical rescue team are not on the front lines of battle, many lives would be lost if not for them. They provide their fellow warriors with a promise to be there for them should they need medical support. Brent tells me, "If they get hurt, they know we'll move heaven and earth to get them back home."

Many of us will never be on the front lines of the orphan crisis. But we are a promise to those who are, and we can act as their support team as they fight the spiritual and physical battle for the lives of orphaned children every day. The biggest mistake we make is thinking our efforts are so "small" they don't really matter. With a right heart and passion, your role as an active member of the body of Christ is anything but small! The many efforts of those who are willing will continue to make a difference, and that's where you are different. You are willing—that's saying a lot!

What Do You Have in Your Hand?

Sometimes we look at a new venture or opportunity and feel fearful that we don't have anything to offer. It's easy to feel this way as we look at the orphan crisis and see the enormity of the problem. Rather than be overwhelmed by the crisis, we need to focus not on what we can't do but on what we can. As we move toward action, like Moses, we have to first look at what we already have in our hands.

Exodus 3 and 4 describe how God called Moses to lead the people of Israel out of bondage in Egypt. Moses felt unprepared to meet the task given to him. But God was extremely patient with Moses. God asked, "What is that in your hand?" In other words, God asked, "What do you have that you can use, Moses?" Moses, having been a shepherd, was carrying a tool of his trade, a shepherd's staff. God instructed Moses to throw his staff on the ground, where it became a snake. This was the first of many spectacular miracles that Moses was able to perform, through God's power, with that shepherd's staff.

So my question to you is, What's in your hand?

When I was working on my MBA, I learned to evaluate businesses and enterprises using a tool called the SWOT analysis, which analyzes Strengths, Weaknesses/Limitations, Opportunities, and Threats. The SWOT analysis can be applied to your own strengths and challenges or to assess a church's or ministry's potential. As we learn from Moses, God can turn what seems like nothing into something amazing. As Christ-followers, we have to slide between the world of God's amazing miracles and the physical world—and sometimes it is impossible to know which is which. It's my philosophy to be as prepared as possible, use all the tools in my tool kit, and then be grateful when God does something far beyond what I ask or imagine. Amazing things can happen when preparation, opportunity, and miracles collide.

So here we go! Grab a piece of paper and do a little brainstorming about what you might bring personally to your strategic orphan-helping plan. Getting the creativity flowing will be a good tool to help you expand your vision.

Strengths

- What do you love to do?
- What do you do well?
- What are you passionate about?
- What professional experience do you have that might be useful in orphan care?
- What are your spiritual gifts?
- What resources do you have? (good people skills, strong communicator, a minivan, a spare room, etc.)
- What is your time availability? (Daily, weekly, monthly?)

Weaknesses/Limitations

- What are your current limitations? (a mother of a newborn, travel three days a week for work, etc.)
- What are current constraints that are not negotiable?
- What do you really dislike doing? What feels like work to you?
- What do you not do well?

Opportunities

- How can you turn what you love to do into something that can help an orphan-care ministry?
- What current opportunities related to orphan care do you know about? Perhaps in your church?
- Do you currently have a relationship with any orphan-care ministries?

- Are there other individuals who might be interested if you were to get something going?
- What are the benefits of being involved in orphan care?

Threats

- Is there any reason you should not be involved in something related to orphan care?
- Will you be putting anyone or any ministry in harm's way by being involved in some aspect of orphan care?

Take a few minutes to pray about what you have written down. You have a unique set of gifts and skills that can make a difference to an orphaned child. Pray that God opens your eyes to the unexpected. Pray that you will be willing to step out in faith even if you don't know where you will end up. This leads us to our first opportunity, prayer.

Prayer

Prayer has to be the first and the most important gift you can give to orphaned children. It seems too simple, like it isn't enough. In reality, prayer is the most productive, powerful, and wonderful gift you can give to a child, an adoptive or foster family, or orphan-care ministry. Prayer is power! The great man of the faith D. L. Moody said, "Every great movement of God can be traced to a kneeling figure."[1] Prayer is the power that can change the lives of orphaned children around the globe. And although prayer is not the power itself—God supplies the power—prayer helps to release the power. You can actively participate in releasing God's power around the world.

Prayer Journal

Start a prayer journal just for orphaned children and the ministries that help them. Be creative with your journal, adding pictures, Bible verses, quotes, dreams, goals, and stories. Sometimes when I sit down with my Bible and journal, I feel like I'm sitting with an old friend. I really enjoy looking back to see how God answered my prayers. It also helps me to stay focused and keep the most important things right in front of me. I also enjoy starting a new journal, anticipating all the exciting things that will eventually fill the pages.

Pray for a Child

You can look up orphaned children on the Internet through ministry and adoption websites and choose a few children to pray for specifically. Information is usually limited online, but you can find out some of the basics, such as country, current situation, and even some of the children's personal likes and dislikes. Pray for their health, safety, and growth. Pray especially that somehow, some way, they will experience God's love. Pray that those orphaned children will ultimately come to know God in a personal way and they will impact the world because of God's hand upon them. You might never know this side of heaven what you did for a child, but one day, you will be greeted by a familiar stranger whose life was made better because you prayed for him or her.

Pray for God's Will

Pray for God's will to be done. Often we pray for a speedy and quick answer, but God's timing is perfect. His process is perfect. His answers are perfect. Sometimes God allows circumstances and people to come into our lives and the lives of others to bring us closer to Him. We should do our best to intervene on behalf of the orphaned child, but we should ask that God would bring about His plan, in His timing, and in accord with His will rather than our own.

Pray for an Orphan-care Ministry

Find a ministry serving orphaned children and pray for that ministry. You can select from the ministry partners on the website or find other ministries online that mirror your heart and passion. Sign up for their ministry newsletter to stay up-to-date with detailed information. Become an advocate, and share that ministry with friends and family to help spread the work of the ministry.

Pray for Orphan-care Leadership

Pray for your pastor, church leaders, and others to be more interested in the orphan crisis. Pray that God would mobilize your church in different ways to become part of the solution. A well-planned note or word of encouragement wouldn't hurt either.

Pray for Others to Join the Cause

Pray for Christians to be opened to God's leading and to open their homes to orphaned children. Pray that more Christ followers will be willing to become foster and adoptive parents or serve as a Safe Family. Pray that people will be willing to sponsor orphaned children through programs that provide food, shelter, and support to kids in need.

There are so many ways you can pray for children and orphan-care ministries. Your availability will allow God to prompt and guide you. Prayer is the most important thing you can do for an orphaned child. In the quiet of your own heart you can unleash the power of God. What a privilege! What a responsibility. What an amazing gift you can give to an orphaned child.

Give Financially

Giving a portion of our financial resources is part of every Christ-follower's worship to God. We have an opportunity to touch children's lives by giving to a church's orphan ministry, sponsoring a child, or supporting an orphan-care organization. If we each give a little, we will make a huge impact.

Dave and I love to give to missionaries and ministries. Sometimes there has been a lot to give and sometimes very little. Whatever the case, we consider our donations with a lot of thought, prayer, and intentionality. It is always a great joy to write the check, address the envelope, and send a gift to a ministry or missionary. Personally I still like to actually write checks. Even when giving online is more efficient, somehow putting that envelope in the mail is part of our treasured tradition.

You might be thinking, This is really a bad time for me to give to any cause. For many of us money is tight. We live in a dynamic and difficult economy, and for many of us it is a toss-up whether we will have a job tomorrow or not. I have to remind myself that when God put His great plan for this earth together and laid it out for us in His Word, He asked us to participate in worship to Him through giving. God knew His children wouldn't always be flush and overflowing with cash. God knew there would be economically difficult times. However, God asks us to give as our worship to Him, in spite of our circumstances, during feast or famine. In many cases such giving is a step of faith. Sometimes the gift will only be a very small amount. The amount is less important than the act of giving itself. Giving requires sacrifice, and that in itself is part of the gift.

On the top of my to-do list today I have written, "Eliminate what doesn't matter!" I don't know where I saw that quote, but it struck home for me in two ways. First, give up those things that are marginal in my life and don't add value to the big picture. Second, in a financial sense, don't spend money on something of no intrinsic value.

Those of us who live in a developed country have choices. Sometimes we will choose to give up what isn't really that important anyway in order to save money for a higher purpose. For example, could you give up gourmet coffee a few times a week to set that money aside to pay for a sponsored child? How about a movie once a month? Are you willing to whittle away a few of life's unimportant things to free up money for what is important? What about making a change jar for orphaned children and asking the family to drop their change in the jar at the end of each day? With a little creativity, you can come up with some ways that will not alter your daily life but could significantly improve the life of an orphaned child.

A friend of mine recently told me about a father in Haiti whose little daughter was very sick. He didn't have the money to take her to the clinic. After trying all he knew to do, he had to watch as she slowly started slipping away. My friend was able to come along at just the right moment to offer assistance to this dad, who was able to get the medical attention the little girl needed. For $12.50, medical treatments saved this child's life. Two days later she was back at home, playing in the yard. Don't ever think that a small amount doesn't make a difference. Money that we would mindlessly spend on lunch saved that little girl's life.

Designated Gifts

Here are some ideas to get you thinking about both big and small ways that you can be part of the orphan solution financially:

Sponsor a foster child to go to camp. (See arrow.org.)

Sponsor a children's home.

Support an orphan-care ministry.

Support a missionary who works with orphaned children.

Donate funds for animals that can be given to orphanages and vulnerable families to provide food and income opportunities. (See Compassion International at compassion.com.)

Donate funds for school supplies, school uniforms, and school books.

Support an orphaned teen in educational pursuits at trade school or college.

Sponsor a Bible program for orphaned children. (Check out Heart for Orphans, a program in the Ukraine, at http://heartfororphans.com.)

Support a family who hopes to adopt. Lifesong for Orphans helps to raise funds for families who are adopting. They have lists of families in the process of adoption and their current financial needs. Donors can contribute directly to a family's adoption need. (See http://bothhands foundation.org.)

Support your church's missions project. Many churches have short-term missions opportunities available for students and for adults to serve orphan-care ministries.

Sell Something

Last year my church was raising money for a community outreach center. Our pastor challenged us to donate money, but not in the usual way, right from our wallets. He challenged each of us to pray about it for a time and choose one item to sell and give that money to the church for the project. This is a great idea that everyone can do. We all have stuff sitting around gathering dust, so it's a win/win situation. We clean out the space and are able to give the money we make to a ministry we care about. Many people prefer online selling options, such as ebay or Craigslist, but there are other outlets as well. Do whatever works best for you.

In-Kind Giving

In-kind giving is a great way to donate items to those in need. However, before you go diving into your boxes to seek out things sitting around your home that are not valuable to you anymore but might be valuable to someone else, here's a word of caution. I once was volunteering with a mercy ship called the Good Samaritan and was driving a group of missionaries back and forth to the grocery store. When I picked up the team, I saw a roll of carpet sitting on the dock by the ship. It was torn, tattered, and filthy, and I assumed it had recently been taken out of the ship to be replaced. I was shocked to find that it was a recent *donation* to the ship. The ship's director commented that although it was nice that someone thought about them, it was a real pain to receive a donation that had to be put directly into their trash once received. The worst part is that they also had to pay extra for the trash pickup to get rid of it. The same missionary told me that someone had once donated *used* tea bags to them. My point? Please don't donate anything you wouldn't use in your own home or on your child. If it is dirty, tattered, or torn, throw it away. If it is clean, unstained, useful, and still in good condition, by all means donate it to someone who can repurpose it. Remember we give to others as if we are giving to God alone. Don't give God your junk—give Him your best! Here are some other ideas of things that you can give from your own home (or purchase and give):

- Unexpired medical and dental supplies
- Clothes
- Shoes
- Backpacks
- Personal care items
- Books and educational materials
- Bedding and mosquito netting[2]
- Toys
- Nonperishable food items
- Furniture (for a local ministry)
- Office equipment
- Computer equipment
- Vehicle

Giving in-kind gifts has gotten a little trickier lately, particularly for international ministries. One ministry told me they used to bring items with them when they flew to different ministry locations, but the new baggage restrictions on international flights have forced ministries to ship rather than try to carry items overseas. But shipping is costly! To ship a box of donated clothing overseas is expensive, so while you might have donated some good items for a ministry, it might cost the ministry something to get the items to the people who need them.

One way to avoid this costly issue is to contact the ministry and ask if the items would be useful. If they are not equipped to manage the shipping situation, your donations could be better suited for a local ministry rather than an international one. If the ministry does need the items, plan to give a little extra cash to provide for shipping the items.

Buy Something You Normally Buy

You purchase things every day that are staples in your home. Some organizations have products for sale that directly benefit an orphan-care ministry. For example, Bolivia's Best Coffee supports several children's homes in Bolivia.[3] Mike and Bonnie Timmer, missionaries with International Teams, moved to Bolivia years ago and decided they wanted to try to create a sustainable ministry model. The implementation of their idea became Bolivia's Best Coffee. Coffee beans are picked in Bolivia and shipped green to the United States. A volunteer with the ministry roasts the coffee, people purchase the coffee online, and the coffee is shipped to their door. People are going to purchase coffee anyway; why not let the purchase benefit an orphan-care organization as well? Although there are many such ideas online, here are a few to get you started:

- Bolivia's Best Coffee. The money from the sale of the coffee directly supports children's homes in Bolivia. http://bolivias bestcoffee.com/
- Tiny Hands Store. Sales of bags, necklaces, bracelets, and scarves benefit women and children in Nepal, India, and Bangladesh. tinyhandsinternational.org.
- Ordinary Hero. Adoptive families receive 40 percent of all sales of products purchased from this site. www.ordinaryhero.org.
- Crafts of Hope. Scarves and hats are made by disadvantaged women and children. All profits go directly to Home of Hope and solely benefit the women and children. craftsofhope.com.
- Beauty from Ashes. Note cards are created and sold by Romanian girls as they age out of the orphanage system. romanian orphanministries.com.

Advocate/Educate

There are so many ways to advocate for the cause of orphaned children, you can choose an advocate style that works with your personality style and the desired demographic.

CASA

Perhaps you have a strong sense of justice and compassion but aren't an attorney or trained professional. Court Appointed Special Advocates (CASA) is a network of 955 programs that recruit, train, and support volunteers to represent the best interests of abused and neglected children in the courtroom and other settings. Advocates help to support and look after the interests of children. Check out casaforchildren.org.

Orphan-care Organization Advocate

Many orphan-care organizations have specific advocacy programs you can join. Some programs are quite organized, while others are more self-directed with training materials. Some of the advocacy programs have specific groups they ask you to speak at; others suggest that you make a presentation to people from your network on behalf of the organization. If you are an up-in-front type of person, you might use your gifts and gather more interest for a particular organization in this way.

Advocate for the Cause

If you have the skills and interest in being a cause-related advocate, many compassion and justice organizations work in policy creation to protect the rights of orphaned children. One active organization is the International Justice Mission (IJM.org), a human rights agency that helps rescue victims of slavery, sexual exploitation, and other forms of violent oppression.

Become an Expert

Become an expert on a specific topic related to orphaned children and be willing to speak on the topic to civic groups, churches, schools, and more. For example, the sex slave trade industry is one that crosses all borders and has reached epic proportions. This issue not only impacts the individuals caught in the slavery but also the families and friends of those held captive. Becoming an expert on the topic can educate others and help with prevention. Orphaned and vulnerable children are especially susceptible to deception; your knowledge and activism can make a difference.

Be an Advocate for Your Church

Does your church already have some type of orphan-care ministry? If so, you could increase exposure to the ministry by being willing to talk with others about it. If your church doesn't have some type of orphan-care ministry yet, you could be a voice to bring the need to their attention. Every church should have some type of orphan-care ministry to help address the global need, but they especially need to be involved with the local need. Helping the fatherless child in your neighborhood might look different from helping the fatherless child in Cambodia, but, rest assured, moms in both places need support and their children need people willing to invest in their well-being.

Be an Advocate/Educator in Your Community

My brother Brian is a gifted communicator. At one point in his career he worked for a large company as the liaison to a local nonprofit organization during a fund-raising campaign. His company donated his expertise to raise funds for the campaign. As he met with different corporations, Brian's enthusiasm and knowledge of the need was compelling, and many gave money to the cause.

Perhaps you too are a gregarious, enthusiastic type who would make a good advocate in your community. There are local clubs, schools, churches, and radio stations in need of presenters, and you could talk about the plight of orphaned children in our world. If you are a gifted communicator who likes a worthy challenge, perhaps this is something for you. If the idea terrifies you, keep reading! There are additional ideas that might fit your personality a little closer.

Host "Orphan Sunday" at Your Church

Orphan Sunday brings about exposure for the orphan crisis right in your own church. Christian Alliance for Orphans facilitates a program called Orphan Sunday (orphansunday.org) that provides videos and written materials at low or no cost to help educate congregations about the needs of orphaned children and encourage involvement.

Alliance president Jedd Medefind shares,

> "How you use Orphan Sunday materials and ideas is limited only by your creativity. It could be simple—a short video shown during a church service, a prayer gathering for area foster youth, or a simple meal at home with families considering foster care or adoption. Some churches organize concerts, fund-raisers, or church-wide meals and experiences. Often a sermon or Sunday school class centers on God's heart for the orphan, and opportunities for engagement are offered in the lobby or at an after-church meeting."

Organize an Educational Event

Many adoption and foster care agencies have seminars to educate and interest families in becoming involved. You can be the host who brings interested people together for an educational or exploratory meeting.

Host an Orphan-care Art Show

One church held an art show for the artists in their congregation in conjunction with a missions conference. It was a great way to encourage people to come out to the missions conference. You could host an art show for orphaned children. Start a club where artists can meet together and over time develop pieces of art related to orphaned and vulnerable children. Eventually the items could be sold at an art show and some of the proceeds given to an orphan-care ministry. Someone from a local adoption and foster care agency or orphan-care ministry might be willing to give a presentation.

Orphan-care Awareness Group Study

Use *The Global Orphan Crisis* in a small group so that other ministry ideas might emerge for your church or the group.

Sponsor a Child as a Group

A Sunday school class or a Christian school classroom can sponsor a child or a children's home. This is a great way to involve children in understanding and supporting the cause of an orphaned child. The Christian school where I worked "adopted" an orphanage in Mexico for one school year. The children from the orphanage were divided up by age, and each classroom sponsored one or several children. They wrote to them throughout the year, sent Christmas gifts, and prayed for them. The children not only learned about the plight of orphaned children but were able to actually do something to help.

Giving Your Time

Volunteering is a rewarding way to serve under-resourced people. Years ago I worked at Willow Creek Community Church with operations in the student ministries department. I had one assistant but needed several more people to get all the work accomplished for the busy ministry. Fortunately, Willow Creek has created a culture of volunteerism, so with relative ease we were able to assemble a team of people with willing hearts and amazing skills. One man with an accounting background took over the daily bookkeeping. Another outgoing woman volunteered to work reception a few half-days a week. Several people volunteered to help with general office work and were on-call to tackle mailings. We had a volunteer team of adults who chaperoned events and loved walking around with walkie-talkies on their belts. These incredible volunteers were the backbone of the ministry and became a valued part of the ministry team.

Administrative Volunteer

I often hear from church and parachurch ministries that they need additional administrative help and can't afford to pay for the extra staff. A great solution is volunteers. Perhaps you really enjoy making travel plans to far-off destinations. This could be a welcome relief to a busy ministry leader who regularly crisscrosses the globe. Or perhaps you really enjoy editing. You could be the volunteer who edits the monthly newsletter. Your willingness to help will be a great source of encouragement to a ministry.

If you are available one hour a week, or eight hours a week, and are willing to support an orphan-care ministry at your church or in your city, you can be a valuable asset to the team. Once you find a good ministry fit, let them know your skills, gifts, and availability. Then, be willing to be a servant and treat your involvement just as if it were a paying job. It is difficult for a ministry to assign tasks to volunteers and then not have them show up. Be consistent, be willing, and work with your whole heart as if for the Lord. You will become an indispensable part of the ministry team and touch the lives of children in the process.

Short-Term or Project Volunteer

Every organization has specific projects that they might need help with. Project work can be a shorter commitment but sometimes more intense. Perhaps an annual fund-raiser happens to fit into your schedule. A friend of mine who was out of work took on the facility management of his church while he looked for a permanent position. It looked good on his resume and kept him busy between jobs. I also have retired friends who travel south most winters and volunteer with a ministry in Orlando for a few months each year. Ab works on building projects, and Rosie helps in the commercial kitchen or wherever needed. Julie is a teacher with summers free. She spends most of the summer helping to run a girls Christian camp and assisting in the kitchen. Last summer she spent a week volunteering at an orphanage in Ethiopia as well. If you are creative, willing, and available, there is a ministry that could use your help. (You can read more of Julie's story in the "Stories of Hope and Healing" in the appendix.)

Host a Fund-raising Event

Fund-raisers are a critical part of most orphan-care organizations. In addition, many families interested in adopting might need to do some personal fund-raising. If you do an Internet search using the words *adoption fund-raising*, you will find dozens of websites with all kinds of great ideas. Below are just a few ideas for raising funds for whatever reason—to sponsor a child, to help friends with an adoption, or to support an orphan-care organization.

- Bake sale. Hold an orphan-care ministry bake sale on a Sunday morning at your church.
- Block party. Set up a donation bin for specified donations, such as medical supplies, children's clothes, and shoes, etc.
- Craft/Art sale. Use your talents and sell your creations to earn money for your favorite charity.
- Garage sale. Pull together items from your friends and hold a garage sale to benefit an orphan ministry.
- Birthday party. In lieu of a birthday present, ask each of your guests to bring a gift for an orphaned child.
- Graduation party. When one graduate requested that all donations go to a specific missionary, more than $500 was raised.

- Host a home-based business party (such as Pampered Chef, Mary Kay, or Tastefully Simple) and donate part of your earnings to an orphan-care ministry.
- Christmas toy swap. Clean up some lightly used toys and have a Christmas toy swap with your friends, donating some toys to families who have adopted, foster Safe Family children, have or are single-parent families.
- Shoe drive for orphaned children. Buckner Shoes for Orphan Souls went from being a Dallas-based shoe drive in 1999 to a nationwide endeavor. Find out how you can host a shoe drive for Buckner. Check out buckner.org.
- Beans and rice fast. Many churches have started asking their congregation to participate in a beans-and-rice fast for a day or a week, saving the money that would have been spent on food and using it to support orphaned children. Some provide daily devotionals and educational opportunities along with the fast.
- Talent Night. Hold a talent night and charge a small admission fee. During the program, have someone give a presentation about the needs of global orphans.

Be a Part of a Large Fund-raising Event

Different from personally hosting a small event, helping with a fund-raiser can be quite an adventure. Perhaps the event is an annual fund-raiser or a onetime event. You might be an organizer, promoter, or a participant in the event; all are important roles for the event's success.

A few years ago I was part of a team that hosted the Ride for Refugees at our church. This event started in 2004 as a small annual fund-raiser in Canada for International Teams (iteams.org) to raise money for their international refugee ministry. The Ride has taken on a life of its own and has spread throughout Canada and the United States, raising hundreds of thousands of dollars every year for refugee ministries.

There are many different rides, runs, walks, golf outings, concerts, etc. that are potential fund-raising events for orphan-care organizations. Being a small part of a larger event can be very satisfying, especially if you enjoy working with like-minded individuals. If you enjoy being a part of a good cause, this might be a good fit for you.

Logistics

Ministry organizations and individual families (single-parent, foster, or Safe families) often can use help moving things! Getting furniture where it needs to go can be a real blessing to a family, and many ministries need help with getting supplies to a person or program. I have enlisted my husband countless times to help with transporting groceries, supplies, and even pizzas to different events.

Work from Home

My friend Mary helps children from her own suburban home. A church in the area asks volunteers to make fleece blankets for children. Mary picks up the fleece from the church, takes it home, crochets a border on each of the blankets, and brings the finished products back to church. The ministry handles the distribution. Sometimes she joins other women for a crochet get-together so she can socialize with other blanket makers, but mostly she makes them at home. A blanket seems a simple thing, but for the child who receives it, it is a warm reminder that he or she is loved.

While traveling in Haiti I actually saw dozens of handmade blankets on children's beds in children's homes. At one children's home a precious little girl had on a handmade dress sewn by a ministry that turns pillowcases into dresses. It was fun to actually see someone's hard work in action.

Many products can be made from home for orphan ministries. Some organizations give specific detailed instructions for what they need. If you are creative or artistic, put your talent to work and create something to help the plight of orphaned children.

Families who participate in the Safe Family program receive no external funding; the volunteer family pays all the expenses. Finding, cleaning, and repairing baby or child furniture could be very useful for a family.

Feel free to enlist the help of children at home or at church as well. Children can add excitement and enthusiasm. Depending on their ages, children can be a big help in many ways. I've seen children help with letter writing, shopping, packing boxes, and making crafts. My niece Kathryn crochets wonderful scarves, washcloths, and other items that become great gifts. As you can see, making items for orphan-care ministries can be fun for the whole family. The ideas are unlimited.

Products to Make at Home

- Knit or crochet. People love handmade gifts, and orphaned children are no exception. Knowing someone took the time to personally create a gift especially for them can be encouraging. Try blankets, scarves, hats, and sweaters (or "jumpers" as my British cousin calls them). Check out KasCare: Aid for AIDS Orphans at knit-a-square.com.

- Dress a girl around the world. One organization came up with an idea to make simple dresses out of pillowcases and other materials for girls who have very little or nothing. See www.dress agirlaroundtheworld.com.

- Make a blanket. Karen Bradley, the owner of Sassy Scrubs, adopted two girls from China and then started making blankets to send to orphanages in China. Karen would enjoy making you part of her blanket-making crew. The blanket instructions and other information is found at www.sassy scrubs.com.

- Bake a cake. An organization called Sweet Blessings Cakes makes birthday cakes for children in poverty. You can make a cake to brighten the face of a child who might not otherwise have a birthday cake. See sweetblessingsbakery.com.

- Make sock puppets or other crafts to send to a children's home. Make a project yourself, or create a kit that a child can complete, and send them to a children's home or orphanage. Get some puppet craft and skit ideas at www.daniellesplace.com.

Resource Network

Many adoptive, foster, and Safe Families need support teams around them, especially for new placements or during stressful times. We often assume these families have the support they need, but that is often far from the case. You can become a part of the family's circle of support. You and your family can be a "go-to" family when they have specific needs or for general support. Here are some specific ways that you can be of service.

Use your professional vocation. If you are a physician, dentist, therapist, auto mechanic, handyman, etc., use your skills to help keep costs down for a family that serves orphaned children. Many families serving in this way have already stretched their dollars to support their ministry so the additional professional help is appreciated. We are placed in positions of influence for a reason. It is a wonderful gift when you are able to use your position, education, and resources for a child or family needing your help.

Offer to babysit for an evening or for a weekend so that the adoptive or foster parents can get a respite.

Become certified to provide respite care for a family with foster children. Typically, a state requires a respite caregiver to have some type of official clearance and training in order to care for a state-placed foster child. If you have a family you would like to help in this area, let them connect you with the person who can help you get started on your training requirements.

Cook a meal for a single working mom or an adoptive or foster family. With some planning you can make extra meals when you are cooking for your family. Freeze the extras so they are ready to give when needed.

Organize a Facebook fund-raiser for a friend who is adopting a child.

Have a shower for a family who has adopted a baby or child.

Christmas Activities

Around the holidays people seem more generous and willing to support a project for orphaned children. Although people are busy close to the holidays, if you start a project in late October or early November, you will likely get a good response. That also leaves enough time to send your gifts to the children before Christmas.

Angel Tree is a Prison Fellowship program connecting parents in prison with their children through the delivery of Christmas gifts. In most cases, local church volunteers purchase and deliver gifts to children on behalf of their prisoner-parent. See angeltree.org.

Provide *Christmas gifts for the children of deployed military.* Every year more than two million children are temporarily left by a deployed military parent. If you live in a community near military bases, this could be an opportunity for you. Christmas gifts, as well as general services, could be a way to serve these children.

Operation Christmas Child, organized by Samaritan's Purse, distributes shoeboxes full of personal care items every Christmas to children around the world. Look for samaritanspurse.org.

Fill backpacks with school supplies. Several organizations provide backpacks with school supplies for orphaned children or children in poverty. Check out missionbackpack.org.

Decorate a mitten tree. Put up a tree in the church foyer or other busy spot, and encourage people to donate new mittens to hang on the tree, possibly including a personal note to send along when the mittens are given to local children or sent to children around the world.

Donate children's Bibles. Bibles can be donated to local adoption and foster care agencies, sent overseas to a children's home, or given to

an orphan-care ministry to use where they have a need.
See www.americanbible.org.

Donate toys and supplies to an orphanage.

Invite a single-parent family to join you for Thanksgiving or Christmas.

Retreat for Ministry Workers

Being in front-line orphan-care ministry can be very exhausting. The need is enormous, the passion is high, and the work is relentless. There is a high potential for burnout. To go the distance in any ministry, workers need to care for themselves in addition to caring for the ministry. One way to encourage and support those in frontline orphan-care ministry is to provide retreat opportunities.

If you have a second home, condo, or vacation house, consider offering the use of the facility to an orphan-care leader or ministry for a few weeks a year. I have heard dozens of wonderful examples of this, and in every case the break was beyond refreshing for the recipients. Perhaps you have a mountainside condo and could let a ministry leader use it for a weekend ski retreat with her family. If you have a large beach house, perhaps you could allow a ministry to use it for a month in the spring or fall, so their staff can take turns with their families for rest and relaxation.

Around the country several retreat organizations provide semi-structured retreats for leaders. If you have a larger home that could accommodate a small group of people, perhaps you could organize retreats for ministry leaders or allow a retreat ministry the use of your home for a month or more to use to serve ministry leaders. One house on a small lake in Wisconsin is run like a bed-and-breakfast. Each Monday the owners welcome up to eight ministry leaders or couples, who stay through Saturday morning. They provide all the meals, with buffet-style breakfast and lunch. Dinner is a special time shared with the host family. During the day the guests can rest, read, play games, watch a DVD, make a craft, hike, boat, or even go on a picnic with a prepared lunch. This particular facility also offers professional counseling and a lot of encouragement by the hosts. The idea is to provide a restful, encouraging environment to refresh a leader's mind, heart, and soul. If you are interested in allowing your home to be used in this way, contact me through the website, and I can help you make the connections.

Additional Ideas

We could fill several books with the countless ways you can contribute to the cause of orphans. Your only limit is your own creativity. Here is a quick-pick list of dozens of ideas that could be one-shot ventures or the basis for an entire ministry. Don't just look at the words on the page, but let these words spur on your thinking to take the ideas even further.

Let your Internet searches work for you, as GoodSearch.com says, "empowering you to change the world through simple everyday actions." Let your Internet searches help make money for an orphan-care ministry. GoodSearch.com is powered by Yahoo! A participating organization receives one cent for every search you perform. Forgotten Voices is already registered, so it is easy to direct donations to them, or you can designate another nonprofit organization. To make the most of this donation program, don't keep forwarding through to the next search, which makes all your searches considered as one search. Close the window and go back to the Good Search home page before you begin your next search. That will keep the pennies ticking. Do the math. I personally rack up about fifty cents on a normal workday. Multiply that by 100 days. If 5,000 people signed up and worked on average as I do, we could donate more than $250,000 each year to orphan-care organizations. It is well worth the few minutes to get it set up.

Blog for a cause. Help spread the word about the global orphan crisis through your blog, if you are a blogger. Some orphan-care programs would like to partner with you to have you spread the word for them as well. Compassion International selects a small group of bloggers each year, taking them on a trip to see their ministry in action so that they can blog about it. Check out compassionbloggers.com.

Give a friend a gift. Give a friend a book about the orphan crisis for a Christmas or birthday gift.

Correspond with an orphaned child. You can be a correspondent even if you can't financially sponsor a child. Many organizations would like their sponsors also to correspond to children. If for some reason the sponsor can't write to the child, some organizations will partner a writer with a sponsor so the child receives both financial and emotional support.

Get your workplace involved. Talk to your employers to see if they would be willing to donate to the cause through a sponsorship or corporate donation.

Send Valentines. Hope Unlimited sends Valentines cards to children in Brazil. If you like to make and send cards this could be the perfect fit for you. Look for hopeunlimitedforchildren.blogspot.com.

Help at a camp. Be a camp counselor, buddy, or even a cook at the Royal Kids Camp for foster children. Campers attend free. The goal of Royal Family Kids is to have every child in foster care in the United States be able to attend a summer camp. See royalfamilykids.org.

Donate your life insurance. Donate your life insurance plan to an orphan-care organization. LifePoint can help you determine whether this is an option for your life insurance policy (lifepointce.org). An organization such as Food for Orphans would be an exceptional beneficiary of a life insurance policy (foodfororphans.org).

Recycle. Recycling used cell phones still worth using helps to earn money for Life in Abundance ministry (liaint.org). Recycling your old print cartridges takes a little extra effort, but every little bit helps (fundingfactory.com)

Run a baby bottle campaign. Buy bottles in bulk and design a paper flyer to go in each bottle telling about your ministry or adoption. Distribute them to friends, family, businesses, churches, schools, daycares—whoever is willing to put their spare change in the baby bottle. Give them one month to fill the bottle and then collect them. One crisis pregnancy center using this idea averages $20–25 per bottle, so the pennies really add up.[4]

Create your own fund-raiser. One family raised funds for their adoption by creating and selling a photography e-course. Perhaps you have an idea of an app or an e-course that you could sell online as well.

A Few Thoughts

As you can see, there are hundreds of different ways to be a part of the solutions for the orphan crisis. All it takes is tenacity, creativity, willingness, and time. Here is the thing: Don't wait for the "right" time. Don't put it on the agenda for tomorrow or next week. Don't wait until after you _____ (fill in the blank!). I don't know about you, but if something is important I keep the task front and center. If something gets into a pile, it could be days or weeks until I get back to it. Do something right away, like implementing the Good Search browser. It makes me smile to know that every Internet search is benefiting an orphan-care organization. Other ventures will require some preparation and will develop over time. Remember the urgency of this crisis. Vulnerable, abandoned, and orphaned children can't wait. A little bit every day will make a difference in the lives of orphaned children. Start today!

QUESTIONS TO PONDER

Take notes about the ideas you've encountered in three categories of response: Love it, Like the Idea, and Hmmm . . . Worth Thinking About.

Love It

_____

_____

_____

Like It

_____

_____

_____

Hmmm . . . Worth Thinking About

_____

_____

_____

ACTION POINT

Pray over the "Questions to Ponder" ideas you jotted down, pick the top two or three ideas God seems to keep bringing to the front of your mind, and do some research. Start dreaming. What are the possibilities?

Lara never intended to adopt, but God expanded her heart in ways she never thought possible. *Mandie Turner, photographer © Mandie Turner*

12

Changing Your
Life to Change
the World

**Defend the cause of the weak and fatherless;
maintain the rights of the poor and oppressed.
Rescue the weak and needy; deliver them
from the hand of the wicked.**
Psalm 82:3–4

Perhaps this book should have come with a warning: Beware! Getting passionate about orphan care could change your life forever! If you've made it this far, you already have a heart that leans toward solutions to the global orphan crisis. That's the beginning of a great adventure, because the Lord works through willing hearts.

Here's how orphan-care advocate Lara Dinsmore describes the way God changed her life to change the world:

When Orphans Become Sons:
An Adoption Story

I always said I'd never leave America for anything. I like warm showers and drive-through fast food and all of the comforts of home. My grandpa is a missions pastor and before every trip he took, I would remind him he was nuts. I was thankful God would never, ever, call me to leave home. Note to self: Don't ever dare God to ask you to step away from comfortable, because He just might.

My journey started when I was student teaching during college. A tiny girl in my third-grade class was in the foster care system. Her parents were both incarcerated, and she was in desperate need of love. She was the first kid in the classroom in the mornings and gave long hugs at the end of each day. School was a safe place for her where she received the love she got nowhere else.

I knew this child needed love, and certainly I had that to give. I began researching fostering and adoption. Ultimately, the foster care and adoption process seemed so daunting, it struck me as one of those things other people did, not me. Fostering/adoption just looked too hard, too expensive, too scary. I thought that if something was difficult it meant God hadn't called me to it.

Fast-forward several years: My husband and I were living the good life by most people's standards, with a nice house, two kids, and a dog. But I felt this longing to be a part of something bigger.

One night I was tinkering around on the computer and ran across a picture that was there by accident. I had borrowed my grandparents' memory card to download some pictures and wound up with pictures from one of their missions trips. This particular picture was of my grandpa ministering to orphans in Burma. I didn't sleep that night.

Had God been calling me? When He said to care for the poor, the orphan, the widow, the sick, the imprisoned, was He talking to me? I had been sauntering through my Christian life, letting myself think He just hadn't "called" all of us to do all that crazy stuff. Weren't some of us just meant to enjoy comfortable lives while attending church on Sunday and giving our 10 percent to the Lord's work?

I wrestled with these questions for weeks. At the core of it was the fact that there was a hurting world outside my front door and I was doing absolutely nothing about it. I realized I had been running from a calling that God had deeply incorporated in me—simply because I thought it would be too hard.

My husband and I began talking about what this meant for our family. We loved being parents. We wanted more children. We wanted to follow Jesus wherever He led us.

Eighteen months later, I sat nervously in a courtroom in rural Uganda with the most beautiful brown-eyed boy in my arms. He was four and a half, just six weeks younger than our biological son. His young life had been difficult, and he had already experienced things no child should.

A winding road had taken us there. We had spent every dime we had to get to him and traveled halfway around the world. Yet we had also built friendships, become involved in orphan-care ministries, fell in love with another country, and grew more than ever before.

Our first days with our new son were a blur. He clung to me for dear life, fearful of everything. Sometimes he'd cry and not be able to tell me what he needed. Sometimes he wanted nothing to do with me and was angry. I held him until he could calm down, not knowing what else to do. Those days stretched me farther than ever before. But when I looked in his eyes, there was no question: He was my son, and I was his mommy. God would heal his heart. I just needed to love him even though he couldn't love me back.

Just a few weeks after being home, our newest son was a different child. We watched the change in his heart as he went from being an orphan to a son. He made eye contact, gave hugs, and started to verbally express what he needed. The raw fear showed itself less. When it did come up he allowed me to comfort and console him.

It seemed like a miracle. Suddenly he was the child he never got to be before. He laughed with his whole body and constantly wanted to play "this little piggy." He spent hours playing with building blocks with his brother. I felt blessed to have a front row seat to the restoration of this little soul.

Today, my younger son is a joy and blessing to the whole family. I still sometimes have to stand back and wonder what in the world I did to deserve to be the mommy of this precious child. And to think there was a time I was so scared of a different continent, the costs, and the adoption process that I almost missed this!

I am not here to tell you that if you follow God wherever He takes you it will be easy. I can almost promise you it will be the hardest journey of your life. It might take you places you thought you'd never go. It might cost you everything you have. Yet the greatest blessings occur when instead of running from the hard calling you run toward it with open arms and complete faith that God will come through.

Commitment Required

For some people anything less than a life-altering commitment is just not enough. Some people are called to change their lives, to step out of their comfort zones, and really accomplish something extraordinary. Perhaps you have realized, for the first time, the plight of orphaned children in our world and are ready to make a change that might impact the rest of your life. Or maybe you have been thinking about this for a while and have finally put all the pieces together. Regardless of how you got here, you have a calling to be different, to live differently, and to make choices differently. Anything done for an orphaned child is a gift, but are you willing to sacrifice whatever needs to be sacrificed to impact a child on a deeper level?

As you dive into this chapter you might see yourself in some of the scenarios or you might come up with your own new and improved path. Let the examples given here be early building blocks for your unique ministry to orphaned children. Don't settle for the status quo or just doing the minimum. Be different, be brave, be amazing!

Missional Living

Most of us have heard the words *missional living*. In essence the term means living a God-focused life of willingness, sacrifice, and intentionality. Missional living is countercultural, like swimming against the cultural current. We tend to have cultural "norms" that are expected of us, but when we choose to live missionally, we intentionally defy convention to focus on what really matters: bringing God's Kingdom to earth.

Remember Claudia from the last chapter? She lives missionally. She chooses to live frugally in order to support her biological children and her sponsored Compassion children. She is willing to give up something to honor God's calling on her life.

Scott and Kerri, my husband's sister and brother-in-law, live missionally. Scott, a science teacher at a Christian school, chose to leave the typical suburban life and start an organic farm in the hope of raising healthier children and having a more holistic and integrated work, home, and spiritual environment. That was massively countercultural. Several years later they now raise or grow the majority of their food, minister to people through health education and encouragement, and are healthier than ever before. Their children are bright, caring, and responsible. Theirs is not a lifestyle for everyone, but I'm proud that they were willing to go against the cultural current to live in a way that mirrors their beliefs.

Similarly, when we choose to live missionally we throw out convention and ask the questions most people are not willing to ask. We do what most people are not willing to do. As my friend Peggy has said to me for years, "Life is not a rehearsal!" This side of heaven, we get one lifetime to use as we see fit. We spend it with intentionality, or we just spend it haphazardly—either way, we have one shot to get it right. What better way to spend it than to live intentionally in harmony with our beliefs.

So what does living missionally have to do with orphaned children? Everything! If you are living missionally, you are willing to prioritize your life in a way that is God-focused and others-centered. God says in His Word that helping orphaned children is important to Him, so it should also be important to us as well.

There are untold opportunities to live missionally and to align your education and career to serve orphaned and vulnerable children in this country and around the world. You don't have to give up what you love and who you are. It makes me cringe when I hear about people who go to school to be in a particular vocation that they love and then decide to set it aside to be in a ministry where they have to start back at square one. While God might call some to do that, it is more likely that God will align your interests, education, and experiences to come together to do something amazing, which might very well be in a vocational or ministry setting. We need all types of people, from all different careers and walks of life, to live missionally and be fully engaged in bringing God's Kingdom to earth.

Richard Stearns, in his book *The Hole in Our Gospel*,[1] talks about his journey from the corporate world to the world of compassion, as he became the president of World Vision U.S. It was certainly not an expected or easy decision, but his life change will impact the lives of hundreds of thousands of children around the world. God has blessed the ministry. Stearns and World Vision have continued to grow as a formidable force caring for vulnerable children. Had Stearns not taken the role with World Vision, that organization may not have grown as it has. God's plans are not thwarted by our lack of response to His call. However, can you imagine what Stearns would have missed had he not taken the leap of faith?

Missional Living with In-Home Child Care: Adoption, Foster Care, and Safe Families

Taking a child into your own home is a life-altering commitment—one with great challenges and wonderful rewards. We've already covered the different ways children might be brought into your home, and getting personal advice from professionals working in adoption, foster care, or Safe Families is the best way to begin to get a feel for what might work with your specific family. In the meantime, pray. Do your research. Talk to those already involved. Allow God to open your heart to His best for your family. Remember that oftentimes when we want microwave results, God gives us slow-cooker answers; His timing is certainly not our own. In spite of the challenges and the setbacks or heartbreaks involved in the process, God wants you to embrace the journey that He has you on. We often try to fast-forward to get to our desired result, but on that fast track we'd miss so much of what God is trying to teach us. God will make His plan happen for your family in His time. As it teaches in so many places throughout the Bible, we are called to trust, embrace, and rest in God's great promises: "Truly my soul finds rest in God; my salvation comes from him. Truly he is my rock and my salvation; he is my fortress, I will never be shaken" (Psalm 62:1–2).

Using Your Profession to Live Missionally

We have touched on using your career from your current zip code to serve orphaned and vulnerable children. But we haven't begun to tap your professional skills as a place to begin brainstorming how, with your commitment, God can use you in places and ways that you never imagined.

There really is a role for everyone. Take the challenge, as I did, and dream about the possibilities. If we were to sit down together and brainstorm a little bit, I bet that within ten minutes we could come up with ten ways that you could use your profession to serve orphaned children. Let's say you are a counselor by profession; let's give it a try. You might:

1. Hold a monthly suppport group for parents of adopted children.

2. Offer a monthly therapy group for adopted teens.

3. Work at a camp for foster children one week each summer, offering your services for one-on-one time with children.

4. Teach a class for foster or Safe Family parents on topics such as boundaries, attachment, or healthy relationships.

5. Offer your services to brief and debrief a ministry team going overseas to help at an orphanage. Emotions are high, and perspective is helpful.

6. Offer a counseling/wellness check-up to a couple considering adopting to help them think through their decision and the impact it will have on their family.

7. Participate on a missions trip to an orphanage or children's home to counsel the ministry leadership and staff and empower them to keep lines of communication open.

8. Find a ministry that works with recovery and restoration in the sex slave trade and be willing to train counselors in helping young women recover from trauma.

9. Volunteer for a week at a ministry retreat for orphan-care leaders and meet with different leaders to avoid burn out in their ministry.

10. Offer counseling and coaching to a foster children aging out of the foster care system, perhaps connecting them to services that might be able to help direct their future.

Now that wasn't too difficult. With more time and a few more people to throw ideas around with, we could come up with dozens more ideas. Now if you are a rocket scientist by profession, it might be a bit harder to come up with as many applications to orphan care, but I expect we'd find out that your likes, dislikes, hobbies, past job experiences, and future aspirations hold many clues to how you could fit in the solutions picture. Don't limit yourself, be creative, challenge tradition, and you *can* come up with a list of possibilities.

If you can't get any traction in coming up with ideas on your own, gather some like-minded people and talk, pray, and dream about it together. If you are an artist, invite all the artists you know to come over for dessert sometime and just enjoy one another, share your passion, and ask for their help to come up with ideas. You'll be amazed at the ideas generated by like-minded individuals.

Travel Required

It is so exciting to see God at work around the world. I enjoy being involved in ministry locally, but my real passion is going overseas and being a part of what God is doing in other parts of the world.

Dave and I were visiting a ministry in Colorado Springs in 1995 and stayed in the home of a Navigators missionary couple. The couple had recently returned from a small town in Siberia where they were seeing a newfound hunger for God and His Word. They felt that the opportunities were tremendous for evangelism and discipleship and were assembling a team to go again the next summer. I had never seen a spiritual hunger like they described, and I felt compelled to see it firsthand. I was moved, intrigued, and ready to go.

The following summer I spent three weeks with a team of seven adults in the university town of Irkutsk, Siberia, engaged in evangelism and discipleship. We each had a translator; mine was Natasha, a young lady who had just graduated from language school. Natasha was petite with long brown hair, big brown eyes, and she was smart, confident, and fearless. Natasha had translated for the team before ours and had recently become a believer. She was hungry for God's Word. Before long I realized that one of the main reasons I was in Siberia was to disciple and encourage Natasha.

In Irkutsk I went to my first children's home. It was a hospital for terminally ill children. The sick children didn't go there to get healed; they went there to die. Many of the children at the hospital had been affected by the Chernobyl accident six years earlier.

In April 26, 1986, the Chernobyl nuclear power plant experienced an explosion of epic proportion that sent radioactive contamination spewing throughout the region. Although the immediate death toll was rather small as far as disasters go—only thirty-one people—the fallout affected millions more. There have been anywhere from 30,000 to 200,000 deaths, primarily due to cancer.[2] Most of the children in the Irkutsk hospital were contaminated by radiation and were in various stages of cancer and disease. With minimal resources, little medication (a hangover from the days of Communism), and no precedence, the skilled doctors were forced to stand by and watch the children slip away.

Natasha and I spent a day with the children at the hospital, trying to encourage them and show them the love of Jesus. Working with Natasha and being able to touch the lives of these children (who have likely long since died) was such a bitter blessing, but one that is burned into my mind and heart. Those children needed to hear about the life-giving salvation that can only come from Jesus. They had no hope for this world, only hope for eternity. This type of experience changes a person. Every Christ-follower ought to have this type of experience. You don't have to go as far as Siberia; there are plenty of opportunities to touch the lives of orphaned children and other individuals in need. If you haven't been on a missions experience in this country or somewhere around the world, please do. It will change you. It will hurt your heart in places you never knew you had, but it will also expand your worldview and make you more effective for whatever God has in store for your future.

I've been with dozens of adults and students as they served in many countries. In every case they came back blessed. To be really honest: some did come back sick, most everyone was exhausted, and everyone had fewer dollars! But in every case the participants were glad to have served and to have been a part of something bigger than themselves.

Personally, I've found these trips remind me that the world doesn't revolve around me—a shocking reality when I went overseas on my first missions project as an eighteen-year-old. Getting to other parts of the world shows me that we live in the richest country in the world and that developed countries are the anomaly—not the other way around. Service trips show me that I need to choose to live counterculturally in my country to make a difference for someone else who doesn't have choices. That makes me want to do better with my resources so I can share them with those who don't have what they need. We have been given a huge responsibility: "From everyone who has been given much, much will be demanded; and from the one who has been entrusted with much, much more will be asked" (Luke 12:48). Are we up for the challenge?

Circling back to the main point: You are skilled, trained, and gifted. Are you willing to use those resources for orphaned and vulnerable children here and around the world? I have a friend who used to say that we are all called to "go" unless God calls us to stay. That's a different take from the conventional view, but swimming upstream is never easy. There are many types of mission and service projects and depending on your skills and experience, there might be specialized opportunities for you to serve around the world.

Medical Skills

A medical mission welcomes help from all types of professionals in the medical field. Years ago my father (now a retired dentist) served on several trips to Haiti and Honduras. You might want to undertake a longer-term commitment of months or years at a clinic. Cousins Steve and Mary Hawthorne have served in missions in Bolivia for more than twenty years with Steve as a local physician and Mary serving in the community in many different ways. Medical missions are critically important ministries that can serve orphaned and vulnerable children. You can collect ideas for possible directions at christianmedical.org and healthenations.com.

Business Skills

Every nonprofit has a business component to the program. If you are an accountant, general businessperson, administrator, or consultant, your skills could make the operations of an organization flow better. If the business side of an organization is not run well, it doesn't matter how important the cause. We have all seen organizations go out of business because of poor management. Offering your skills for a short-term project could be helpful for a ministry organization as well as life-changing for you.

Building, Trades, and Architecture

Phil and Emily have been serving in Africa for several years. Both grew up in Africa as missionary kids and now are back in Uganda, where Phil uses his architectural degree to design and build bridges, children's villages, hospitals, and more. Phil uses the skills of volunteers to plan and implement his projects. Sometimes a short-term team of building professionals will travel to Africa to investigate or design the project. Other times builders, carpenters, plumbers, electricians, and other individuals go overseas to actually build the projects. There are many building opportunities around the world. It wouldn't take you long on the Internet to find one that desperately needs your services. My friend Jeff traveled back and forth to Haiti and Mexico for several years as a general contractor and built several projects, including a children's home, a school, and a church. Willing workers are dedicated and irreplaceable.

No matter what your training or skill set, it won't take long to find someplace where you can serve. If your vocation doesn't lend itself to serving, perhaps your hobbies do. At the very least, floors need mopping and dishes need cleaning—and most of us could help in that way.

Start a Business

Whether you applaud it or are terrified by it, we live in a global economy. Ten years ago we could debate if being part of the global community was a good thing or not. That is no longer an option. Now we have to adjust our ideas to ignore international business (to our detriment) or embrace the reality of a world economy and take advantage of the opportunities. Embracing the global economy can be utilized to produce missional business opportunities to benefit many people, including orphaned children. From a purely economic aspect, creating jobs in a poverty-stricken area can turn vulnerable children and families into stable families. From a spiritual perspective, if the parent is introduced to the lifesaving knowledge of Jesus through an employer's godly example, he or she can change the spiritual trajectory of the family as well. And changing a family changes a community.

In the last decade the concept of business as missions has come into its own. People intentionally build businesses here in the United States or around the world with the twofold purpose of conducting business to the glory of God and touching people's lives for Jesus. There is often a blending of economic, social, and spiritual elements in the business's stated goals.

Business as missions can take many forms. For some entrepreneurs the company they create might support a nonprofit ministry, like Bolivia's Best Coffee acting as the financial engine for an orphanage. Other companies might provide jobs, creating an environment conducive to spiritual growth opportunities. Another company might simply seek to create commerce and employ local people to assist in the venture. Consider the possibilities! Someone might even create a business that could train orphaned teens in skills that could head them toward careers to support them throughout their lifetimes.

Roy and Liz (not their real names) lived and worked in a country in Asia where it is not acceptable to talk about the love of God or to be missionaries, but the people of that country are in great distress and in need of jobs and services. Roy started several NGOs, clinics, and businesses that benefit the people in numerous ways even while they provide a platform to tell people about God. Although Roy and Liz are no longer living in that country, they still run the organizations from outside the country using both nationals and non-nationals for the daily operations. They have made a tremendous difference in the lives of many people in spite of the danger to their own.

If you are a businessperson or have the desire to be one, business as missions could be a way for you to be involved with serving orphaned children. Check out businessasmissionnetwork.com. Allow God to open the doors of opportunity. You'll be amazed at the results.

Starting an Orphan Ministry: Dreams to Reality

Some little girls dream of being a princess. Others dream of being a mommy. Since she was eight years old, Hilliary Anderson had dreams of starting a home for vulnerable children.

Years later, while finishing up a college internship on a trip to Kigali, Rwanda, with a friend, Megan Swanson, these two young women did the unthinkable and started developing friendships with young street boys. As it often happens, God's plans for these women was much bigger than just a trip to Africa. They met Chantal Umutesi, an accomplished professional woman with a degree in travel operations and language. Amazingly, Chantal also had a childhood dream of one day starting an orphanage. God blended their dreams, and several months later Hope for Life Ministry (HFLM) was born.[3]

All three women had their plans "interrupted." Now, only a few years later, they have a staff, a board of directors, a home in Kigali, and more than twenty-four children in their residential program. Both Hilliary and Megan travel back and forth to Africa to continue the work, while Chantal, the Children's Director, keeps all the parts moving harmoniously. All of the children's stories are breathtaking, but Muhawe's story is nothing short of miraculous.

Elijah Muhawenimana (Muhawe) was only five months old when rebels killed his mother while he was strapped on her back. His mother's killers took the baby and laid him in the bush, where he spent four days until people passing by heard his cries. He was sent to the western province of Rwanda to grow up at his cousin's house because his widowed father was forced to move to Kigali, the capital, to try to earn money. When Muhawe was around eight years old, he started behaving badly and his cousin refused to care for him anymore. His father took him to Kigali to live with him, but Muhawe could not tolerate living in deep poverty and ran away to begin life on the streets. His nickname on the streets was *Rwaranunemeye,* meaning "rejected by death."

Living on the street is difficult in any city, but living in a poverty-stricken city in the heart of Africa makes it even harder. Muhawe begged for money and food, lived in an abandoned building, and started taking drugs. Occasionally he went to Hope for Life Ministry to bathe, wash his clothes, and have a meal. When Muhawe became very sick with malaria, the staff at HFLM took him to the hospital, got him medication, and let him recover at HFLM. Muhawe came to the center as a timid, fragile, and sick young boy, but after only a short time he became gentle and kind and even started smiling.

Now Muhawe smiles for almost any reason. He is a happy boy who has impressed the staff with his humility and servant attitude. In July of 2010, Muhawe added a few words to Hilliary's blog, saying, "This is Muhawe. I am twelve years old. I pray for you so that you can continue to help us at HFLM. I ask God that He'll let you be able to visit HFLM someday. I also thank God because He changed me and took me away from the street and now I've stopped taking drugs. Please continue to pray for me. I also thank God because I used to have bugs living in my feet and now they are gone!"[4]

These days, Muhawe has dreams too. He wants to be a pilot or a driver. He is happy. He is surrounded by a community that loves him. He is loved. All this is possible thanks to three young women who were willing to allow their lives to be "interrupted" in order to bring hope to those who had none!

Start Small, Think Big

Starting an orphan-care ministry is an enormous step, and yet hundreds, perhaps even thousands, of people have done just that in recent years. Look for a need, come up with a creative way to meet that need, and enlist the help of others. Start small, and see if it starts to grow into something bigger.

Perhaps you are a single mom and notice other single parents in need of some specific type of encouragement. Even starting a support group with provided babysitting at your church would be something that could encourage another single parent.

Perhaps you are a computer techie who spends much of your time in a distant country on business. During your time off perhaps you could find an orphan-care ministry somewhere in the area that needs tech support. You might volunteer your time several times a year to keep their computer systems up to date. Or perhaps your company will donate lightly used equipment to the organization, and you can install it for them. If this works out well, perhaps you could replicate the idea and make a ministry out of it somehow.

Using Ingenuity and Technology
to Improve Children's Lives

Technology is fascinating to me. I like adapting old ideas in new ways. I am especially excited when ideas improve people's lives in unexpected ways. Aquaponics is a technique used thousands of years ago but has lately gathered new interest due to its simplicity and productivity. Aquaponics is growing fish and plants together in an integrated system. In a soil-less hydroponic-type system (plants grown in water), the fish waste from the water tanks provides nutrition for the plants, and the plants provide a natural filter for the water. The result of this unique relationship is the production of fresh organic vegetables and fish. This system utilizes a small portion of the water required for conventional farming and grows larger vegetables in half the time. This concept is used in smaller systems for the home gardener or on a large-scale industrial size to provide food for hundreds.

Several years ago a handful of students at the Milwaukee School of Engineering were in a Bible study together. The group wanted to create a senior design project that would meet their academic criteria, be productive, and glorify God. The team came up with the idea of designing an aquaponics system for an orphanage in Haiti. Their system became known as Project Grow.

Faith Orphanage, the recipient of Project Grow, is located in Jacmel, Haiti. In a resource-poor environment, growing food in an economical and healthful way is critical. With Project Grow the orphanage is able to provide nutritious vegetables and high-quality protein for their children on a consistent basis. All this was made possible because a group of engineering students wanted to create something that mattered.[5]

This example is just the tip of the iceberg. In the northern part of Haiti an aquaponics company from Wisconsin worked with missionaries to create an industrial-sized system to feed hundreds of people. Let's take that one step further. Can you imagine a team of engineers coming up with a self-sustained program that not only provides food but could also come up with ways to create self-sufficiency in other areas as well? Perhaps they could develop systems that could access water and purify it by eliminating potential disease.

Power is another utility that is nonexistent or unpredictable in many parts of the world. We met Jarrett at a children's village in Haiti. Jarrett is an engineering student who has worked in agriculture and who just happened to be in Haiti for a few weeks while our team was visiting. Young and technologically savvy, Jarrett has come up with a plan to convert the unreliable electric power at the Village to a solar system. Because of the consistent sun and high cost of the current power, Jarrett believes converting to a solar system would save two-thirds of the power cost over the next twenty years. He is willing to put up all the labor and only needs the costs for the conversion equipment. His enthusiasm was contagious. If I had the resources, I would have written him a check on the spot. These and other ingenious ideas can, and will, make serving orphaned children a little easier.

Microloan Programs

Microloan programs are typically small loans given to impoverished and disadvantaged people in order to start an income-generating venture. Many of the recipients are women in impoverished countries who have no other way of earning money. Microloan programs show an amazingly high repayment rate. The typical repayment rates are usually from 95–98 percent, meaning that the risk involved for the loan is minimal, and the same money can be used and reused to benefit the lives of many.

Tirzah International implements a microloan program for women. Their name comes from the Bible in Numbers 27. Tirzah and her sisters were the daughters of a man named Zelophehad. Zelophehad died, leaving the daughters unable to inherit, as was the custom of the day. The daughters, brave and undaunted, went before Moses and other leaders and asked them to grant them their inheritance in spite of the current laws. Moses sought God's guidance, and God said to Moses, "What Zelophehad's daughters are saying is right. You must certainly give them property as an inheritance among their father's relatives and give their father's inheritance to them" (Numbers 27:7).

Readers in Bible times would have found the leadership's treatment of the orphaned daughters countercultural—and even today it is still countercultural in some cultures for women to inherit money. This passage that shows God's judgment about caring for women on their own serves as an inspiration to Tirzah International as they seek to enable oppressed women in tangible ways, such as microloans.[6]

I met with Emily Voorhies, the director of Tirzah International, over a cup of coffee on a crisp fall day outside Colorado Springs, Colorado. Emily has been in ministry for more than twenty-five years, the last ten as leader of the worldwide network of women that eventually came to be called Tirzah International. Emily is passionate about the plight of women, especially women who are widowed and have to fend for themselves. Emily feels that so many times a widow can feel invisible, powerless, and vulnerable: "Widows in the Bible are not named; they are just called widows." In impoverished situations a widowed woman with children in tow has the heartbreaking reality of watching her children suffer along with herself.

Tirzah's microloan program gives women the ability to break the generational cycle of poverty—and a chance to meet with the life-changing love of Jesus as well. Emily's passion for women comes through when she says, "It is so exciting to see women grab hold of their destiny in Christ." Undaunted by the enormity of the task, Emily added, "Every life change is a victory."

Emily and I talked for nearly two hours nonstop, and she really echoed my heart in wanting to see women around the globe realize their worth in Christ. Emily feels that no woman, regardless of her station in life, should be marginalized. Emily's goal and passion is to free women in the name of Jesus and be able to teach them their worth in Christ as daughters of the King. Emily desires to see other people become aware of the plight as well: "God never created human beings to be about themselves. That is a quest for unhappiness.... People need significance and belonging." Significance is accomplished when one gives up her own rights to serve another.

Microloans help widows and others to break free from poverty. By developing a microloan program, or just supporting one already in existence, we can continue to change the lives of women and children.

Rescuing and Recovery—Not for the Faint of Heart

The sex-slave industry is so vast, there are many ways to attempt to help restrain that evil in the world—but none is easy or without consequences. Some organizations rescue young girls out of brothels. Others provide housing, counseling, and rehabilitative services. Some organizations such as WAR International (Women at Risk) even try to help the girls learn a trade or skill and guide them toward a career. The impact of this kind of trauma is life-altering, and the recovery for these young girls is long and difficult and has a high failure rate. With the love of Jesus and the help of trusted adults, there is hope but no easy fixes. As Somaly Mam, a woman rescued from the Cambodian sex slave trade says, "It takes five minutes to rescue a girl, and then the hard work starts."[7] Perhaps you have unique skills that could serve in this difficult but much-needed area of rescue and recovery.

So Much More

Choosing to make life-altering changes is difficult, sometimes scary, but worth the effort. But I hope your aspirations have started you thinking down paths that you have never considered before.

It rained the entire time when I visited the Wears Valley Ranch,[8] a children's home near Pigeon Forge, Tennessee. But the rain didn't dampen the enthusiasm of Pastor Jim Wood, the founder and director of the ranch. We toured the campus, had dinner with his wife, Susan, and four of their seven children, and talked for hours over the course of two days.

The dream of the children's home started when Jim was just a teenager, well before he met his wife. Now, four decades later, he has been building the ministry for twenty years and has served more than 175 children at the ranch positively impacting thousands of other children, families, young adults, and others in the process.

The ranch is a hundred acres of rolling green pasture and wooded mountainside. Jim and the staff have created a truly holistic environment that ministers to the whole child. There is a school on the property, and the children receive a solid education tailored to their specific educational needs. There are four homes—two girls' homes and two boys' homes—that can accommodate up to thirty-two children with rooms for a houseparent couple and two young adult mentors in each of the homes. The ranch has animals, gardens, and a new aquaponics greenhouse that will supply fresh fish and vegetables year-round. The ranch is also in the early stages of building a chapel onsite that will have an attached welcome center housing a donated art collection from resident artists.

God placed this dream in the heart of a young man years ago, and through Jim's faithfulness in listening to and obeying God and sharing his vision with others, this amazing facility has helped introduce children to Christ and mend their broken hearts and spirits for more than two decades. When Pastor Wood's days are finished on this earth, his dream will be passed on to others who will carry the baton forward to yet another generation. Now imagine this: What if Pastor Jim heard God's call to start a children's home, but was too scared, broke, or busy to follow through? Yes, God could have used someone else to carry out the plan, but Pastor Jim would have not received the blessing of being a bigger part of God's plan.

This is my question to you: What is God placing on your heart right now? What is He prompting you to do? Is there something, even something unlikely, that God wants you to be a part of?

Jim gave a great illustration that really spoke to me. He said that it is when we give God a blank check to our heart and life, He will work through us for His greater purpose. When we give conditions and stipulations on how, when, and where we want to be used, we are defeated already. Are you willing to give God a blank check? That is a difficult decision. It means not only giving over those things that are easy, but those things that are difficult as well.

Parting Thoughts

Over the last few years I have intentionally offered my heart and life to God to use as He sees fit. I've been a Christ-follower for years. I've even been in ministry off and on for most of my life. But I was sensing the need to give over my whole life, to completely open my hands to God. In other words, to write God a blank check.

Something unexpected happened to me while I was in Haiti. Halfway through our trip we were on a hilltop touring a Loving Shepherd site where several children's homes were under construction. Standing alone on the hilltop I felt the Lord ask me, "Are you willing to follow Me?" To that, I responded, "Of course." I had prayed many times that God would guide my steps and had offered Him my blank check. Then God asked me, "Are you willing to move to Haiti to serve Me?" Immediately I started listing all the reasons why that wouldn't work— my husband would never do that. I couldn't leave my dog, Kody. It is way too hot here. I don't have anything to offer. What could I possibly do here? Within seconds I almost had to laugh at myself because the excuses were so close to my mind I didn't even need to stop to think of them. The idea of moving to Haiti seemed quite ridiculous, and I walked off to join the rest of the group on the tour.

A few minutes later, just before we headed back to Port-au-Prince, we huddled together as a team to pray for Loving Shepherd and our host, Jan. But before we prayed, one of my teammates asked Jan if he needed a construction guy and a writer/meeting planner couple. He meant Dave and me. I was shocked. I looked at him strangely. Why would he say that? One of my other teammates jumped right on the bandwagon and offered me up as well. The conversation quickly shifted, and then Clayton led us in prayer. As he was praying I felt the Holy Spirit again whisper, "If I call you to Haiti, are you willing?" A little overwhelmed, I started to cry.

During the rest of the trip, my excuses were slowly chipped away. One missionary friend told me how she regularly brings her dog back and forth between the States and Haiti. Then, when I came back to the cold Chicago weather, I really missed the Haiti heat.

Although much time has passed since that experience, I'm still trying to sort it out. Dave and I have talked about it, but there is no clear path. I'm just wondering if God was testing my willingness to follow through with my blank check offer, or if He really does have a ministry in mind for us in Haiti. I know I fell in love with the orphaned children, the Haitian people, and the dedicated workers serving there. In many ways, living in Haiti would be less comfortable than my suburban existence, but I find myself thinking about Haiti often. I still don't know what we would do, or if it is even a possibility for Dave and me, but I do know I have learned not to offer God that blank check unless I'm willing to actually let Him cash it!

For now, I have to go back to the basics: Obey the last direction I know for sure God has asked of me. Without a shadow of a doubt, His last instruction to me was a call to advocate for orphaned children around the globe. I know I'm supposed to help encourage, educate, and influence people to join with me as solutions to the orphan crisis. And I know that God wants you, in some way, to be part of that solution as well.

Change of Heart

Orphaned children around the globe need people who are willing to write a blank check to God in order to help in their time of need. This check will enable children to have some of life's essentials such as food, clothing, shelter, and clean water. This blank check can also be one that provides educational opportunities, career development, and potential jobs. This check can be one that tells orphaned children about the love of God and can transform a child's life both now and for eternity. This check—your check, your willingness—can bring you untold blessings that are only experienced when you are willing to follow Christ, even to the ends of the earth. So are you ready to answer the call? Are you willing to step out in faith? The choice is yours.

Thank you for the privilege of walking with me on this amazing journey to understand the global orphan crisis and to prayerfully consider your role as part of the solution. I pray that God will continue to touch your heart and life, that He will be real to you, and that God will empower you to make a dramatic difference in the world, especially in the life of an orphaned child. To God be the glory!

QUESTIONS TO PONDER

1. Do you feel that you are living missionally—in other words, living a life consistent with your beliefs?

2. If you are living missionally, what does that look like? If you are not yet living missionally, what do you need to change to be more intentional with your life, family, work, ministry, and walk with God?

3. Have you ever offered to write God a blank check? What would that look like for you?

4. As you looked at this chapter, what thoughts or ideas inspired you?

5. What thought or feeling you have experienced while reading this chapter is something you don't want to forget?

ACTION POINT

Many ideas simply fade away because they're not taken to the next step, the action plan. Because of what you know now, take some time to write out your ideas about how to positively impact the orphan crisis. Then make an action plan of what steps need to be taken to accomplish your goals.

This little boy couldn't stop smiling during naptime under a hand-made blanket. Pray that he will learn to depend on God to build in him strong character for a lifetime and that God will provide family relationships that will build in him strong character to last a lifetime. *Diane Lynn Elliot, photographer © Diane Lynn Elliot*

Stories of Hope
and Healing

Can a mother forget the baby at her breast and
have no compassion on the child she has borne?
Though she may forget, I will not forget you! See,
I have engraved you on the palms of my hands.
Isaiah 49:15–16

I want to share some of the inspiring stories of the many amazing people I met on my journey to understand the orphan crisis. These people, from all walks of life, have chosen to live out their faith and calling to meet the needs of orphaned children in different ways. I hope you will be as inspired by these stories as I have been.

Many years ago on a trip to India, God impressed the need for compassionate intervention for impoverished, orphaned, and abandoned children on Lovie Phillips' heart. More than three decades later, she and hundreds of others inspired by her reach around the globe to answer the cries of orphaned children. *Bill Wegener, photographer © God Loves Children*

The Cry of the World

Lovie Philips, founder of God Loves Kids, Christian Communications Commission

God Loves Kids ministry has always believed that the way to change the world is one life at a time. One way to change a life is through small sacrifices that add up to *big* results in the life of a child!

I am often asked why it is important to reach children. We learn from statistics that 85 percent of all personal salvation decisions happen before the age of eighteen. The more startling fact is that 80 percent of those decisions are made between the ages of four and fourteen.[1] These statistics remind us that if we are to win the world, we must begin by turning our hearts toward the children. We must win the lost while their hearts are still within reach.

Even though I have always had a heart for children, I never really thought about it in terms of missions, and I certainly never thought about starting a ministry to reach the children in foreign lands. It was that first trip to India many years ago that affected me so deeply and was the beginning of God Loves Kids child sponsorship program in 1974.

I can still visualize miles and miles of those extremely large cement pipes lying beside the roadway from the Calcutta airport to the church we were visiting. I was amazed to see a family living in almost every one of those pipes. I have never seen so many people anywhere. You could hardly walk on the streets because there were so many people.

I will never forget the thousands of children begging on the streets. Each child in such need. Each child needing God's love.

I will never forget passing the garbage dump and seeing children digging for a scrap of food—an apple core, orange peel, chicken bone, or anything at all they could eat. Each day the church took their mobile kitchen to the garbage dump to give the children a piece of bread and a cup of milk. We were told this was probably all these children would have to eat the entire day.

I will never forget the day our car could not continue to move because of so much traffic. It was a sweltering hot day and the old car had no air conditioning, so the windows had to be completely open. We had been told many times that we should not give anything to anyone on the streets or we would be surrounded and unable to move. While we were waiting, three little boys approached our window and started begging for food. One of the boys was missing the lower half of one of his arms. It was just a ragged nub. Our driver sensed that we really desired to give something to the boys, but knowing we would be mobbed if we did, he kept shaking his head at us. When the boy saw that we were not responding, the one boy pushed his little ragged nub through the window almost touching my husband's face. He looked him right in the eye and said, "Love me, Mister; love me. Love me, Mister." We had to turn our heads to keep him from seeing us cry. At that point, my husband, Syvelle, said to me, "We are hearing the cry of the world."

I will never forget being taken to the place where they burned the bodies of those who died on the streets the night before (many live and die on those streets). Our host looked at me and said, "Does this bother you?" Though it was a sad sight, I said, "No, not really, for it is too late for them; it is for the living that I weep." I kept praying, "Oh Lord, how can we ever reach these people? There are millions of them." It was while I was crying out to the Lord, almost in despair, that I heard the sweet small voice within me saying, "You reach them one at a time—yes, one at a time."

I will never forget the contrast in the children we saw on the streets and those who were in the church school. These were children who had sponsors to financially support them, who made it possible for the church to provide them food, medical care, and an education. Even more importantly, they had the opportunity to learn that there is a Father God who loves them. What wonderful news for a child who at one time was taught to believe he might come back as a rat or bug or whatever! You could see the joy of the Lord in their lives—such a contrast to the despair you saw in the children on the streets.

I will never forget when we went to the church very early one morning to watch 1,000 kids being fed the only meal they would get that day. The signs of malnutrition were so evident in their little bodies and we were told that at least 40 percent of them had tuberculosis. The church told us they would like to take more of these children into the school but they did not have the funds.

I certainly will never forget taking Syvelle by the hand, as we looked at each other with tears streaming down our cheeks and said to one another, "We must do something about this!" That day the child sponsorship program under Christian Communications Commission was born. Oh, we didn't realize it right then! We thought we would just share what we had seen with a few friends and get ten or fifteen of them to sponsor a child.

Soon we had the fifteen, and then we had a hundred! I didn't know a thing about running a sponsorship program, so I asked the Lord for help. I learned that availability is more important than ability. If we have all the ability in the world but don't make it available to the Lord, what does it accomplish?

I never imagined that so many years later, we would still be helping children through the Calcutta missions church and in ten other locations. What a joy it is to visit the orphanage/schools and see the changes in the children's lives. Children who were once destitute are now pastors, teachers, nurses, village chiefs, evangelists, singers, and mechanics.

I will also never forget that I cannot accomplish this mission alone. Without the support of people locally, across the country, and internationally joining with us, none of those children's lives would have been changed. Thank you for helping us to answer the cry of the world, one life at a time.

Reprinted with permission from the April 2006 God Loves Kids sponsor newsletter. Used by permission of Lovie Phillips, president www.God loveskids.com.

Ngim is one of the many children who touched Katie's heart as her Youth With A Mission team served in Cambodia. Katie found that being willing to make a difference in the lives of orphaned children changed her. *Katie Dyer, photographer © Katie Dyer*

A Mission of Love

Katie Dyer

From April through June of 2011, I was on a team with twelve other people and had the opportunity to travel from Youth With A Mission's (YWAM's) base in Kona, Hawaii, to another base in Battambang, Cambodia. One of our focuses while in Battambang was to serve at an orphanage that housed thirty children. The children ranged between the ages of four and fifteen.

When we arrived at the orphanage, we were shocked to see the conditions these children live in. They all shared one room with only five bunk beds with no mattresses and one destroyed mattress lying in the middle of the floor. There were rusty nails lying right outside their door, broken glass around the yard, and a massive beehive in the ceiling of their gazebo. After talking briefly with the man who ran the orphanage, it was apparent he was not pouring into these children's lives other than doing the bare minimum. The children simply needed to be loved, and the facility needed work.

We quickly noticed that the children fought a lot and had no sense of discipline. They punched and pinched, screamed and cried, and did not share any of the crafts or items that we brought for them. To be honest, after that visit, many of us were so discouraged we didn't feel like returning, so we prayed. God gave us vision for transformation and hope.

Each day we gathered for half an hour to pray before leaving for the orphanage. Our team prayed that God would pour out His love on these children. We prayed that the man's heart would be changed and his eyes would be opened to see the needs of the kids. We also prayed that the children would be able to see their identities in Christ.

While at the orphanage, our team taught Bible stories and used coloring pages relating to the stories. We played games, sang songs, and taught how to be kind to one another. Nothing we did was complex or a huge revelation from God. We simply loved.

It truly is amazing to see how love brings transformation. Love breaks down barriers and softens hearts. By the end of our time one of the little boys who always pinched a girl on our team sat next to her and placed his head on her shoulder. The man running the orphanage also opened up a little, and we were able to encourage him about some of the needs of the children.

This orphanage is not an isolated case. There are so many children in the world living in these conditions, and worse. God is calling us to step out and see the world with open eyes. He is calling us to love.

Written by Katie Dyer. Used by author permission.

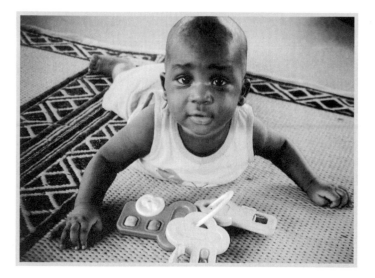

Baby Fidèle lost his mother and now receives temporary care at an orphanage in Chad. After growing up in Africa as a missionary kid, Lisa returned to Chad to work. *Lisa Haberkamp, photographer © Lisa Haberkamp*

My New Family

Fidèle's story told by Lisa Haberkamp,
Béthanie Children's Home, Chad, Africa

My name is Fidèle. I was a little more than a month old when my father brought me to Béthanie. It was a new place with many different people, sights, and smells. Dad, my aunt, and my uncle all said goodbye and that they would visit me often; then they left. Someone with funny color skin took me in her arms and spoke to me gently in a language I couldn't understand. I got a bath and was fed. I cried a little, but for the most part I was brave. Change and loss has been a part of my life, which brings me to why I am here.

I was born on the 29th of April 2011. During this time there was a meningitis epidemic in N'Djamena—the capital of Chad, where I live.

Unfortunately, my mom got meningitis and passed away on the 18th of May, leaving my dad with a newborn plus my four brothers and sisters. He works at the local high school and didn't know how he could keep his job plus take care of us, especially me. Without my mother to feed and take care of me, I was highly at-risk. Not only does the formula I need cost more than my family can afford, but without my mother's breast milk, I wouldn't get the antibodies I would need to survive in Chad's harsh environment. My dad didn't know how to best care for me. My aunt took care of me right after my mother died, but she has four young children of her own and ran into the same problems as my dad. They were almost out of hope when they heard about Béthanie, a small orphanage run by a French/Swiss organization called Betsaleel. They brought me to Béthanie and asked if I could stay. I was accepted, and my family immediately brought me to my new home.

I am now almost five months old, and I have come to love my little home away from home. I live in a house with fifteen other babies ranging from a week to a year old who have also lost their mothers. There is never a dull moment where I live! When I'm not sleeping or eating, I enjoy studying the faces of my friends, being held by one of my three Chadian "aunties," and listening to the big kids play. There are also a few French, Swiss, and American ladies who visit throughout the day as well. My family comes and visits me often, as they promised they would. They enjoy seeing me grow, and I enjoy a little taste of my old home. I look forward to once again living with them when I'm three years old.

Béthanie is an orphanage for young, at-risk children like me. All of us have lost our mothers, but like me, everyone here still has some sort of family. Béthanie's purpose is not to take us away from our families but instead to accompany us and our families through this difficult time. Once we're older and stronger, and once our families are in a better situation, we can return to our families. Once I am back with my family, friends from Béthanie will visit me until I am twelve years old. They want to make sure that I get the medical attention I need and that I am able to attend school.

My family once again has a hope and dream for my life. They know it is only through God's faithfulness that I still live and am a healthy, growing boy. That is why they named me Fidèle, which means Faithful. I am thankful to God for my friends and family here at Béthanie. My story started out harsh, but because of God's love, I now see hope.

Written by Lisa Haberkamp. Used by author permission.

After a missions trip to Ukraine, a professional couple stepped out in faith to adopt these three girls from a Ukrainian orphanage. This act of love birthed a ministry that continues to inspire others to adopt and change the lives of many orphaned and abandoned teens in the Ukraine. *Phyllis Ward, photographer © Phyllis Ward*

Heart for Orphans
Nancy Hathaway, Heart for Orphans

"Nancy, wake up. We're almost there." My husband, Steve, shook me awake. I had just spent a restless night, only to finally doze off just before dawn. I had been awake most of the night crying out to God for guidance. The train compartment where we slept had been hot and oppressive, with shouting and doors slamming at each station. I had a nervous stomach and couldn't relax.

We were on an overnight train from Kiev to Berdyansk, a small seaside city in southern Ukraine. Our train compartment was a strange mix of leather seats and lace curtains, and the air smelled of coal and vinegar.

With a brisk knock on the door a babushka brought us tea from the samovar in the hall. I lifted back the lace curtain and wiped the steam off the window. The snow and ice glistened in the soft morning light just like a scene out of *Dr. Zhivago*. We pulled into the station, and there was a sea of gray faces with furry hats and bulky coats swarming the platform. It was then I had the overwhelming thought, "Today I'm going to meet someone who will be part of our lives for the rest of our lives. She will be our daughter, and her children will be our grandchildren.

We got off the train and made our way through the crowd, trying to keep up with our translator. The ancient PA system cackled Russian announcements and then played a patriotic anthem. As we loaded our bags into the tiny taxi, I thought that I should be excited, but all I felt was afraid.

When we got to the orphanage, I was so nervous I was shaking. Our escort took us to the director's office and brought several children in to meet us, one by one. The very first child we met was Natalie, a cute nine-year-old with big green eyes and a bubbly personality. She recited a poem in Russian about a butterfly, and she was so animated my heart melted. I began to cry. I knew immediately that she was our daughter! Later, when the director told her she was chosen, she was so excited she clung to us and immediately started calling us Mama and Papa.

We'd hardly been home a few months when Steve started talking about going back for another child. At first I wasn't interested. I was still exhausted and adjusting to life with our new daughter. We certainly couldn't afford it, but I agreed to pray about it. A few days later Natalie began to talk to us about her friend Angelina. She told us Angelina cried when she told her that she was being adopted and leaving the orphanage. But Natalie said, "Don't worry. I'll ask my new mama and papa if they can come and get you, too!" So nine months later we found ourselves on that same overnight train from Kiev to Berdyansk.

When we met sweet Angelina, she was so tiny we were shocked that she was nine. She was shy and precious and had a soft, whispery voice. What we didn't realize was that we would also meet another friend, Elisabeth, and decide to adopt her as well. Elisabeth was thirteen, smart, athletic, and beautiful. She later told us that all she ever wanted was a family, and she had been praying for years and had almost given up hope. Although we tried to adopt both of the girls on that trip we were only able to take Angelina home with us and ended up having to wait three more months before we could go back for Elisabeth. Three months later, as we flew out of Kiev airport, Elisabeth looked out of the window and began to cry. I put my arm around her and asked if she was sad or scared at leaving. She said, "No, Mama, I am very, very happy!"

So how did we get here? We had never intended to be the parents of three adopted girls. Life was good; Steve and I had active lives, busy careers, and a grown son. We were empty nesters and thought we were content to just enjoy life. Instead, we both felt restless. I had spent twenty plus years in television as an actress and producer, but in recent years I had lost my passion for my work. I just didn't have the drive and excitement I once had. God was changing my heart and priorities. Steve and I began to pray that God would use us and that He would refocus our attentions on things that were important to Him, and He did.

During the next several years the seeds of adoption were planted in our hearts, and through various circumstances we were drawn to the Ukraine. In the late '90s there were about 800,000 kids in private and state-run orphanages, and almost as many kids living on the streets. The need was great. After a two-week missions trip to the Ukraine, we knew God had called us to adopt from the Ukraine.

Steve and I have been so blessed! Our lives are richer and a little crazier too. Everyone has adjusted so well, and we are closer than I ever thought possible. Sometimes I think back to how I almost let my fears stop us from adopting and how much I would have missed had we let the fears take hold. Sometimes we have to be willing to walk through scary places in life, but it is ultimately for His good. We took a step of faith, praying that God would be glorified through our obedience, and we were blessed beyond our wildest imaginations.

What is also amazing is that our adoption calling spurred on others to adopt older children as well. Little by little God touched people's hearts and orphaned children were placed in forever homes. When we let God take control and follow His plan, it is far beyond what we can see and understand. In our plans we intended to adopt one child. But God planned to bless hundreds of children.

The vision for Heart for Orphans was born in the early 2000s when other adoptive parents and I began meeting together. We incorporated in 2007, with the vision to open transition homes for teen orphans who have aged-out of the orphanage. These kids would otherwise be living on the streets or caught up in the sex-trafficking world. Today we have six homes and several more in the works. God continues building the ministry to orphaned teens, and we are seeing incredible changes in their lives. The extra blessing is that because of the change in the teens' lives, the communities are changing as well. Except by God's orchestration, there is no explanation for the miracles that have happened since we took our step of faith so many years ago. When we are obedient to what God calls us to, as unexpected as they may seem, God will bless us and multiply the blessing to others as well.

Adapted from Nancy Hathaway's blog, www.heartfororphans.com. Used by permission.

God calls each Christ-follower to care for orphaned children in some way. In addition to touching the lives of adopted children locally, Julie enjoyed a short-term missions trip to an orphanage in Ethiopia. *Julie Barrett, photographer © Julie Barrett*

God's Call to Serve Orphaned Children

Julie Barrett

For as long as I can remember, orphans have had a special spot in my heart. A few years ago, I was looking through a box of Christmas books from my childhood. I came to one I clearly remember being a favorite. As I flipped through the pages, I remembered that it was a fantasy tale that included a talking stuffed animal, a little orphaned girl who finds a home for Christmas, and a mother who had a longing in her heart for a special little girl even before she knew her. Perhaps that was the beginning of my journey that God used to develop in me a heart for orphaned children.

Throughout my life I used to ask God things like, "I know I care about orphans, but do You want me to be involved in some way to specifically care for them?" or "Do you care if I'm involved with orphaned children?" But over the years as I have studied Scripture, read orphan-care and adoption books, and talked with friends, my questions shifted from, "Do You want me to be involved in caring about orphans?" to "How do You want me to be involved in caring for orphans?"

Scripture is clear about the topic of caring for orphans. Through my adoption through Jesus Christ, I was adopted as God's child. Because of this love, I should be a first-responder in the orphan-care crisis. Really, there is no question to my involvement in caring for orphans. As a believer, I can't selectively abandon parts of Scripture because they seem difficult or because I don't know what to do. I sensed God speaking directly to me and felt compelled to respond. Perhaps you have found the same thing. While our responses won't always look the same, the important thing is that we are willing and open to the Spirit's leading.

So what should my involvement with orphaned children look like? I'm a single, young, twenty-something woman. How could God use me to make a difference in this huge worldwide crisis?

God is bigger than my fears and insecurities. God is looking for a willing heart. A friend encouraged me to be open to one step at a time and to just see where God leads me. Since that time I've been involved in touching the lives of orphaned children in many different and sometimes unexpected ways.

Sometimes it looks like taking my friends' adopted daughter to a movie or inviting her for a sleepover. Sometimes it looks like encouraging a friend who is considering going on a missions trip to care for orphans. Sometimes it looks like giving financially toward a family in the process of adoption. Sometimes it looks like having intentional conversations with people about God inviting each of us to be part of His adopted family. Sometimes it looks like writing a note to encourage a friend waiting for her adoption paperwork to go through. Sometimes it looks like going to an adoption website in my home state and praying specifically for children who are waiting for adoptive parents. Sometimes it looks like praying for orphaned children around the world who are especially vulnerable to exploitation for the simple reason that they're orphans.

As I started to let go of my fears and insecurities and allow the Spirit to guide my heart and actions, I came across a challenging quote on a friend's blog. The friend is in the process of adopting two children from Ethiopia. The quote is by Bill Johnson, the pastor of Bethel Church in Redding, California. He says:

> Part of our problem is this: We are accustomed only to doing things for God that are not impossible. If God doesn't show up and help us, we can still succeed...His righteousness/character is not built into us by our own efforts. It is developed when we quit striving and learn to abandon ourselves completely to His will...If the Holy Spirit is to be free to move in our lives, we will constantly be involved in impossibilities. The supernatural is His natural realm.[2]

Accepting the biblical challenge to care for orphaned children can feel overwhelming, impossible, and confusing, especially if we try to do it in our own strength. There is a fear that if we take the risk, God might not show up. However, we don't need to wonder whether or not God is going to show up. God loves orphaned children far deeper than we can ever imagine, and he isn't going to abandon us in our obedience.

So what does the future look like for me in regard to caring for orphaned children? I don't exactly know. I will continue to ask God to soften my heart and make myself available. Regardless, I'm honored and grateful that God would use me to be a part of His greater purpose.

Written by Julie Barrett. Used by author permission.

Ellie is the much-loved daughter to a missionary family in Athens, Greece. Through the process of adopting Ellie from China, doctors discovered that in addition to having been malnourished, she also had cerebral palsy. The McCrackens felt God's affirmation to proceed with the adoption resulting in countless blessings for the family every day. *Scott McCracken, photographer © Scott McCracken*

Ellie's Story

Scott McCracken, International Teams,
Athens, Greece

Our family has been sharing the gospel through International Teams in Greece with refugees through proclamation and demonstration. Refugees are coming from the Middle East, Far East, Eastern Europe, and Africa. In the last fifteen years, they have been mostly refugees from Islamic countries and regions (i.e., Iran, Iraq, Kurdistan, Afghanistan, Sudan, Somalia, Turkey, etc.). Because of Greece's strategic location it is a "gateway" to the West. We started a Greek-registered nonprofit here called "Helping Hands" and have done a number of different ministries to help meet physical and spiritual needs, such as a drop-in center (where they drink tea, play table games, and watch videos), many different feeding programs, refugee camp visitation, language classes, computer classes, Bible studies for seekers and for believers, discipleship and leadership programs, children's ministries, shower ministry, shelter ministry, prison ministry, clothing distribution, weekend retreats, establishing ethnic fellowships, special needs distribution (disposable diapers, shoes, sleeping bags, etc.), hospitality ministry, friendship, advocacy, etc.

Vicky and I made the decision to adopt before we were married. Actually, since my wife and I were kids, long before we knew each other, we wanted adoption to be part of our family planning. In spring of 1990, when we lived in Austria and our first biological child, Kendra, was six months old, we started the adoption process from Romania. We even went to an orphanage there and chose the child we wanted. However, it didn't work out in the end, and we moved to Athens in September of that year and spent the next several years having another three biological kids. Finally, at the end of 2000 we realized we weren't getting any younger and decided we should get moving on the adoption process if it was ever going to happen while we still met age restrictions.

We chose an agency and started by looking into China, but we did not meet certain requirements at that time. So we looked into the Philippines and South Korea (both of which would not allow children to be adopted into families with more than three biological kids), and finally Vietnam, where adoption looked as if it would be relatively quick and easy. However, after we submitted all our paperwork and were waiting, Vietnam changed its laws about international adoptions. They were good laws, but the U.S. would not sign off on them as they were involved in human rights issues and this was a political playing card. After waiting about three years for this to be resolved, we revisited the China possibility and learned the previous restrictions no longer applied. So we removed our application from Vietnam and began the process for adoption from China. It was supposed to take twelve to eighteen months and ended up taking close to two and a half years.

We had a full house and a full life, and we were all very excited about the idea of adding a little Chinese girl to our family, but some of us were also growing skeptical after such a long process and so much waiting. However, when we received the call in early March of 2007, we were all ecstatic to learn that little Hao Nan Dang (who would later become Ellie MingYun McCracken) was available and in apparently relatively good health. She was malnourished and weighed only eleven pounds at twelve months old, but that was not unusual for many Chinese orphans. They told us we could come get her a couple months later in May.

Because we were missionaries living in a foreign land on a limited income with no idea what Greece would have available for a special needs child, we had made it clear that we were not interested in a special needs child. However, one month after we were notified of Ellie's availability, the agency called again to say that a doctor had examined her and had concerns that there may be brain damage of some kind, not simply the results of malnutrition. She was too young to diagnose but it could be something minimal or something further along the spectrum of severe cerebral palsy. We needed to prepare to adopt a special needs child or let her go to a couple who had made this request. If we let her go, we would receive a new referral within two weeks. We asked for a week to pray, think, and talk with our family.

Within twenty-four hours God showed us in a number of ways that this child was His gift for us. On the day we received the phone call about Ellie's medical condition, Vicki woke up in the night and tearfully said to the Lord, "I don't know if I can give her what she needs." The Lord's voice immediately replied, "But I can give you what you need." Vicky felt God meant that He would provide the grace, provision, and wisdom Ellie would need and that she needed to trust in His sovereignty.

Parenting isn't for everyone. Parenting adopted kids isn't for everyone. Parenting adopted kids with special needs isn't for everyone. But one thing we are sure of: Where God guides, God provides! We have been blessed beyond belief with the love and joy that has come into our family through Ellie, and while it hasn't always been easy, it has always been good!

Looking back, we are glad we didn't know that the adoption process would take six-plus years, or we probably would not have followed through.

The Scriptures are clear that both caring for orphans and adoption are God's ideas. What better way to care for orphans than for God's people to adopt them and make them a full part of their families, just as He has done with us?

We sometimes spend a lot of time and energy trying to figure out God's will about so many things. The Scriptures show that orphans have a special place in the heart of God. He must be pleased when we invest time and other resources in sharing this piece of His heart. When we step out in faith to join Him in His mission, in spite of our fears, worries, inadequacies, economic challenges, insecurities, impure motives, and ignorance, He leads us, changes us, provides for us, and accomplishes in and through us His purposes for our good and for His glory.

Adapted from an interview with Scott McCracken. Scott, his wife, Vicky, and their five children are missionaries with International Teams in Athens, Greece. Used by permission.

Printers Ratiba is a boxing coach to many boys, after his own painful journey of loss led him to leadership working with vulnerable boys. *Cherie Bulger, photographer © Cherie Bulger*

Printers Ratiba: His Story

Cherie Bulger

"I now have to stand for myself and be a man."

In July, 2002, an after-school ministry was started for children in the squatter community of Zandspruit, twenty kilometers outside the city limits of Johannesburg, South Africa. The ministry was designed to give children a safe place to play and to be kids in the midst of a community plagued by violence, abuse, poverty, and sickness. The after-school ministry, a joint effort of two South Africa churches, solicits sponsorships to pay the school fees and for school uniforms to ensure all its children attend school, and provides two hot meals to students each weekday. The program ministers to children's physical, spiritual, emotional, and relational needs. Nine years after its beginning, the ministry serves 250 children from Zandspruit and has grown to include a preschool and a high school ministry.

Printers Ratiba was eleven years old, and his brother, Lucky, was six when they started to attend the after-school ministry in 2002. Printers and Lucky lived in a shack with their mother, with no father active in their lives. Printers had lived in the community of Zandspruit since he was born. In 2006 when Printers was fifteen years old, his mother was tragically killed in a taxi accident. She died from her injuries after weeks in the hospital. Printers and Lucky were left alone to fend for themselves, with no immediate family to assist them. They had no parents, or anyone, to take care of them. Printers can easily recall his specific thought from that season when he was fifteen: "I now have to stand for myself and be a man."

During this time Printers gave his heart to Jesus. Printers had grown up going to church with his mother and had been learning about Jesus at the after-school ministry. He knew he would need help from God in order to take on this challenge. When the ministry became aware of his situation, it intervened by providing food parcels, clothing for the boys, a bed, blankets, and other assistance when needed.

Printers made the transition into the high school ministry and was a faithful participant. The following year, Printers and some other high school students were selected to help lead a holiday club for the primary school children of the after-school ministry. Printers demonstrated real leadership ability all week as he interacted with his small group of children. His group loved having him as their leader.

Printers turned nineteen in 2010, and he found himself struggling with his school studies. He had repeated tenth grade twice and could not manage to move to the next grade. Printers began attending the high school ministry less and less as he felt like he didn't fit in since he was older than the other students and not progressing in his studies. Leaders in the ministry encouraged Printers to keep coming and to take on the role of an apprentice leader. This would keep Printers connected to the ministry he loved, while at the same time grooming him to be a small group leader in the future.

At nineteen, Printers was considered an adult and needed to find ways to earn money to provide for his and his brother's basic needs. Part of his survival plan included adding two additional sleeping rooms to his shack so that he could rent them out and generate income. Printers sent Lucky to live with extended relatives in another South African province, in order to keep Lucky in school and give him a better future. This was a painful decision, as Printers was then truly all alone, but Printers knew he had God.

Later Printers was asked if he would be interested in being mentored by Mohai, an adult leader in the after-school and high school ministries. Mohai would show Printers how to become a boxing coach and mentor Printers on how to influence young boys in a positive way. The vision was to equip Printers so that he could coach and run the sport on his own. The high school ministry (*Impumelelo Phambili*, a Zulu phrase meaning "we are achieving forward"), paid for Printers to attend and train at a professional gym. In 2011, Printers was offered a paid coaching position with the ministry. Now, in the squatter community of Zandspruit every Monday through Friday from 4:30–5:30 p.m. Printers can be found with his group of schoolboys, practicing their sport of boxing. The ministry has empowered Printers to take responsibility and ownership while providing for himself.

On a recent sunny, spring day, Printers was standing in front of seven schoolboys sitting on the ground looking up at their coach. As they listened intently, Printers shared words from his own experience: "Don't be afraid to share and speak out about your problems. I was once your age too. And just like many of you who don't have mothers, I don't either. If you are struggling, pray. Jesus is everything. He will hear you. Go to Jesus for everything. The key to success is only through Jesus. Jesus won't let you down." With that, Printers closed in prayer as the boys huddled around him.

Printers speaks those words with confidence and truth as he is a living testimony of "Jesus not letting him down." Printers was asked how the after-school and high school ministries have made a difference in his life. Printers shared, "If the ministries had not been there, I would not get knowledge or advice of good and right decisions." For the leadership team of both the after-school and high school ministries, what has been most exciting about walking this journey with Printers has been how God has brought him full circle. Printers is giving back and serving in the very ministries that helped to shape him, to introduce him to a growing relationship with Christ, and to equip him to serve others. The leadership team's dream and desire is to see more young guys and girls come back and serve in the ministries that served them.

Printers was asked if he had any words to share with those who might read his story. You bet he did. "Life is not all about who you are. Life is all about knowing Christ. Christ will lead to good things in your life."

Written by Cherie Bulger. Used by author permission.

Recommended Reading

Adopted for Life by Russell D. Moore and C.J. Mahaney. Wheaton, IL: Crossway Books, 2009.

The Bottom Billion by Paul Collier. Oxford University Press, 2007.

Castaway Kid: One Man's Search for Hope and Home by R.B. Mitchell. Carol Stream, IL: Tyndale House Publishers, 2007.

The Connected Child by Karyn B. Purvis, David R. Cross, and Wendy Lyons Sunshine. Chicago: McGraw-Hill Professional, 2007.

Dangerous Surrender by Kay Warren. Grand Rapids: Zondervan, 2008.

Fields of the Fatherless: Discover the Joy of Compassionate Living by Tom Davis. Colorado Springs, CO: David C. Cook, 2008.

Half the Sky: Turning Oppression into Opportunity for Women Worldwide by Nicholas D. Kristof and Sheryl Wudunn. New York: Random House, 2009.

Hands and Feet by Audio Adrenaline. Ventura, CA: Gospel Light, 2007.

Hello, I Love You by Ted Kluck. Chicago: Moody, 2010.

The Hole in Our Gospel by Richard Stearns. Nashville: Thomas Nelson, 2009.

Journey to the Fatherless: Preparing for the Journey of Adoption, Orphan Care, Foster Care and Humanitarian Relief for Vulnerable Children by Lawrence E. Bergeron. Bloomington, IN: WestBow Press, 2012.

Just a Minute by Wess Stafford. Chicago: Moody, 2012.

Kisses from Katie: A Story of Relentless Love and Redemption by Katie J. Davis and Beth Clark. New York: Howard Books, 2011.

Launching an Orphan Ministry in Your Church (with DVD) by Jason Weber, Paul Pennington, and Dennis Rainey. Little Rock, AR: FamilyLife Publishing, 2009.

Living on the Edge by Chip Ingram. New York: Howard Books, 2009.

The One Factor—How One Changes Everything by Doug Sauder. North Lauderdale, FL: 4Kids of South Florida, 2008.

Orphanology: Awakening to a Gospel-Centered Adoption and Orphan Care by Tony Merida and Rick Morton. Birmingham, AL: New Hope Publishers, 2011.

A Passion for the Fatherless: Developing a God-Centered Ministry to Orphans by Daniel J. Bennett. Grand Rapids, MI: Kregel, 2011.

Passport through Darkness: A True Story of Danger and Second Chances by Kimberly L. Smith. Colorado Springs, CO: David C. Cook, 2011.

A Place to Call Home: Wears Valley Ranch by Susan M. Wood. Kearney, NE: Morris Publishing, 1999.

The Poor Will Be Glad: Joining the Revolution to Lift the World Out of Poverty by Peter Greer and Phil Smith. Grand Rapids: Zondervan, 2009.

Relentless Hope: Extracting the Precious from the Worthless by Beth Guckenberger. Cincinnati, OH: Standard Publishing, 2011.

The Second-Half Adventure: Don't Just Retire—Use Your Time, Skills & Resources to Change the World by Kay Marshall Strom. Chicago: Moody, 2009.

Start Something That Matters by Blake Mycoskie. New York: Random House, 2012.

Too Small to Ignore by Wess Stafford. Colorado Springs, CO: Waterbrook Press, 2007.

When Helping Hurts by Steve Corbett and Brian Fikkert. Chicago: Moody, 2009.

The White Umbrella: Walking with Survivors of Sex Trafficking by Mary Frances Bowley. Chicago: Moody, 2012.

The Word of God calls us to reach out to orphaned children. What practical implementation will you make to be the hands of hope to these precious ones? *Bill Wegener, photographer © God Loves Kids*

Scriptures Related to Orphans and Fatherless

Scriptures are taken from the NIV translation, with bold added for word emphasis.

*When you are harvesting in your field and you overlook a sheaf, do not go back to get it. Leave it for the foreigner, the **fatherless** and the widow, so that the Lord your God may bless you in all the work of your hands.*
Deuteronomy 24:19

*When you beat the olives from your trees, do not go over the branches a second time. Leave what remains for the foreigner, the **fatherless** and the widow.*
Deuteronomy 24:20

*When you harvest the grapes in your vineyard, do not go over the vines again. Leave what remains for the foreigner, the **fatherless** and the widow.*
Deuteronomy 24:21

*When you have finished setting aside a tenth of all your produce in the third year, the year of the tithe, you shall give it to the Levite, the foreigner, the **fatherless** and the widow, so that they may eat in your towns and be satisfied.*
Deuteronomy 26:12

*Do not take advantage of the widow or the **fatherless**.*
Exodus 22:22

*My anger will be aroused, and I will kill you with the sword; your wives will become widows and your children **fatherless**.*
Exodus 22:24

*For the Lord your God is God of gods and Lord of lords, the great God, mighty and awesome, who shows no partiality and accepts no bribes. He defends the cause of the **fatherless** and the widow, and loves the foreigner residing among you, giving them food and clothing.*
Deuteronomy 10:17–18

*So that the Levites (who have no allotment or inheritance of their own) and the foreigners, the **fatherless** and the widows who live in your towns may come and eat and be satisfied, and so that the Lord your God may bless you in all the work of your hands.*
Deuteronomy 14:29

*And rejoice before the Lord your God at the place he will choose as a dwelling for his Name—you, your sons and daughters, your male and female servants, the Levites in your towns, and the foreigners, the **fatherless** and the widows living among you.*
Deuteronomy 16:11

*Be joyful at your festival—you, your sons and daughters, your male and female servants, and the Levites, the foreigners, the **fatherless** and the widows who live in your towns.*
Deuteronomy 16:14

*Do not deprive the foreigner or the **fatherless** of justice, or take the cloak of the widow as a pledge.*
Deuteronomy 24:17

Then say to the Lord your God: "I have removed from my house the sacred portion and have given it to the Levite, the foreigner, the fatherless and the widow, according to all you commanded. I have not turned aside from your commands nor have I forgotten any of them."
Deuteronomy 26:13

"Cursed is anyone who withholds justice from the foreigner, the fatherless or the widow." Then all the people shall say, "Amen!"
Deuteronomy 27:19

You would even cast lots for the fatherless and barter away your friend.
Job 6:27

And you sent widows away empty-handed and broke the strength of the fatherless.
Job 22:9

They drive away the orphan's donkey and take the widow's ox in pledge.
Job 24:3

The fatherless child is snatched from the breast; the infant of the poor is seized for a debt.
Job 24:9

Because I rescued the poor who cried for help, and the fatherless who had none to assist them.
Job 29:12

If I have kept my bread to myself, not sharing it with the fatherless.
Job 31:17

*If I have raised my hand against the **fatherless**,*
knowing that I had influence in court.
Job 31:21

But you, God, see the trouble of the afflicted; you consider
their grief and take it in hand. The victims commit
*themselves to you; you are the helper of the **fatherless**.*
Psalm 10:14

*Defending the **fatherless** and the oppressed, so that mere*
earthly mortals will never again strike terror.
Psalm 10:18

*A father to the **fatherless**, a defender of widows, is God in his holy*
dwelling. God sets the lonely in families, he leads out the prisoners
with singing; but the rebellious live in a sun-scorched land.
Psalm 68:5–6

*Defend the weak and the **fatherless**; uphold the cause of the*
poor and the oppressed. Rescue the weak and the needy;
deliver them from the hand of the wicked.
Psalm 82:3–4

*They slay the widow and the foreigner; they murder the **fatherless**.*
Psalm 94:6

*He [the Lord] upholds the cause of the oppressed and gives food
to the hungry. The Lord sets prisoners free, the Lord gives sight to
the blind, the Lord lifts up those who are bowed down, the Lord
loves the righteous. The Lord watches over the foreigner and sustains
the **fatherless** and the widow, but he frustrates the ways of the wicked.*
Psalm 146:7–9

*Do not move an ancient boundary stone or
encroach on the fields of the **fatherless**.*
Proverbs 23:10

*Wash and make yourselves clean. Take your evil deeds out of my sight;
stop doing wrong. Learn to do right; seek justice. Defend the oppressed.
Take up the cause of the **fatherless**; plead the case of the widow.*
Isaiah 1:16–17

*Your rulers are rebels, partners with thieves; they all love bribes
and chase after gifts. They do not defend the cause of the
fatherless; the widow's case does not come before them.*
Isaiah 1:23

*Therefore the Lord will take no pleasure in the young men,
nor will he pity the **fatherless** and widows, for everyone is
ungodly and wicked, every mouth speaks folly. Yet for all this,
his anger is not turned away, his hand is still upraised.*
Isaiah 9:17

*To deprive the poor of their rights and withhold justice
from the oppressed of my people, making widows
their prey and robbing the **fatherless**.*
Isaiah 10:2

*Like cages full of birds, their houses are full of deceit; they have become rich and powerful and have grown fat and sleek. Their evil deeds have no limit; they do not seek justice. They do not promote the case of the **fatherless**; they do not defend the just cause of the poor.*
Jeremiah 5:27–28

*If you really change your ways and your actions and deal with each other justly, if you do not oppress the foreigner, the **fatherless** or the widow and do not shed innocent blood in this place, and if you do not follow other gods to your own harm, then I will let you live in this place, in the land I gave your ancestors for ever and ever.*
Jeremiah 7:5–7

*This is what the Lord says: Do what is just and right. Rescue from the hand of the oppressor the one who has been robbed. Do no wrong or violence to the foreigner, the **fatherless** or the widow, and do not shed innocent blood in this place.*
Jeremiah 22:3

*"Leave your **fatherless children**; I will keep them alive. Your widows too can depend on me."*
Jeremiah 49:11

We have become fatherless, our mothers are widows.
Lamentations 5:3

*In you they have treated father and mother with contempt; in you they have oppressed the foreigner and mistreated the **fatherless** and the widow.*
Ezekiel 22:7

*Assyria cannot save us; we will not mount warhorses. We will never again say "Our gods" to what our own hands have made, for in you the **fatherless** find compassion.*
Hosea 14:3

*Do not oppress the widow or the **fatherless**, the foreigner or the poor. Do not plot evil against each other.*
Zechariah 7:10

*"So I will come to put you on trial. I will be quick to testify against sorcerers, adulterers and perjurers, against those who defraud laborers of their wages, who oppress the widows and the **fatherless**, and deprive the foreigners among you of justice, but do not fear me," says the Lord Almighty.*
Malachi 3:5

*I will not leave you as **orphans**; I will come to you.*
John 14:18

*Religion that God our Father accepts as pure and faultless is this: to look after **orphans** and widows in their distress and to keep oneself from being polluted by the world.*
James 1:27

Share Your Solutions at GlobalOrphanCrisis.org

This adorable little lady was orphaned but now is being cared for, educated, and loved with God's love in a foster family with eleven sisters. *Diane Lynn Elliot, photographer © Diane Lynn Elliot*

Do you have a heart of compassion for orphaned children? Have you done something to make a difference in the life of a child and are willing to share your story? I'm looking for solutions to inspire and motivate others to serve orphaned children around the globe. I'd love to hear what you have to say! For my blog, gallery tour schedule, photographs, and missions trips, please see the website for more details: www.globalorphancrisis.com.

—Diane

Photographer Credits
and Biographies

Matthew A. James

© Bill Wegener, photographer

Matthew is a down-home Texas gentleman who is a telecommunications engineer by trade, but his real passion is for people and photography. Over the years God has given him opportunities to inter- twine these two elements to produce impressionable im- ages. "From a young age I've always had a camera in my hand," Matthew says. "My mother was the right-brained creative artist, and my dad was the highly technical left-brained individual. Having each of these two traits helps me to not only visualize how I want to capture a moment, but it gives me the confidence to be technically proficient as well."

In 2007 Matthew traveled with "God Loves Kids" in Uganda and Rwanda. Although the primary objective for the trip was to visit or- phanages and photo-document each of the orphans in hopes of getting them sponsored, this experience was a life-changing one he would do again in a heartbeat. The cover photograph is just one of the many pow- erful pictures that were a result of that trip. Matthew currently lives out- side of Dallas, Texas, with his wife and twin boys.

Jeffrey Weeks

© Marla Weeks, photographer

For more than twenty years Jeff has worked as a litigation and personal injury attorney. But his passion has been his family, working with the teens, photography, and a growing interest in missions. Combining these passions he has set out to create compelling photographs that communicate the need for Christian missions involvement around the world. Jeff and his daughter Waverly have a blog where he displays some of the images he has taken over the last several years in hopes of inspiring others toward missions involvement (www.showthestory.com).

Jeff has the unusual personality combination of being driven, creative, and compassionate all at the same time, and for him it works perfectly. Jeff lives in Colorado Springs, Colorado, with his wife, Marla, and three teenage children—Morgan, Waverly and Sawyer.

Bill Wegener

© Matthew A. James, photographer

With a background in design, Bill is the founder of Colorenlargement.com and holds the company to high standards to provide quality work and customer satisfaction for every order. His drive and determination have helped him hone his photography skills, and he has become an exceptional photographer.

Art and photography have been a passion of Bill's for decades. His desire to create compelling images was taken to new heights as he traveled with "God Loves Kids" and two other missions organizations to nineteen different countries including Africa, India, and South and Central America. From this experience Bill found that he derives great inspiration from seeing people who love God and sacrificially serve others.

Bill is an honest and humble man who sums up his life in one powerful quote: "Anything good that has happened in my life is all due to Jesus Christ, jumping into the middle of it and giving me a reason to live. Short of that—well, it's not worth discussing."

Diane Lynn Elliot

© Debbie Ruzga, photographer

Diane has been interested in photography since college but never took it seriously until the wonderful era of digital photography. After a long career in meeting planning and administration in the mid 2000s, she was ready for a change and put away the notebooks and picked up the camera. Since that time she has honed her photography skills and works professionally in communication as both a writer and photographer.

Diane says, "One of my greatest joys is to help the viewer feel the emotion I felt when capturing the image. I want the viewer to get lost in the magnificence of the moment." This statement becomes even more profound when capturing the beauty, heartbreak, and hope of orphaned and vulnerable child. "Rather than to just see a hurting child, I long to see the hope that can be given as compassionate people bravely engage in the drama to help lift children out of hopelessness."

Select photographs can be viewed at http://www.globalorphan-crisis.com.

Acknowledgments

"Follow God's example, therefore, as dearly loved
children and walk in the way of love,
just as Christ loved us and gave himself up for us
as a fragrant offering and sacrifice to God."
Ephesians 5:1–2

Thank you to my husband, David, who has been a great source of encouragement, strength, and advice during all my adventures for the last thirty-plus years. You have enriched my life more than any other person on this planet, and I love sharing life with you.

Thank you to the Marquette, Elliot, Barrett, and Gray families for being wonderful cheerleaders. I especially appreciated those who prayed for me to have the right words to say and for safety on my travels. Thank you for believing in me.

Thank you to several dear friends who have stood by me, supported and prayed for me, gave me ideas, challenged me, had long phone conversations with me, and met me for lunch or coffee when I needed to bounce ideas off someone. Thanks for listening!

Thanks to the Haiti team: I will always remember our great discussions, Maggie Mohr's open arms for orphaned children and her massive bug bites, Clayton Wood's helpful processing and the laughs provided with his boy-scout preparedness (i.e., the always-essential emergency mask and snorkel), Debbie Ruzga's sweet spirit that draws people in and leaves them wanting more, and Susan Plough's great questions and deep thoughts.

Thanks to the Peru team: My heart was touched by Morgan Sutter's compassion for every child, and I love traveling and laughing with my sweet niece, Corrie Wielenga. Thank you both for all your technological skills and pack-mule support.

Thank you to the many, many inspiring people and ministries we visited in both Haiti and Peru, especially to our hosts Christen Morrow, Barbara Walker, Lucien Michel, and Jan Gutwein. Your hospitality was outstanding and your knowledge and wisdom profound. I thank God for your ministry, your work, and your dedication.

A special thanks to the many people I interviewed and who sent in stories and photographs. Thank you for your willingness to be part of the solution to the global orphan crisis. Your openness and contagious hearts for orphaned children and for God was inspiring. Your wonderful ideas have made this book so much richer.

To the professional photographers who graced this book with breathtaking photographs: your passion for orphaned, abandoned, and vulnerable children is remarkable. Thank you for capturing the heart of the matter and allowing me to share your inspiring work.

To my friends and colleagues at Moody Publishers, thank you. Your remarkable team makes me look better than I deserve. Your enthusiasm is contagious, your compassion for the orphaned child inspirational, and your support every step of the way outstanding. It has been a pleasure serving with you these many months. My work with Moody won't be complete until there is a travel stamp in the passports of Holly Kisly, Deborah Keiser, Tracey Harris, and Annette LaPlaca when they join me on a missions project somewhere in the world to serve orphaned children. I look forward to that day.

For my dear friends who have gone above and beyond, I'm so grateful. Morgan Sutter, thank you for expanding the cause as we reach out through media. Marni Wielenga and Sherry Capes, thank you for reading every word and making sure we put our best foot forward. Chris Capes, thank you for the behind-the-scenes work that makes the finished product look oh, so good. Beryl Glass, it is fun creating projects with you; I love your design work. You read my mind, then create masterpieces out of my stick figures. Thank you, friends and family, who allowed me to impose chapters on you and who provided very helpful feedback: Jennifer Glacken, Larry and Janet Gray, Lynn and Craig Marquette, Mike Moffitt, Dr. Ernest Taylor, and many others.

Thanks to the compassionate individuals who carried the global orphan torch well before my involvement and will carry it into the future long after I'm gone—Dina Ackermann, Dixie Bickel, Julia Chuquitaype, Tom Davis, Sister Gladys, Jedd Medefind, Joyce Moffitt, Ed Schwartz, Doris Storz, Matt Storer, Pastor Jim and Susan Wood, Emily Voohries, and so many others. Thank you for your longstanding commitment to children and love for the Lord. You, along with social workers, foster and adoptive parents, child care workers, attorneys, policy makers, pastors, ministry leaders, and countless others, have given your lives to meet the needs of orphaned and vulnerable children, protecting them during their darkest time. Your dedicated service is humbling. Thank you for the eternal investment you have made in the lives of children.

Thank You, God, for providing Your Word, which gives us clear instructions about caring for orphaned children. You fearfully and wonderfully created each child. You know every child by name. You see every tear and hear every cry. Make Your path clear to each person who calls on Your name and is willing to engage in the fight for the world's neediest children. Thank You for loving us in spite of our sin and providing a way to You through the sacrifice of Your Son. Thank You for giving us the hope and promise of a future with You in heaven, where there will be no more pain, no more tears, and only joy and praising for all eternity. To God be the glory!

Notes

Introduction

1. Unicef, "At a Glance: Haiti," www.unicef.org/infobycountry/haiti.
2. UNICEF, UNAIDS, and WHO. Children and AIDS: Fifth Stocktaking Report. 2010.
3. Ibid.

Chapter 1: The Orphan Crisis: A Cause Bigger Than Ourselves

1. UNICEF, UNAIDS, and WHO. Children and AIDS: Fifth Stocktaking Report. 2010.
2. Orphan's Hope, "Our Vision," www.orphanshope.org.
3. Leslie, Lifesong for Orphans, "Little Ephrem," www.lifesong.squarespace.com.

Chapter 2: On Becoming an Orphan: Contributing Factors

1. Mahbub ul Haq, creator of the Human Development Index, quoted in Sakiko Fukuda-Parr, "The Human Development Paradigm," *Feminis Economics* (2003), 301–317.
2. Tearfund, "What Are These?" www.tearfund.org, updated March 2012.
3. "Human Development Index and Its Components," statistical tables Table 1, *Human Development Report 2011*, 127–130. www.hdr.undp.org.
4. United Nations World Food Program (WFP), Oxfam, UNICEF, cited at www.poverty.com.
5. World Hunger Education Service, "2012 World Hunger and Poverty Facts and Statistics," updated December 4, 2011. www.worldhunger.org.
6. Avert, "Global HIV and AIDS estimates, 2009 and 2010," Worldwide HIV & Aids Statistics, 2011. www.avert.org.
7. Avert. "Worldwide HIV & AIDS Statistics Commentary." Accessed June, 2011, www.avert.org.
8. Ibid.
9. World AIDS Orphans Day, "Charles," The Orphans Crisis: AIDS Orphans Stories. Accessed June, 2011. www.worldaidsorphans.org.
10. World Health Organization, "Maternal Deaths Worldwide Drop by Third," September 15, 2010. www.who.int/mediacentre/news.
11. "Maternal Mortality in Central Asia," *Central Asia Health Review (CAHR)*, June 2, 2008.
12. Nils Dulaire, *Promises to Keep: The Toll of Unintended Pregnancies on Women's Lives in the Developing World* (Washington, DC: Global Health Council, 2002).
13. World Health Organization, "Maternal Deaths Worldwide Drop by Third," September 15, 2010. www.who.int/mediacentre/news.

14. Julia Adamson, "Natural Disasters of 2010," Natural Disasters@suite101, December 25, 2010. http://julia-adamson.suite101.com.

15. Ibid.

16. Ibid.

17. Jenny Inglee, "Mexican Drug War Orphans 10,000 Children in One Year." Take Part, June 16, 2010. www.takepart.com.

18. Catherine Bremer, "Special Report: Mexico's growing legion of narco orphans," Reuters, October 6, 2010. www.reuters.com.

19. World Data Center, "State Fragility Index." www.wdc.org.ua.

20. World Bank Institute, "The OVC Situation," *The OVC Toolkit for SSA*, 12. www.worldbank.org.

21. World Vision report, 2001, quoted in "Children at Risk," Stand 4 Kids. Accessed May 5, 2012. www.stand4kids.org.

22. All Girls Allowed, "Frequently Asked Questions." www.allgirlsallowed.org.

23. Patricia Lone, "Commentary: Keeping girls in school." www.unicef.org.

24. Malavika Karlekar, "The girl child in India: does she have any rights?" *Canadian Woman Studies*, March 1995, quoted in Adam Jones, "Case Study: Female Infanticide," Genderwatch 1999–2000. Accessed May 5, 2012. www.gendercide.org.

25. John-Thor Dahlburg, "The Fight to Save India's Baby Girls," *Los Angeles Times,* February 22, 1994. http://articles.latimes.com.

26. Housing Works, "Haiti One Year Later: A Call to Action!" Accessed May 5, 2012. www.housingworks.org.

27. Restavèk Freedom, "Restavèk: The Persistence of Child Labor and Slavery," *Universal Periodic Review,* October 14, 2011. http://ijdh.org/wordpress.

28. Ibid.

29. Ibid.

30. Restavèk Freedom. www.restavekfreedom.org.

31. UN Women. "The United Nations Fourth World Conference on Women," point 268 (September 1995). www.un.org/womenwatch.

32. Stanley K. Henshaw, "Trends in Abortion and Contraception: Global Overview," Guttmacher Institute, Seville, Spain, October, 2010. www.fiapac.org/media.

33. Counseling Services, Kansas State University, "Dysfunctional Families: Recognizing and Overcoming their Effects," 1993, 1997. Accessed May 5, 2012. December 12, 2011. http://www.k-state.edu/counseling.

34. Ibid.

35. Heart for Orphans, "The Problem." Accessed May 5, 2012. http://heartfororphans.com.

36. This undocumented story comes from knowledgeable orphan-care providers.

37. International Society for the Prevention of Child Abuse and Neglect, "Executive

Summary," *World Perspectives on Child Abuse: An International Resource Book, ninth edition* (June 2010). www.ispcan.org.

38. BBC News, "Study reveals global child abuse," October 12, 2006. http://news.bbc.co.uk.

39. Ibid.

40. Canadian Children's Rights Council, "Fatherless Children in Canada." Accessed May 5, 2012. www.canadiancrc.com.

41. International Disability and Development Consortium, "Report of Rights for Disabled Children," *Seen and Heard* (October 1997), quoted in Randy Alcorn and Joni Eareckson Tada, *Why, O God? Suffering and Disability in the Bible and the Church* (Wheaton, IL: Crossway, 2011), 317.

42. Rehabilitation International, "Children with Disabilities: Global Priorities," a report prepared for the UN Special Session on Children, January 1, 2001. www.reddiscapacidad.org.

43. Pew Charitable Trusts 2010, *Collateral Costs: Incarceration's Effect on Economic Mobility*. Washington, DC: The Pew Charitable Trusts, 2010.

44. Erik Eckholm, "In Prisoners' Wake, a Tide of Troubled Kids," *The New York Times* (July 4, 2009). www.nytimes.com.

45. Daniel Tencer, "One in 28 US kids has a parent in prison: study," The Raw Story, September 29, 2010. www.rawstory.com.

46. Michelle Chen, "Parents in Prison, Children in Foster Care," Gotham Gazette, July 2009. http://www.gothamgazette.com/article/socialservices/20090720/15/2968.

47. Ibid.

Chapter 3: The Dangers Orphans Face

1. BBC News, "Romania and Bulgaria join the EU," January 1, 2007. http://news.bbc.co.uk.

2. Liana Muller, "Romania's Way into the EU," European Studies Vienna, August 16, 2002. www.iet.ntnu.no/~ralf/muller/pubs/romEU.pdf.

3. USAID, "Haiti—Earthquake and Cholera: Fact Sheet," May 3, 2011.

4. *The World Almanac and Book of Facts 2011*, quoted in the Texas Tribune, Monday, December 27, 2010. www.ourtribune.com.

5. USAID, "Haiti—Earthquake and Cholera: Fact Sheet," May 3, 2011.

6. Centers for Disease Control, "Cholera in Haiti: One Year Later," October 25, 2011. www.cdc.gov.

7. Joseph Guyler Delva, "Death Toll in Haiti's Floods, Mudslides Rise to 23," Reuters, June 8, 2011. www.reuters.com.

8. Holden, "How much money has been given and spent for Haiti earthquake relief? Putting the numbers in perspective," Give Well, January 10, 2011. http://blog.givewell.org/2011/01/10.

9. Blue Planet Network, "The Facts About The Global Drinking Water Crisis." Accessed May 2012. http://blueplanetnetwork.org.

10. Ibid.

11. Ibid.

12. World Vision, "About Hunger," accessed May 2012. www.worldvision.org.

13. World Food Programme, "Hunger Stats," accessed May 2012. www.wfp.org.

14. Judy Mandelbaum, "This side of starvation: The mud pies of Haiti," Open Salon, January 19, 2010. http://open.salon.com.

15. International Food Policy Research Institute, "2010 Global Hunger Index: The Challenge of Hunger: Focus on the Crisis of Child Undernutrition," October 2010. http://www.ifpri.org.

16. International Justice Mission, "Africa." Accessed May 2012. www.ijm.org.

17. Cassandra Jardine, "Telegraph Christmas Charity Appeal: It all began with a meal on a minibus," *The Telegraph*, January 15, 2009. www.telegraph.co.uk.

18. Center for Healthcare Strategies, "Health Screening and Assessment for Children and Youth Entering Foster Care," November 2010. www.chcs.org/public.

19. American Women's Club of Oslo, "Health Care in Norway," AWCOslo, November 15, 2009. www.awcoslo.org.

20. Crunkish, "Top Ten Deadliest Diseases in the World," January 22, 2008. http://crunkish.com.

21. Boston University, "Accute Respiratory Infection," Online IH877 Textbook 2010. Aaccessed May 2012. https://bu.digication.com.

22. AVERT, International HIV and AIDS charity, "What is AIDS?" Accessed May 2012. www.avert.org.

23. UNAIDS and the World Health Organization, "Sub-Saharan Africa: Fact Sheet," November 21, 2005. www.unaids.org.

24. SOS Children's Villages, "AIDS Orphan Facts, Figures and Statistics." Accessed May 2012. www.sos-usa.org.

25. Avert, "AIDS Orphans." Accessed May 2012. www.avert.org.

26. Compassion, "Environment Facts." Accessed May 2012. www.compassion.com.

27. Henrylito D. Tacio, "Asia's Looming Water Crisis," May 2, 2009. www.gaiadiscovery.com.

28. World Health Organization. "Tuberculosis," March 2012. www.who.int.

29. Centers for Disease Control, "Progress in Global Measles Control and Mortality Reduction 2000–2007," December 5, 2008. www.cdc.gov.

30. Ibid.

31. She Is Priceless, "Help Wanted: Learn." Accessed May 2012. www.sheispriceless.org.

32. National Underground Railroad Freedom Center, "Invisible: Slavery Today." Accessed May 2012. www.freedomcenter.org.

33. International Justice Mission, "Social Justice Curriculum for High School Students." Accessed May 2012. www.ijm.org.

34. Margaret A. Healy, "Child Pornography: an international perspective," Computer Crime Research, August 2, 2004. The quote within the extract comes from a U.S. Senate report, "Child Pornography and Paedophilla: Report made by the Permanent Subcommittee on Investigations," U.S. Senate, 99th Cong. 2d Sess. 34, 1986. www.crime-research.org.

35. Family Safe Media, "Pornography Statistics." Accessed May 2012. www.familysafemedia.com.

36. Nicholas D. Kristof and Sheryl Wudunn, *Half the Sky: Turning Oppression into Opportunity for Women Worldwide* (New York: Random House, 2009), 36.

37. U.S. Department of State, "What Is Trafficking in Persons?" Trafficking in Persons Report 2010. www.state.gov.

38. International Justice Mission, "A False Controversy: Law Enforcement and the Sexual Exploitation of Children and Trafficked Women," October 7, 2009. www.ijm.org.

39. For more about Bacha Bazi, see www.onemillionvoices.com.

40. Kristof and WuDunn, 83–84.

41. Ibid., 84.

42. Stand 4 Kids, "Children at Risk," 2010. Accessed May 2012. www.stand4kids.org.

43. U.S. Department of State, "What Is Trafficking in Persons?" Trafficking in Persons Report 2010. www.state.gov.

44. North American Council on Adoptable Children, "Research on Institutional Care of Vulnerable Children." Accessed May 2012. This article quotes studies from the 1940s, 1950s, and 1960s, as well as recent studies. www.nacac.org.

45. International Christian Adoptions, "International Program." Accessed May 2012. www.4achild.org.

46. Skyward Journey, "Orphan Statistics." Accessed May 2012. http://skywardjourney.wordpress.com.

47. Ibid.

48. Ibid.

49. Ibid.

50. Childhood Well-being Research Centre, "Safeguarding Children: a comparison of England's data with that of Australia, Norway, and the United States," 2010. Accessed May 2012. www.lboro.ac.uk.

Chapter 4: The Orphan Crisis in Developed Countries

1. United Nations Development Programme, "Human Development Index and its components," November 2, 2011. http://hdr.undp.org.

2. Ibid.

3. Ibid.

4. Ibid.

5. Ibid.

6. Jeffrey D. Bachs, "Globalization: Capitalist Exploitation or Global Prosperity?" Culture & Poverty, September 27, 2010. http://perspectives-on-poverty.blogspot.com.

7. United Nations Development Programme, "Human Development Index and its components," November 2, 2011. http://hdr.undp.org.

8. Spectrem Group, "Even as Millionaire Households Climb to 8.6 million in 2011," March 21, 2012. www.spectremgroup.com.

9. Frank Newport, "This Christmas, 78% of Americans Identify as Christian," Gallup Wellbeing, December 24, 2009. www.gallup.com.

10. Bob Smietana, "Statistical Illusion," *Christianity Today*, April 1, 2006. www.christianitytoday.com.

11. United States Census Bureau, "Income, Poverty, and Health Insurance Coverage in the United States: 2010," September 13, 2011. www.census.gov.

12. United States Census Bureau, "Poverty Thresholds," September 13, 2011. www.census.gov.

13. Jennifer Wolf, quoting a report from the U.S. Census Bureau, in "Single Parents Statistics," About.com. Accessed May 2012. http://singleparents.about.com.

14. Ibid.

15. Answers.com, "Single-Parent Families," Accessed May 2012. www.answers.com.

16. "Worldwide Divorce Statistics," Divorce.com. Accessed May 2012. www.divorce.com.

17. "The States with the Highest Divorce Rates," 24/7 Wall St., August 25, 2011. http://247wallst.com.

18. Amanda May Dundas, "Going It Alone: The Trend in Single Motherhood," Care.com, March 9, 2011. www.care.com.

19. Maggie Fox, "New Report Finds Unplanned Pregnancy Rates Are on the Rise," NationalJournal, August 24, 2011. www.nationaljournal.com.

20. Answers.com, "Single-Parent Families." Accessed May 2012. www.answers.com.

21. Stop Trafficking, "Human Trafficking May Be Closer to Home Than We Think." Accessed May, 2012. www.antitraf.net.

22. Defense Institute of International Legal Studies, "New Trafficking in Persons Module," May 31, 2005. www.diils.org.

23. Stop Trafficking, "Child Trafficking Statistics." Accessed May 2012. www.antitraf.net.

24. PEW Charitable Trusts, "Foster Care Reform." Accessed May 2012. www.pewtrusts.org.

25. Adopt America Network, "Waiting Children: Waiting for a Family Is the Longest Wait of All." accessed May 2012. http://adoptamericanetwork.org.

26. SOAR Youth Ministries, Knoxville, Tennessee. www.soaruponwings.com.

Chapter 5: The Orphan Crisis in Emerging Countries

1. See the chart on p. 116.

2. ReportLinker, "Peru: economy statistics and industry reports," April 23, 2012. www.reportlinker.com, and *USA Today Money*, "Unemployment rate falls to 8.6% in November," December 2, 2011. www.usatoday.com.

3. CNN, "Forced Labor Fuels Development, *U.S. Report* finds," June 4, 2012. http://articles.cnn.com.

4. United Nations Development Programme, "Human Development Index and its components," November 2, 2011. http://hdr.undp.org.

5. Ibid.

6. World Bank, "China 2030: Executive Summary." Accessed May 2012. www.worldbank.org.

7. Orphan Outreach, "Countries We Serve." Accessed May 2012. www.orphan outreach.org.

8. United States Census 2010, "Interactive Population Map." Accessed December 2011. http://2010.census.gov.

9. Missionary-Blogs, "Cambodia Christian Missionary." Accessed May 2012. www.missionary-blogs.com.

10. Ubuntu Africa, "HIV/AIDS and Children." Accessed May 2012. www.ubafrica.org.

11. The Economist, "The War on Baby Girls: Gendercide," *The Economist*, March 4, 2010. www.economist.com.

12. Beth Nonte Russell, "The Mystery of the Chinese Baby Shortage," *New York Times,* January 23, 2007.

13. Reuters, "13 million abortions in China each year: report," July 30, 2009. www.reuters.com.

14. Anastacia Mott Austin, "The 'Lost' Girls of Asia," Buzzle.com, August 2, 2007. www.buzzle.com.

15. Ibid.

16. United Nations Development Programme. "New Report: Asia-Pacific has one of the world's worst gender gaps," March 8, 2010. http://content.undp.org/go/newsroom/2010.

17. BBC News, "India's Unwanted Girls," May 22, 2011. www.bbc.co.uk.

18. Ibid.

19. Ibid.

20. Steve Corbett and Brian Fikkert, *When Helping Hurts* (Chicago: Moody , 2009).

Chapter 6: The Orphan Crisis in the Least Developed Countries

1. Christiane Badgley, "Cameroon: Pipeline to Prosperity?" PBS, June 7, 2010. www.pbs.org.

2. Ibid.

3. United Nations Development Programme, "Human Development Index and its components," November 2, 2011. http://hdr.undp.org.

4. USAID, "Haiti—Earthquake and Cholera: Fact Sheet," May 3, 2011.

5. Jeff Swicord, "January Earthquake Displaces Many Haitian Children," *Voice of America*, April 12, 2010. www.voanews.com.

6. Matayo Moshi, "The Sleeping Catastrophe: HIV/AIDS in an Already Devastated Haiti," Council on Hemispheric Affairs, February 18, 2010. www.coha.org.

7. Robert Kennedy, "5 Facts About Private Schools in Haiti," About.com. Accessed May 2012. http://privateschool.about.com.

8. Benjamin Steinlechner, "A new government program aims to provide a free education for all Haiti's children," UNICEF, October 21, 2011. www.unicef.org.

9. Robert Kennedy, "5 Facts About Private Schools in Haiti," About.com. Accessed May 2012. http://privateschool.about.com.

10. Information about Chadasha and Loving Shepherd ministries can be found at www.chasdasha.org and http://loving-shepherd.org.

11. Save the Children, "Haiti." Accessed May 2012. www.savethechildren.org.

Chapter 7: Bringing God's Kingdom to Earth: God's Plan for Spiritual Adoption

1. Ruth Bovard, interview in Traverse City, Michigan, January 31, 2011.

2. Guttmacher Institute, "Facts on Induced Abortion in the United States." August, 2011. www.guttmacher.org.

3. Wes Stafford and Michel W. Smith, *Too Small to Ignore* (Colorado Springs, CO: Waterbrook Press, 2007), foreword.

4. John Piper and Desiring God staff, video presentation, "Adoption Is Greater Than the Universe," October 25, 2010. www.desiringgod.com.

5. Ibid.

6. Used by permission of Nichole and Aaron Marshall, missionaries in Cape Town, South Africa. Written May 16, 2010; permission granted February 26, 2011.

7. Pastor Darren Whitehead, "Kingdom Come," sermon, Willow Creek Community Church, August 21, 22, 28, and 29, 2010.

8. Dallas Willard, in a televised interview with John Ortberg about Willard's Book *The Divine Conspiracy: Rediscovering our Hidden Life in God* (New York: HarperCollins Publishers, 1998).

9. Baylor University, "God's Hands, God's Feet." Accessed March 10, 2011. http://www.baylor.edu.

Chapter 8: Jesus Loves the Little Children

1. Adapted from Dennis Bratcher, "The Book of Deuteronomy: Introduction and Overview," *Harper's Bible Dictionary* (New York: HarperCollins, 1995). www.crivoice.org.
2. George M. Stulac, *James* (Downers Grove, IL: InterVarsity Press, 2010), 85.
3. International Standard Bible Encyclopedia, "Justice," Bible History online. Accessed May 2012. http://www.bible-history.com.
4. Holly [anonymous surname], Our Adoption Journey blog, in a book review of Tom Davis, *Fields of the Fatherless: Discover the Joy of Compassionate Living* (Colorado Springs, CO: David C. Cook, 2008). Accessed May 2012. www.ourheart-fororphans.blogspot.com.

Chapter 9: Moving Orphaned Children toward Permanence

1. United Nations Department of Economic and Social Affairs Population Division, "Guidelines for improving data on child Adoption 2010." Accessed May 2012. www.un.org.
2. BBC, "Religions: Christianity." Accessed May 2012. www.bbc.co.uk.
3. VisionTrust, "About Us." Accessed May 2012. www.visiontrust.org.
4. Tirzah International, "Our One Year Anniversary." Accessed May 2012. www.tirzahinternational.org.
5. UNICEF, "UNICEF's position on Inter-country adoption," July 22, 2010. www.unicef.org.
6. Andrea Poe, "United States and UNICEF wage war against international adoptions," *The Washington Times*, August 3, 2011.
7. World Health Organization, "Community Home-based Care in Resource-Limited Settings," 2002. www.who.int.
8. Joanne Feldmeth, Relationship Recovery: Developing a Biblical Theology of Foster Care, ML583 Global Leadership, Professor: Dr. Wilmer Villacortes, September 2, 2011, Fuller Seminary.
9. Project 1.27, "About Project 1.27." Accessed May, 2012. http://project127.com.
10. Lydia Home, "Safe Families for Children." Accessed May 2012. www.safe-families.org.

Chapter 10: This and That: Improvements, Creativity, and the Global Church

1. Hartford Institute for Religion Research, "Fast Facts." Accessed May 2012. http://hirr.hartsem.edu.
2. Adherents.com, "Major Religions of the World Ranked by Number of Adherents," August 9, 2007. www.adherents.com.
3. Frontier Harvest Ministries, quoted in About.com. Accessed May 2012. http://christianity.about.com.

4. Manuel Bojorquez, "Mission group uncovers fraud, child trafficking after Haiti quake," October 28, 2011. www.wsbtv.com.

5. Christian Alliance for Orphans, www.christianalliancefororphans.org.

6. Small-business-forum.net, "Words of wisdom from James Dyson." Accessed May 2012. www.smal-business-forum.net.

7. Toms Shoes, www.toms.com.

8. Blake Mycoskie, interviewed at Willow Creek Community Church weekend service, August 2011.

Chapter 11: Making a Difference in an Everyday Way

1. Quoted in Ron Hutchcraft, *A Life That Matters* (Chicago: Moody, 2007), 81.

2. Check out Sweet Sleep at www.sweetsleep.org.

3. Bolivia's Best Gourmet Coffee. http://boliviasbestcoffee.com.

4. http://yestoadoption.blogspot.com.

Chapter 12: Changing Your Life to Change the World

1. Richard Stearns, *The Hole in Our Gospel* (Nashville: Thomas Nelson, 2009).

2. Reuters, "Factbox: Key Facts on Chernobyl Accident," March 15, 2011. www.reuters.com.

3. Hovde Foundation, "Kigali, Rwanda." Accessed May 2012. www.hovdefoundation.org.

4. Check out Hilliary Anderson's blog at http://hillsblog.com.

5. Rick Barrett, "Helping to grow hope," *Journel Sentinel*, December 28, 2010. www.jsonline.com.

6. Tirzah International, "Our One Year Anniversary." Accessed May 2012. www.tirzahinternational.org.

7. *The Age*, "Former sex slave fights illegal trade," June 22, 2010. www.theage.com.au.

8. Wears Valley Ranch, www.wvr.org.

Appendix

1. Similar statistics can be found in many places, including Dr. Sam Doherty, *Children: A Biblical Perspective* (Lisbon, Ireland: Child Evangelism Fellowship Book Division, 2011), foreword. www.cefbookministry.com. However, Barna Research Group suggests slightly lower numbers, with about two-thirds becoming believers by age eighteen. See the Barna Group, "Evangelism Is Most Effective Among Kids," October 11, 2004. www.barna.org.

2. Bill Johnson, *A Life of Miracles* (Shippensburg, PA: Destiny Image Publishers, 2011).